AF361316

Paradoxes of
Postcolonial Culture

SUNY series,

Explorations in Postcolonial Studies

Emmanuel C. Eze and Arif Dirlik, editors

Paradoxes of Postcolonial Culture

Contemporary Women Writers of
the Indian and Afro-Italian Diaspora

Sandra Ponzanesi

STATE UNIVERSITY OF NEW YORK PRESS

Published by
STATE UNIVERSITY OF NEW YORK PRESS, ALBANY

© 2004 State University of New York

Printed in the United States of America

For information, address State University of New York Press,
90 State Street, Suite 700, Albany, NY 12207

Production, Laurie Searl
Marketing, Michael Campochiaro

Library of Congress Cataloging-in-Publication Data

Ponzanesi, Sandra, 1967–
    Paradoxes of post-colonial culture : contemporary women writers of the
Indian and Afro-Italian diaspora / Sandra Ponzanesi.
        p. cm. — (SUNY series, explorations in postcolonial studies)
    Includes bibliographical references and index.
    ISBN 0-7914-6201-3 (acid-free paper)
    1. Indic literature (English)—Women authors—History and criticism.
2. American literature—South Asian American authors—History and criticism.
3. English literature—South Asian authors—History and criticism.   4. Italian
literature—Women authors—History and criticism.   5. East Indian American
women—Intellectual life.   6. Immigrants' writings—History and criticism.
7. East Indians—England—Intellectual life.   8. Emigration and immigration
in literature.   9. Africans—Italy—Intellectual life.   10. East Indian
Americans in literature.   11. Postcolonialism in literature.   12. Women and
literature.   I. Title.   II. Series.

PR9488.P66   2004
820.9'9287'0954—dc22
                                                                                    2004045295

10   9   8   7   6   5   4   3   2   1

To my family.

For teaching me

The value of roots.

The One Who Goes Away

There are always, in each of us,
these two: the one who stays,
the one who goes away—
                    —Eleanor Wilner

But I am the one
who always goes away.

The first time was the most—
was the most
            silent
I did not speak,
did not answer
those who stood waving
with the soft noise
of saris flapping in the wind.

To help the journey
coconuts were flung
from Juhu beach
into the Arabian Sea—
But I saw beggars jump in
after those coconuts—a good catch
for dinner. And in the end
who gets the true luck
from those sacrified coconuts?

I am the one
who always goes away.

Sometimes I'm asked if
I were searching for a place
that can keep my soul
from wandering
a place where I can stay
without wanting to leave.

Who knows.

Maybe the joy lies
in always being able to leave—

But I never left home.
I carried it away
with me—here in my darkness
in myself. If I go back, retrace my steps.

I will not find
that first home anywhere outside
in that mother-land place.

We weren't allowed
            to take much
but I managed to hide
my home behind my heart.

Look at the deserted beach
now it's dusk—no sun
to turn the waves gold,
no moon to catch
the waves in silver mesh—

Look
at the in-between darkness
when the sea is unmasked
she's no beauty queen.
Now the wind stops
beating around the bush—

While the earth calls
and the hearth calls
come back, come back—

(*continued*)

I am the one
who always goes away.

Because I must—
with my home intact
    but always changing
so the windows don't match
the doors anymore—the colours
clash in the garden—
And the ocean lives in the bedroom.

I am the one
who always goes
away with my home
which can only stay inside
in my blood—my home which does not fit
    with any geography.

—Sujata Bhatt, from "The
Stinking Rose," 1995

Contents

Acknowledgments

This book could not have existed without the support of many institutions, colleagues, and friends. Most of it could have not existed without the creativity of the writers, who have nourished me with their beautiful words and unbreakable spirit. I particularly thank Sujata Bhatt for allowing me to use her poem in the foreword. In a few words, she manages to encapsulate many of the critical questions I address in this book. And also Maria Viarengo, Ribka Sibhatu, Sunetra Gupta, and Bharati Mukherjee for their personal exchanges.

I owe great debt to Rosi Braidotti for her intellectual vigor and constant stimulation and for playing such a vital role in this project. Maaike Meijer helped me to discover the pleasure of the text and the subtle twist of narratology. I benefited greatly from her acumen and dedication. I would also like to thank all my colleagues at the Women's Studies Department at Utrecht University for their collegiality and rigor: Rosemarie Buikema, Berteke Waaldijk, and Gloria Wekker along with Sarah Bracke, Esther Captain, Joana Passos, and Rutvica Andrijsevic. Others from Utrecht University also took part in this adventure: Wiljan van den Akker and Frans Ruiter of the OGC (Research Institute for History and Culture) along with the Italian government and the NWO (Netherlands Organisation for Scientific Research) have made this project possible.

My enduring gratitude goes to the Belle van Zuylen Institute at the University of Amsterdam for having provided me with the space and the generosity to finalize my quest. My gratitude goes in particular to Frances Gouda, a precious and vivacious companion in gendered colonial/postcolonial intricacies and Pamela Pattynama for her literary insights and interest in cultural studies, and to Gary Price for his sharp critical eye. A warm thanks to all graduate "Bellies," past and present, in particular Sonja van Wichelen, Sybille Lammes, Catherine Lord, and Amade M'charek.

Other people who have followed my scholarly development and influenced me in many different ways are: Rajeswari Sunder Rajan and Graham Huggan for having carefully read and commented on the manuscript; Stephen Gundle for having provided so many useful insights into Italian cultural history; Rober Fraser for his postcolonial erudition and wit; Susheila Nasta, Melashri Lal, and Tabish Khair for their profound knowledge of the South Asian diaspora; Graziella Parati and Armando Gnisci for their pioneering work on Italian migrant literature; Maria Pia de Angelis, Giovanna Franci, and Vita Fortunati for their important guidance at Bologna University and David

Forgaçs at Sussex University; and finally, Yolanda Rodriguez Pérez, Paola Marchionni, Ghirmai Negash, Daniela Merolla, Monica Jansen, and Joost Raessens for being wonderful scholars, friends and more than that.

It is almost impossible to name all the persons who have been dear to me and accompanied me on the different journeys that have created my own diasporic life outside the theme of the book. Mention, however, must be made of Arjen Burghoorn for his long loving support, and of Pascale Sutherland for her editing across cities, seasons, and languages and most of all for her friendship filled with laughter.

My final dedication goes to my family: to my parents for having supported all my choices and dislocations unconditionally, to Luana for being a loving and unfailing sister, and to my nieces Giulia and Elisa, for whom I wish diasporic lives of their own.

Introduction

If history creates complexities, let us not try to simplify them.
—Salman Rushdie, *Imaginary Homelands*

This book has been generated by many interwoven histories: real and fictional, local and diasporic, histories of women on the move, of refashioned nations, and of transnational crucibles. These histories/stories—whether told in an empowering language (English) or in a minor one (Italian)—necessitate a revisitation of current postcolonial theories. Focusing on contemporary writings by Indian and Afro-Italian women writers in the diaspora, this book explores the conundrum of the present global world. In these writings issues of belonging, identity, and creative expression emerge with renewed force, raising new questions about the location of production and consumption as well as the position from which interpretations and classifications arise. These writings and the questions they raise reveal the changed relation between cultural, historical, and political events and their representations, between the residual ideologies of colonialism and their impact on present society, and between the text and its context.

This book traces the contours of the discourse on postcolonialism, highlighting its complexities and complicities, from the standpoint of feminism and of writers in minority languages. During the last decade, postcolonialism has been a rapidly sprawling field of studies, a successful banner under which various discourses gather, including minorities studies, Third World feminism, and Third World intellectual diaspora. However, as Ania Loomba warns, the term *postcolonialism* risks being seen as "shorthand for something fashionably marginal" (Loomba, 1998: XII), and academics such as Anne McClintock criticize the euphoria around the term, accusing it of being too "prematurely celebratory" (McClintock, 1995: 13). Thus the spectacular diffusion of postcolonial studies goes hand in hand with the increased anxiety about its highly theoretical framework and political evasiveness. This is due to the fact that postcolonial studies is mainly characterized by a constant critique of its own premises rather than a systematic and compact approach to the staging of the colonial encounter. Furthermore, the pressing reality of new global dynamics challenges postcolonial intellectuals to think beyond the premises of their original quest. The major impasse generated by the field itself concerns the viability of the postcolonial paradigm for the assessment of disparate sociopolitical realities that were generated in the wake of different colonial legacies, were marked by diverse forms of anticolonial struggles, and are now characterized by divergent interventions into neocolonial policies.

The undisputed role of the English language within the postcolonial debate and literatures signals the need to address these neocolonial allegations in their manifold articulations. Since language is embedded in power relationships, it is crucial to address the source of present linguistic hierarchies and the effects that these protracted colonial hegemonies have on the representation and consumption of cultural difference.

One of the historical reasons for the dominance of the English language within the field is obviously linked to the colonial literary response to the British empire. Postcolonial literatures are in fact often considered as part of the "syllabus reform" programs of English departments (Gandhi, 1998: 146). In order to dislodge this persistent center-periphery dichotomy, the discourse on postcolonialism needs to be shifted towards literatures expressed in other languages. This shift highlights one of the most visible pitfalls of postcolonialism—the reignition of a totalizing discourse, the abolition of which was a priority of the postcolonial agenda. It further indicates that new policies of publishing and distributing still privilege the English language, which is at present linked to the pivotal role that North America plays in the new global dynamics.

Therefore, the main objectives of this book are twofold. On the one hand, to undermine the monolithic nature of the postcolonial debate by emphasizing its politics of fragmentation. On the other hand, to analyze a new corpus of Italian multicultural literature that resuscitates an obscure chapter of Italian history: that of colonialism. By comparing the burgeoning tradition of women writers of the Indian diaspora to new writings by Afro-Italian migrant women, a set of dissymmetrical relationships emerges that accounts for different colonial, linguistic, and market economies. The investigation of these relationships is central to this book.

Indian writers, for example, are no doubt the "jewel in the crown" of postcolonial literature, whereas the Afro-Italian writers are doomed to play a minor role within the postcolonial literary discourse because they have inherited the "wrong" colonizer. This confrontation brings to light how language encodes power relations. While certain writers are marginal within discourses structured according to the center-periphery dichotomy, they are dominant within other postcolonial lineages.

However, to emphasize the discordant and dissymmetric aspects of postcolonialism is not the only goal of this book. The aim is also to reveal the commonalities among women writers who experience a common condition of diaspora, even though it is dictated by different colonial histories that result in different postcolonial aftermaths. In order to establish lateral affiliations, the trope of diaspora is used to bring divergent histories under the same spectrum of analysis.

Diaspora is, in fact, both a material condition of dislocation and a postmodern intellectual notion that expresses existential dispersion. In both cases it indicates a postnational space where, as Avtar Brah writes, multiple subject positions are juxtaposed, contested, proclaimed or disavowed; where the permitted and the prohibited perpetually interrogate; and where the accepted and the transgressive imperceptibly mingle even while these syncretic forms may be disclaimed in the name of purity and tradition.[1]

Diasporic spaces allow for the representation of those who straddle two or more cultures, languages, and ethnicities and offer a way of rethinking postcolonialism as blurring the lines of national enclaves.

However, the notion of diaspora does not do away with gender inequalities. On the contrary, it makes them more acute and urgent since women must negotiate the conflicting politics of home and abroad, of tradition and emancipation, and of ethnic belonging and metropolitan fusion. The itinerary of women is therefore, as Paul Gilroy writes, both "rooted and routed" (Gilroy, 1993: 3), a myriad process of cultural fissures and fusions that must be constantly situated and embodied.

The aim of this study, then, is to assess the dissymmetrical relocation of these two cultures—Indian and Afro-Italian women—without presuming that their locations in time and space or their modes of representing the postcolonial experience are equal or interchangeable.

This book complicates the postcolonial condition by adopting a comparative approach to postcolonial literatures by women of different traditions and language (English and Italian). It focuses on the intersections of their themes, modes, and genres yet avoids screening different cultural and linguistic realities through the same lenses. The two groups of writers are disparate even as they are linked by the common experience of having undergone the oppression of colonialism. This book emphasizes their common experience of identity formation under the conditions of diaspora, as their identities are uniquely shaped by the categories of gender, class, and ethnicity.

My approach grants autonomy to the work of each author as it represents post-colonial gendered discourse. I analyze one text per author, the text I feel most significantly highlights the author's intentions and reveals the problematic issues raised by the postcolonial paradigm. The first part of the book is entirely devoted to Indian literature and the second to Afro-Italian literature. Each part has an introductory chapter, followed by four chapters in the first part and by three chapters in the second part, each dealing with a different author or aspect of the postcolonial condition. While the chapters can be read separately—each chapter has its own theme and mode of approach—this does not mean that they stand apart from each other. On the contrary, they are meant to be read together in order to establish how difference is constructed from diverging historical, political, and cultural locations.

Each chapter is subdivided into smaller sections in which the narratological analyses of the novel taken into consideration are intertwined with specific theoretical issues arising from the text. By giving narrative body to theory, questions of gender and ethnicity, literary genres, nationhood, and diaspora are illustrated and investigated.

Chapter 1, "Touchstones," broaches all the issues which crisscross the whole book. The issues are contextualized to illustrate a postcolonial dissymmetry. Chapter 2, "The Exuberance of Immigration," looks at Indian women writers of the diaspora through the analysis of Bharati Mukherjee's *Jasmine* (1989), a novel on immigration. This chapter emphasizes both Mukherjee's celebration of fluid identities and the incoherences of her assimilationist credo. Chapter 3, "The Shock of Arrival," an analysis of Meena Alexander's memoir *Fault Lines* (1993), examines whether Alexander's reiterated ontological uprootedness is used as a rhetorical strategy or dictated by the difficulty of tracing a feminist genealogy where multiple identities can be simultaneously represented. The problem or representation is further discussed in chapter 4, "Alienation and Narration," which deals with Sara Suleri's unusual autobiography, *Meatless Days* (1989). In it the author traces the genesis of Pakistan from the matrilineal point of view. Through the analysis of this text the implication of gender in the construction of a national discourse is deconstructed. Chapter 5, "Floating Myths," concludes the part on Indian writers with a discussion of Sunetra Gupta's *Moonlight into Marzipan* (1995). In this novel Gupta reinterprets and subverts traditional Western myths from a feminist and postcolonial standpoint. This chapter traces how mythology is often deployed to oppress or misrepresent women, minorities, and other marginalized social groups.

The first part on the Indian novels is then followed by a second part on Afro-Italian literature. Given the very novelty of these texts within Italian culture, a more in-depth analysis of the colonial/postcolonial relationships between Italy and the Horn of Africa is sketched in order to understand the reasons for the belated appearance and recognition of postcolonial literature in Italian. For these reasons the second part opens with a programmatic chapter, chapter 6, "A Short Story about the Italian Empire," which briefly reviews the short-lived Italian colonial adventure in order to establish how a different form of colonization has influenced the tumultuous phase of decolonization in the Horn of Africa (Eritrea, Ethiopia, Somalia—areas still experiencing internal wars) and how this history has affected the emerging Italian multiculturalization.

Chapter 7, "Daughters of Empire: *Métissage* and Hyphenated Identities," explores the legacy of Italian colonialism through various histories of *métissage*, as narrated by Erminia dell'Oro in the novel *L'Abbandono: Una Storia Eritrea* (1992) and Maria Abbebù Viarengo's extracts "Andiamo a Spasso?" (1990). The trope of *métissage* raises the issue of how ethnically blended identities—the fruit of specific sexual colonial politics—challenge the racial divide and confront the colonizer even now with his own mutability. Chapter 8, "Living in Translation," concentrates on Ribka Sibhatu's multicultural children's book *Aulò: Canto-Poesia dall'Eritrea* (1993). It illustrates how literature can function as resistance, especially in a country such as Eritrea, which underwent a struggle for independence for thirty years. It further investigates how the translation of a Third World text makes the issue of cultural authenticity all the more complex.

The last chapter, 9, "Voices in Pain: Once We Were Warriors," deals with the issue of female infibulation as presented in literary texts, principally in Sirad S. Hassan's essay-novel *Sette Gocce di Sangue: Due Donne Somale* (1996). This chapter focuses on the theoretical debates surrounding the issue of female mutilation, which divides feminists into two camps, Western interventionists and Third World self-determinists. Even though both fronts believe that the practice must be eradicated, they profoundly differ about how to wage the war against it.

Through the thread of many different narratives, voices, and landscapes this book reconstructs some postcolonial histories/stories that otherwise might have remained unheard. But the scope is also to envisage possible future traditions, which are already present in the here and now waiting to be detected. It seems fitting to conclude this introduction with a quote from Italo Calvino's *Invisible Cities*:

> from my words you will have reached the conclusion that the real [history] is a temporal succession of different [stories], alternatively just and unjust. But what I wanted to warn you about is something else: all the future [histories / stories] are already present in this instant, wrapped one within the other, confined, crammed, inextricable.[2]

Chapter 1

Touchstones

You have navigated with raging soul far from the paternal home, passing beyond the seas' double rocks and now you inhabit a foreign land.

—Medea

THE HYPE OF POSTCOLONIALISM

The terms *postcolonial, postcolonialism,* or *postcoloniality* address and express the different modulations of postimperialism. Postcolonial literature in particular reflects all these variations because literature constitutes the contact zone between society and its representation through language. In this literature theories and politics meet to defy and subvert previous colonial hierarchies. Postcolonial literature thus constitutes a fruitful and contentious field of studies, which is not devoid of internal frictions or paradoxes.

Postcolonial critique nourishes itself upon its inherent contradictions. This marks the vitality of the field but also highlights the highly speculative nature of its practices. Being one of the most interesting interventions in cultural theory since the linguistic turn, postcolonialism neither presents itself in easy packaging nor offers ready-made solutions for the issues raised and investigated. To be aware of the arbitrariness of linguistic meanings is, in fact, not sufficient to dispel the hegemonic nature of language itself. Writing in the language of one former metropolitan power instead of another automatically relocates the role of postcolonial literature in the global market place. This is because the historical traces that connote colonial relations not only influence but also determine the position that new cultural productions acquire in an age of late capitalism. Language has become a commodity in itself and it marks the positioning of literature along the diffused and complex lines of colonial dynamics.

For example, within academia the study of postcolonial literature tends to be an expansion of English department curriculum,[1] and this paradoxically recenters postcolonial literature around the rubric of the English language. This confirms Anne McClintock's anxiety that the postcolonial paradigm narrows down intellectual investigations not only around the rubric of European history but—even more limiting—around the British canon. This has been amply demonstrated by the many studies focusing on British India and on "the empire writing back" from India as the ad hoc peripheral location. By privileging the British context, postcolonialism reproduces one of the main paradoxes whose abolition was at the center of the postcolonial agenda.

Given the impact of British colonialism in India and the politics of institutionalization of the English language through a systematic educational system,[2] it is no coincidence that the strongest response comes from India, the jewel in the crown, and that as a consequence the deep interest in postcolonial literatures initially stemmed from English literature departments. Literatures "out there" were, in fact, not merged within the standard curriculum, but were introduced through a special course entitled "Commonwealth Literature." The term has itself been highly criticized because, as Salman Rushdie said in his *Imaginary Homelands*, "Commonwealth Literature does not Exist"[3] unless as a ghetto of the standard British curriculum. Authors like V. S. Naipaul,[4] a Caribbean writer of Indian ancestry, were considered as hovering between established Western literary genres and ideas and their critiques. Naipaul's elaborations on the complex nature of travel literature and its implication for the spirit of empire preceded much of Said's critique expressed in *Culture and Imperialism* (1993). Yet he defended the values of Western civilization as the only source of enlightenment and progress. His obtaining the 2001 Nobel Prize for literature surprised the world as much as the writer himself since he is notorious for his politically incorrect statements about Third World countries that often overshadowed the appraisal for his brilliant and sparse prose. Naipaul is a Third World writer who longed to be at the center of the empire. He pursued his career in order to redeem himself from the narrowness of the peripheral mentality of his native country, and he strove to become a universal writer and interpreter of the world through his sharp and cynical pen. Traveling from Port of Spain, Trinidad, to Oxford University in the fifties, V. S. Naipaul's itinerary is the prototypical colonial intellectual odyssey.

Naipaul directs his harsh criticism at people from the former British colonies, endorsing a far more Eurocentric view than even the ex-colonizers would dare to express, by saying, for example, that the colonized are like monkeys pleading for evolution. However, despite the arrogant attitude that reveals his tormented relations with his roots and his insecurities within the hosting country, he mobilized the territory between center and periphery, indelibly changing the view on both, and therefore substantially contributing to the postcolonial debate.[5]

Nowadays postcolonial studies (a rephrasing and political complexification of the old term "Commonwealth studies") have redeemed themselves from any status of marginality. It is a booming field that addresses common preoccupations arising from the process of decolonization and the search for alternative national and cultural identities. In this book the term *postcolonialism* will be embraced as an overall category in order to analyze different postcolonial conditions within the same framework. The politics of fragmentation is emphasized in order to avoid the risk of totalization and homogenization that is endemic to the postcolonial discourse. This perspective allows, for example, to compare different postcolonial traditions such as the Anglo-Indian and the Afro-Italian while respecting their specificity. Using gender and ethnicity as categories that cut across different geopolitical locations, the focus will be on how women writers represent identity in their works and on how the experience of transnationalism affects and creates problems in these representations. This comparative approach brings to the fore a set of asymmetric relationships in which language, hegemony, and diaspora play a crucial role. These are all issues at the heart of postcolonial critique but will be dealt with from a very specific positioning—that of minority literature.

THEORETICAL CONTENTIONS

> More complex terms and analyses, of alternative times, histories and causalities, are required to deal with complexities that cannot be served under the single rubric of post-colonialism.
>
> —Anne McClintock, "The Angel of Progress"
> in *Imperial Leather*, p. 13

The serious yet productive dispute surrounding the historical ground, the theoretical breadth, and the cultural implications of postcolonialism's hyphenated formula has not generated any precise theory or method. What is at stake for this contentious field of studies is the enactment of alternative ways of reading and writing that exploit the fertile tensions between different approaches and discourses.

Historically speaking, the term *postcolonialism* refers to the consciousness arising after colonization from the countries that were once colonized and are now independent. These countries engage in subversive, resistant politics that call for the preservation of difference rather than assimilation to the West. Assimilation represents a transcultural fusion modeled on the dominant cultural patterns. Postcolonialism implies the reversion of the role of the postcolonial from an object that is scrutinized and spoken for into a subjective role in which the postcolonial represents her/himself and speaks back. However, there is no consensus as to when this postcolonial consciousness historically started, before or after independence, or whether this is an accurate term to describe the condition of so many Third World people who did not share the same colonizer. These people, in fact, use different imposed languages, are located in different geographical areas, differ in race, ethnicity and sex, and vary in their opportunities for migration.[6]

Due to its heterogeneous and diffused character, postcolonialism is therefore not devoid of internal contradictions. The term, in fact, "closes as many epistemological possibilities as it opens" (Suleri, 1995: 136). However, under the rubric of postcolonialism, it would be useful to distinguish postcolonial theory from postcolonial politics. The first refers to poststructuralist critique of Western epistemology, whereas the second refers to Marxist philosophies that embrace oppositional thinking.

The first is more of a transhistorical mode (Edward Said: 1978, 1993, 2000; Trinh T. Minh-ha: 1989; Homi K. Bhabha: 1990, 1994; Paul Gilroy: 1987, 1993, 2000; Sara Suleri: 1995; Stuart Hall: 1997, 2001; McClintock: 1997; Gayatri C. Spivak: 1988, 1990, 1993, 1999; Ania Loomba: 1998; Robert Young: 1990, 1995; Graham Huggan: 2001; Robert Fraser: 2000). The second approach entails a historical and materialist interpretation (Anthony Appiah: 1992; Ajiaz Ahmad: 1992; Chandra T. Mohanty: 1991; Fredric Jameson: 1991; E. San Juan Jr.: 1995, 1998; Gayatri Spivak: 1988, 1990, 1993, 1999; Gyan Prakash: 1995; Arif Dirlik: 1994; Gandhi Leela: 1998; Benita Parry: 1972, 1997; Elleke Boehmer: 1995; Michael Hardt and Tony Negri, 2000). However, the two perspectives are clearly more imbricated with each other than this subdivision would suggest, and the one cannot exist without the other. As Leela Gandhi writes, "The postcolonial critic has to work toward a synthesis of, or negotiation between, both modes of thought" (Gandhi, 1998: IX).

Nonetheless, the more historicist approach has been slowly submerged by increasingly fashionable poststructuralist jargon, which often runs the risk of becoming self-referential and of erasing the materialist and political specificities of postcolonial realities. This can be damaging when the mannerism of terminology obfuscates the political agenda of a group with a weaker cultural identity, as in the case of Italian postcolonial writers. To avoid an improper use of postcolonial discourse, it is important not to divert the attention from the historical specificities that create its complexities and its riveted paradoxes. Furthermore, the tangible reality of globalization requires a quick reorientation of the postcolonial critique towards the forces of capitalism that subsume geographical peripheries and market difference as a new exotic commodity (Huggan, 2001). In this respect Marxist theorists are seeking revenge against those "culturalist critics" who have brought postcolonial studies to so many historical distortions and theoretical evasions. However, a text such as *Empire* by Michael Hardt and Toni Negri (2001) that claims to recenter postcolonialism around issues of globalization, tends to align the Third World with the old Marxist notion of the working class, thereby reigniting oppositional thinking between globalization as the invisible monster that came in the wake of colonialism and the Third World. In so doing, such approaches only partly address the complexity generated by late capitalist formations and the role that cultural difference plays in it.

For the sake of clarity some of the major issues at stake in postcolonial thinking will be highlighted here in order to indicate the specific position taken in this book within the eclecticism of the debate. A brief excursus between the two streams of postcolonial thought indicated above is necessary to detect major critical interventions and to elaborate on some of the negotiations suggested. Anne McClintock, for example, states that there is some basis for finding the term *postcolonialism* suspicious because it is too celebratory of the so-called end of colonialism. However, we must also watch out for the return to nostalgic myths of origin. If, on the one hand, there is the risk of a spurious universalization of the term, there is, on the other hand, the danger of a return to clear-cut politics of binary oppositions.

It is necessary therefore to focus on what we mean by the term and how we want to make it operational. The term should not be considered as a dogmatic entity but as a critical tool that needs to be used with careful discrimination. This care is all the more urgent if we do not want to locate the Third World discursively, an essentialism which in turn loses the cutting edge of postcolonial critique. As Stuart Hall has written "it is only too tempting to fall into the trap of assuming that, because essentialism has been deconstructed *theoretically*, therefore it has been displaced *politically*."[7]

In this respect Ella Shohat's question is important: she asks whether the postcolonial mark the ruptural point between two epistemes in intellectual history or whether it refers to the strict chronologies of history *tout court*.[8] Here the term *postcolonialism* will be used to interpret the intense subversive practice that has taken place at the end or before the end of colonial empires. This alternative practice arose not only to assess the cultural and political aftermath of colonialism but also to reinscribe representation according to a postcolonial perspective. Therefore, postcolonialism qualifies itself as a resistant set of strategies which aim at reversing the supremacy of the West over Third World countries.[9] Here Prakash's quote comes in useful, since he makes the hyphen in postcolonialism superfluous, nonetheless accounted for:

> post-coloniality as an aftermath, as an after—as a location formed in the fragile functioning of colonialism. Post-coloniality in this sense does not reinterpret either the transcendence or the reversal of post-colonialism, and it sidesteps the language of beginnings and ends. Containing a link to the experience of colonialism, but not contained by it, post-coloniality can be thought of as a form of realignment that emerges *in medias res*, critically undoing and redrawing colonialism's contingent boundaries.[10]

If we consider postcolonialism in a strict historical perspective, we tend to agree that it was generated at the end of colonial empires. However, if we approach it as an ideological and intellectual awareness that has characterized the uprising of colonial countries from political and cultural domination, then we have to agree that postcolonialism started before the date of independence. In this case independence itself has to be seen as the coronation of the postcolonial state of mind and not as the beginning of it. Nonetheless, even though the Yale critic of Pakistani origin Sara Suleri understandably manifests her irritation at being endlessly labeled as postcolonial (she asks, in fact, "when will we cease to be treated as an otherness machine?"[11]), the term retains a useful quality. It critically demarcates the realignment of hegemonies that are far from being undermined.

For these reasons, the concept of postcolonialism will be abandoned as a self-contained and descriptive concept, and shifted towards its use as an analytic and discriminatory tool. By indicating the trajectory from global to local in theory and literature, the focus here will be on the present capacity of transnational cultures to open up to new possible visions for the future. Thus the term will be used both in its strictly historical specificity, as the Indian critic Aijaz Ahmad does, and in its transhistorical mode, which addresses new global dimensions as Gayatri Spivak does. The qualification of the *post* is intended both as epistemological and as chronological, but most importantly as an indicator of the transformations at stake in global dynamics.

Despite the monumental contribution of postcolonial theorizing to subverting and displacing simplifying dichotomies between metropolitan centers and colonial peripheries—with the alleged cultural stereotypes and biased representations—post-colonial practices inherently reinstate the binary oppositions upon which its critique is constructed. The risk of postcolonialism becoming a self-referential category is very much alive today. The risk lies in the cross citations of major thinkers and key issues, often leading to pure misinterpretation or misreading, which become disengaged from specific and situated analyses. It furthermore consists in the over theorizing of identity issues, which often leads to empty rhetoric with no clear and direct political impact and which dangerously deprives minority groups of their language of oppression and impinges upon a more activist side of postcolonial raison d'être.

Furthermore, the self-celebratory character of postcolonialism's innovative force often leads instead to the use of a highly inflated jargon that is obscure not only to people within the field, but also to those subaltern subjects who are supposedly the main agents of the whole postcolonial enterprise. This last aspect, the huge gap between intellectual discourse and the "postcolonial natives," has provoked most of the reiterated reprimands against the legitimacy of postcolonial studies, whose high level of theoretical sophistication often leads to frustration even among its proselytes. In fact, some Third World intellectuals have made postcolonial issues their very own warhorse so as to obtain prominent positions within Western academia. In so doing they become complicit with the Western establishment they set out to undermine, and they exploit the cause of truly disenfranchised minority groups for their own reward.

Scholars such as Arif Dirlik write, in fact, that the term *postcolonial* is part of a poststructuralist, postfoundationalist discourse:

> Deployed mainly by displaced Third World intellectuals making good in prestige "Ivy League" American universities and deploying the fashionable language of the linguistic and cultural "turn" to "rephrase" Marxism, returning it "to another First World language with universalistic epistemological pretensions."[12]

However, Dirlik adds an interesting twist to the material/epistemological debate by being one of the first critics to remind us of the necessary connection between postcolonialism and global capitalism. This related argument is more substantial, and it focuses on the fact that "postcolonial" grossly underplays "capitalism's structuring of the modern world."[13] Post-colonial discourse, he says blankly, is a "culturalism."[14] He agrees with the critics who attack postcolonialism as relying too heavily on literature and creating a "discourse" that shrinks to "texts" (Loomba, 1998: 96), meaning that textuality dominates social analyses and relies too much on its formulaic nature. The refrain lurking within these recent critiques of the term is linked to the extreme flexibility of the term *postcolonial* which has come to function as a fashionable commodity in itself. This is also linked to the prominent position in its deployment of academic intellectuals of Third World origin who, in the name of postcolonial critique, have come to act as pace setters in cultural criticism.

While some of the attacks against postcolonialism are petulant and tiresome, others are constructive and account, in part, for the renewal of postcolonialism. To the first category belongs a quarrel generated by a highly competitive academic market that instigates its own ritualized battlefield. These attacks are critically inconsistent because they conflate postcolonial categories of thought with biographical reductionism and would therefore better be positioned in the realm of celebrity tabloids than serious academic journals. However, to the second category belongs a critique of great relevance since it refers to the implicit question of authenticity, of who is entitled to speak for whom as a "competent informant" (Spivak, 1999: 330), and who can translate the double inscription of empire to the world at large.

This more serious critique concerns the overlooked role that capitalism plays in the rearticulation of global dynamics. The harshest criticism as stated comes from those postcolonial critics of Marxist orientation who blame a particular strand of postcolonial thinking for embracing the post-structuralist linguistic turn and thereby for turning the postcolonial agenda into a mere intellectual exercise with no historically informed and politically motivated referents. Postcolonialism resonates with the conceptual needs of global relations caused by the shift of the world capitalist economy and must therefore address the increased complexity both at a theoretical and political level. But how fair is it to blame the whole postcolonial caravan for such disregard? Is the focus on globalization supposed to emblematize postcolonialism's swansong, or is it on the contrary its regenerative force? Many postcolonial critics have already inflected their analyses with a serious evaluation of the internationalization of financial markets and information flows (Arjun Appadurai, 1996; Saskia Sassen, 1999; Gayatri Spivak, 1999; Manuel Castells, 2000).

The study of colonization as an event of global significance is essential for various reasons: first, for the understanding of the current restructuring of capitalism as a global force and the role of multinational corporations; second, for the understanding of the impact of migration as a form of human movement that is not only dictated by transculturation and hybridization of identities but also by the relocation of labor forces; and third, for the understanding of the impact of digitalization and new media technologies that lead to the construction of new virtual communities. Globalization therefore must be seen as a historically informed momentum that finds its source in colonial relations, though its increased complexities are no longer reducible to colonial divisions, if they ever were. Critics such as Gayatri Spivak (1999), Chandra Talpade Mohanty (1991), and Anne McClintock (1997) have not only reiterated the importance of postcolonial thinking for the critique of new neocolonial formations, but also the crucial role that gender plays in the rearticulation of difference at a global level. Feminism has played a monumental role in the postcolonial rethinking of crucial categories of thought such as marginality, agency, and voice.

This self-criticism signals not the need to abandon postcolonialism as an outdated frame of analysis too engrossed in its colonial nostalgia. It signals instead the need to reorient postcolonialism towards more pressing issues dictated by transnational economies, issues that are usually only partly considered under new headings such as multiculturalism, globalization studies, ethnic minority studies, or Third World development studies. In the past the sociological import clearly overshadowed the cultural significance of postcolonial literatures. Countering this imbalance requires a new analysis capable of dealing with both the text and its cultural contexts, as intersections in time and space and not as fixed entities, and revising categories of interpretation, evaluation, and categorization along new unprecedented routes.

Given the anxiety surrounding the term *postcolonial* here, the focus will be on detecting deviations or certain inner contradictions that could make the term more productive and politically responsible while also making it reflect the existing dissymmetrical relationships. High profile is therefore given to the internal imbalances present within the postcolonial discourse itself. This consists in rejecting postcolonialism as a monolithic discourse and embracing it as a succession of multiple histories linked to the shifts in the world capitalist economy. The comparison between female writers of the Indian diaspora and Italian female writers from the Horn of Africa attempts such a detour and re-routing. The comparison of these authors across their significant differences is grounded in their common historical experience of colonization and life in the diaspora as gendered racialized subjects negotiating local values and global identifications.

LITERARY INTERSECTIONS

An analytical approach to postcolonialism has a double binding function. On the one hand, the postcolonial framework brings two streams of diasporic women's writings under the same spectrum of analyses in their commonalities. On the other hand, it emphasizes the internal contradictions, thereby highlighting how cautiously postcolonialism must be used in order to be employed at all.

We should not forget Stuart Hall's warning that "societies are not post-colonial in the same way and . . . in any case the post-colonial does not operate on its own but is in effect a construct internally differentiated by its intersections with other unfolding relations."[15] Hall goes on to explain that a more careful discrimination is needed between different social and racial formations. The result is that countries like India or Eritrea are not postcolonial in the same way.

Hall's statement is crucial to understanding the nonmonolithic aspect of postcolonialism while acknowledging its indisputable capacity to address a wide range of shared topics, not only concerning the peripheries of the empire but also the very heart of it. It is from this angle that the differences and convergences between British and Italian colonialism will be analyzed—differences and convergences that have created very different postcolonial conditions, but that remain postcolonial nonetheless.

The focus therefore is on the literary production by two specific streams of postcolonial women writers: an established collection and a new corpus. This comparison highlights how power relations are dispersed and contradictory. Focusing on women writers is important because the issue of gender has not been sufficiently analyzed in the definition of transnational identity. From a comparison between the more polished, flamboyant work by women of the Indian diaspora and the scattered, embryonic production by Afro-Italian migrant women writers, gender emerges as an analytical category in different historical and spatial locations. The outcome is a dissymmetrical rearticulation of gender with other axes such as colonial history, language, and condition of transnationalism.

This approach is in itself clearly both conventional and contentious. On the one hand, it is in line with most traditional aspects of feminist studies. It reassesses and reevaluates omitted and misrecognized women's writings by endorsing gender analysis and by constructing alternative feminist genealogies. On the other hand, at the same time that is is reinforced, the traditional approach of discovering and assessing female voices is also dismantled. This practice of subversion within strategies of restitution is conveyed by showing first that postcolonial women's writings recreate hierarchies of power within themselves (which is their criticism of colonial and patriarchal dominion), and second that other minor postcolonial female literatures, such as Italophone writings, open up spaces that have been resistant both to feminism and canonical literatures such as the Italian. This space of resistance allows people of "lesser" traditions to acquire agency to express their creativity.

DIASPORA

Because of these cultural transitions, changes in space have become more important than transitions in time. While in modernism the element of time was central (its fragmentation, the celebration of nonlinearity, time as chronology [*chronos*] as different from the personal time in the stream of consciousness [*kairos*]),[16] in our postmodern era, time becomes ancillary to the much more dominant and expansive notion of space. According to Fredric Jameson, our psychic experience and our cultural languages are today dominated by categories of space rather than the modernist categories of time.[17]

Space can nowadays be easily manipulated or contracted thanks to technology, forms of transport, and mass tourism, and as a consequence boundaries and territories become blurred. Different spaces begin to overlap with each other as terrains become scattered and fragmented. The notion of memory (as in Virginia Woolf or Proust) is overshadowed by a proliferation of space-bound metaphors that express the existential and emotional distress of uprooted and migrant people. Notions such as diaspora (Avtar Brah, Stuart Hall, Paul Gilroy, Lavie Smadar, Ted Swedenborg, Elazar Barkan), borderlands (Anzaldua), edges (hooks), margins (Spivak), in-betweeness (Bhabha), rhizome (Deleuze), exile (Said), and nomadic subject (Braidotti) all emphasize theories of space as a way of describing the postmodern condition. But they are also called upon to express the exhilarating and exciting experience of global travelers, privileged cosmopolitans, and jet setters. Within the category of literary diaspora the two senses—distress and elation—seem to merge. Playing out between center and periphery, the literatures of the diaspora naturally highlight many of the conflicts and paradoxes that characterize our "global village," proclaiming affiliation with the global while asserting their representation of the local.

The notion of diaspora is used here not only to detect postnational spaces—which allows people of "lesser traditions" to emerge—but also to trigger many postulates of postcolonialism as a totalizing discourse.[18] Its specificity with respect to other spatial tropes consists in retaining its implications both as a concrete history of dispersal and expropriation (Jewish, African, Indian) and as a transhistorical mode that expresses a cultural and intellectual stance with respect to nationhood, citizenship, and metropolitan assimilation. New conceptual maps need, in fact, to be drawn in order to account for the erosion between the nation-state and new cultural hybrid identities.[19]

The old idea of diaspora has become a very viable concept to express the state of minorities and migrants. Thus the notion of diaspora allows to connect concrete past histories of colonization to modern global phenomena of migration. This requires the intersection of postcolonialism with the politics dictated by multinational capitalism.

However, before making this connection, it is necessary to sketch a brief review of the historical nature of the term *diaspora*. Originally the term diaspora referred to the collective trauma caused by the banishment and exile of Jewish communities. In a second stage the word also came to signify the dispersal and genocide of Armenians and the coercive uprooting of African people for slavery. More recently, the term has marked the condition of indentured labor in the previous century. This concerns, for example, Indian people enrolled as a work force, once slavery was abolished, to build railways or to work on the plantations in other British colonies. There are also other forms of diaspora such as the imperial diasporas, trade diasporas (Chinese and Lebanese), and cultural diasporas, as in the case of the Caribbean, which is considered the multi-ethnic site par excellence since different forms of diaspora (slavery, imperial, indentured labor, and trade) have intertwined there.

In our late millennium, diaspora has assumed a postmodern tint. It evokes globalized and transnational forces of world economy, international migrations, global cities, cosmopolitism and localism, and deterritorialized social identities. It is therefore a term that can account for "multiple subject positions," as Homi K. Bhabha (1994, 269–72) and Avtar Brah (1996) write, since we need to focus on interstitial moments and processes where difference is articulated. In this respect, postcoloniality and diaspora are synonymous terms since both express aspects of placement and displacement. Postcoloniality emphasizes the global rearticulation of nations and cultures after a condition of colonization, whereas diaspora emphasizes a territorial scattering of national identity throughout human history.

Both terms are encompassed in the notion of migrant literature, a literature that is "unhomely," and this very quality of dispossession—a kind of haunting by otherness—is migrant literature's great strength (Bernheimer, 1995: 8). However, the mobility of the mind allowed by the phenomenon of migration, and with it a separation from tradition and obligations, is not a process devoid of pain and alienation. The problem of occupying a cusp between tradition and modernism, past and present, or peripheries and cosmopolitan life, is the quintessential chore of diasporic people. The phenomenon of diaspora calls for reimagining postcolonial area studies and developing units of analysis that enable us to understand the dynamics of transnational culture and economic processes, as we challenge the conceptual limits imposed by national and ethnic/racial boundaries.[20]

Stuart Hall (1992), for example, describes the result of this process as producing "cultures of hybridity" since cultural identities are emerging that are "in transition," drawing on different traditions at the same time without assimilation or total loss of the past. Therefore, the growth of these cultures within new diasporas created by the colonial experience and the ensuing postcolonial migrations are very central to the postmodern debate.

However, the critic Kevathi Krishnaswamy rightly warns about the "excessive figurative flexibility (of) the metaphorization of post-colonial migrancy (which) is becoming so overblown, overdetermined, and amorphous as to repudiate any meaningful specificity of historical location or interpretation" (Krishnaswamy, 1995: 128). Krishnaswamy is afraid of too easy a fusion between postmodernism and postcolonialism that would empty politically charged words such as "exile" and "diaspora" of their histories of pain and allow them to be deployed to express a wide array of cross-cultural phenomena. He fears that difference would be reduced to equivalence, and syncretism interchanged with diversity, leveling the subversive subalternity in any and all. However, he agrees that the "figure of migrancy indeed has proved quite useful in drawing attention to the marginalized, in problematizing conceptions of borders, and in critiquing the politics of power" (Krishnaswamy, 1995: 128).

In order to preserve subalternity and avoid simplifications the postcolonial authors analyzed here are positioned within the debate on diaspora according to their contribution to the reproduction of hierarchies.

POLITICS OF LANGUAGE

For the writers who straddle two or more cultures, such as those in the diaspora, the language used for creative purposes is of the utmost importance. The use of one colonial language instead of another in diasporic writings conveys an immediate hierarchical relocation of literature. Writers in English can rely on a broad network and on a vast readership, whereas Afro-Italian writers risk being doubly erased by colonial policy and by neocolonial powers that privilege English in the new global economic transactions.

For our purpose it is very important to remember Italian Marxist Antonio Gramsci's concept of hegemony and how it can be applied to the analysis of postcolonial reproduction of hierarchies. The most vexed questions arising from the comparative approach presented here are connected to the use of alter*native* languages as a way of both reframing the globally known category of the postcolonial and outlining dissymmetrical relocations of cultures. Gramsci formulated the notion of hegemony as being achieved via a combination of "force" and "consent" and therefore cutting through social classes.

Some writers and theorists of Marxist orientation have argued that African literature, for example, must be written in indigenous African languages to resist linguistic colonization. One of the most famous cases is provided by the Kenyan writer Ngugi wa Thiong'o who chose to stop writing in English, turned to Gikuyo "to decolonize the mind" (Wa Thiong'o, 1986) from the ideological apparatus of empire, and used the vernacular as a political act of resistance.[21]

For the postcolonial debate the issue of language is a rather irksome one, since it has served as a site of controversy even as it remains postcolonialism's most exciting and stimulating aspect. The focus of this comparison is to show how writers who use different languages, English and Italian, generate different impacts and consequences for the revision of the literary canon, the empowerment of Third World women, and the relocation of cultural centers. These effects occur because language encodes power relations, a vital assumption explored by Gramsci.

Gramsci analyzed the political character of language and accents. Language conveys power differences, and this is made apparent, according to Gramsci, in the attempt of the dominant class to create a common cultural climate through the imposition of a national language. Linguistic hegemony involves the articulation of signs and symbols that tend to codify and reinforce the dominant viewpoint:

> Thus, Gramsci argued that there existed a close relationship between linguistic stratification and social hierarchization, in that the various dialects and accents found within a given society are always rank-ordered as to their perceived legitimacy, appropriateness, and so on. Accordingly, concrete language usage reflects underlying asymmetrical power relations and it registers profound changes which occur in the cultural, moral, and political worlds. . . . Gramsci also felt that the maintenance of regional dialects helped peasants and workers partially to resist the forces of political and cultural hegemonies.[22]

Transferring Gramsci's discourse on Italian regional accents (with particular reference to his native Sardinia and the Italian South) to world languages, we can detect the profound political character of postcolonialism as a mainly

Anglocentric discourse. It also highlights the role of the English language as the most powerful protractor of the imperial hegemony. The British Empire was, in fact, not only the most expansive as far as settlement and penetration was concerned, but also the one with the greatest linguistic impact. Imperialism has laid the groundwork for globalization by making English the lingua franca for international exchange. The role of English as the world's leading language is not only to be attributed to the extensions of the British Empire and its minutiose enterprise in the organization of schooling and institutionalization in English, but also to the neo-imperialist role of the United States, technically speaking also a former British colony. This intersection between colonial aftermath and capitalistic neo-imperialism has definitely established English as the normative international language (with all its ideological implications) and thereby rendered the other languages minorities (called "dialects" in Gramsci's analysis). This is demonstrated by the monolinguistic discussion which has taken place around postcolonialism. Not only is the language of the "empire (that) writes back to the centre" (Salman Rushdie: 1982: 8) English, but the literature analyzed for the demolition of the Western canon is also in English. However, the postcolonial asset is widely differentiated as far as colonial aftermaths and linguistic heritages are concerned. Using the English language as a medium of communication, for example, definitely provides more possibilities than using other minor, formerly imperial languages such as Portuguese, Italian, or Dutch, to offer few examples. Within the postcolonial discourse of resistant thinking the literatures expressed in English grant themselves the privilege of attracting wider interest, a global readership, and the support of international publishing houses located in strategic cosmopolitan centers such as London, New York, New Delhi, and Toronto. These possibilities go hand in hand with the garnering of flashy international literary prizes (such as the Nobel Prize, Booker Prize, Commonwealth Prize, Pulitzer Prize, and Neustadt Prize for Literature[23]) and the corresponding media coverage and critical reviews. The locations that use English are not only the ex-colonial centers but also neocolonial ones, like the United States.[24]

In India, for example, despite the strength of nationalism, English continued as a literary language after independence, and it remained the official language along with Hindi. Although the use of English is mainly confined to the middle classes, it can cross regional boundaries to address a national—albeit élite—audience. Yet, many argue that English has effectively been "Indianized" or "nativised" through the incorporation of vocabulary, idiom, and even syntax from the regional languages since most writers are bilingual or trilingual. The "E" English, as the Queen's English is called, or Standard Received English (SRE),[25] has been transformed into many "englishes," and the small "e" is used to identify all the forms of english spoken in former colonies and around the world. In India it becomes Indian-english, or Hinglish (Hindi-English), or

Benglish (Bengali-English), or Englees (basic English). This is the silent subversive strategy adopted by Anglo-Indian writers to get rid of the label "Made as England," Rushdie's pun to express the uncritical cultural adhesion of the Indian élite to the British model. Furthermore, many people in India prefer to use English rather than Hindi as a vehicular language. The latter is, in fact, imposed by the central government in Delhi upon the many other regional languages such as Urdu, Bengali, Tamil, Malayalam, Telegu, or Marathi. Therefore, paradoxically enough, English, the language of the masters, acquires a resistant and subversive function within India since it is used by the minority groups against the hegemonizing role of the central state.

However, English not only has a subversive function within India but also within the British literary canon. This proliferation of "englishes" mimic, as Bhabha would say, the language of the master, depriving it of its original political and ideological supremacy. Through the abrogation and appropriation of the English language Anglo-Indian writers enact a strategy of cultural decolonization. The very survival of Royal English as such becomes tied to certain classes as opposed to the more lively and creative use of English among the so-called social marginalities who through linguistic adaptation and metamorphosis reinvent the very notion of the English language. This reinvention can be seen in the explosion of literature in English from Scotland, Ireland, and Wales.

This analysis of the "englishes within" has shifted the center of the debate from the monopolistic function of British English to other imperial languages. The success of the Indian Women Writers tradition, for example, has directed attention towards the emergence of new forms of literary antagonism that were more hidden, since they concerned writers who were less articulate and less capable of standing up for their own rights. The shift in Indian diasporic literature mentioned here, from minor towards major literature, has allowed Indian writers to increasingly reterritorialize their identity by deterritorializing that of the dominant group. For example, the work of Hanif Kureshi around race and postcoloniality explores the complex mechanism of politics, sexuality, culture, race, and capital in the British-Pakistani diaspora, articulating his hybridity and deconstructing the concept of Britishness. The achievement of major status of some postcolonial literatures—read "Anglo-Indian literature"—has left the position of minority status vacant. This has been filled by those struggling minorities (other postcolonialities, other women, other ethnicities) who, thanks to the successful struggle already carried out by previously minor postcolonial literatures that have become major, can now shine in reflected light and claim a literary authority of their own.

It is therefore time to analyze how other minor colonial languages, such as Italian, are affected by the emerging postcolonial literature. The different linguistic policy followed by the Italian government during its colonization of the Horn of Africa and the modalities of decolonization in those countries partly explain the huge gap between the time of Italian colonization at the beginning of the twentieth century and the emergence of the Italian postcolonial literature only at the end of the same century, fifty years after independence. The diffusion of the Italian language at the institutional level was hardly encouraged during the period of colonialism. Schooling in Italian was furthermore prohibited for the natives after they reached the fifth grade. So unlike the British prolonged educational system in India, the Italian system imposed the language only at a superficial level. In contrast, in Eritrea, the *colonia primogenita* (first born), which had structurally been under Italian influence since 1880, the use of Italian was wide spread and even today elderly people speak it with great fluency. After the defeat of the Italians in Africa in 1941, Eritrea became a British protectorate, and in 1962 after a much contested and fatal U.N. treaty, it was annexed to Ethiopia as one of its sixteen provinces. The Mengistu dictatorial Marxist regime completely eradicated the use of the Italian language in Eritrea, since it symbolized Eritrea's independent status (a nation that was created by the Italians through the colonization of territories historically belonging to Ethiopia) and Eritrea's sense of cultural superiority, which was in partly due to the Italian infrastructural investments in the area. Therefore, there is no continuity in the Italian linguistic colonial legacy, especially for the younger generations who are those who usually migrate to Italy. This history explains the belated emergence of an Italian postcolonial tradition. Immigrants from the Horn of Africa must often learn the language from scratch, and thus a consistent and self-confident tradition can only be expected from a second or third generation of immigrants, as was the case in the United States with the emergence of an Italo-American literary tradition.

Writers from Africa have just begun to write down their existential experience in Italian, often using French as an intermediary language. The fragile identity which characterizes these Afro-Italian writings is destined to slowly change the character of Italian literature from monolinguistic towards multilinguistic and multicultural. Derogatory terms like *vu cumpra* (would you like to buy), referring to immigrant sellers on the Italian sidewalks who cannot speak without an accent, are destined to be replaced by a plurality of accents, not only from the south, as Gramsci's resistant strategy proposes, but from many other cultural heritages.

The goal of this book is therefore to bring to light how hegemonic structures recompose themselves within the postcolonial debate, and to show how the shift in power continues to privilege some cultures to the detriment of others. Hidden within the subversive discourse of postcolonialism are structures of power that need to be detected and analyzed. Hegemonies are relational, and within the postcolonial debate, which distinguishes itself by its oppositional politics, its anti-hegemonic struggle, and democratization process, there are hierarchies of power. These reproduce themselves not only in the relation between center and peripheries, colonizers and ex-colonized, but also among margins, among minorities, and among different peripheries and different ex-colonized subjects, producing not a leveling of hierarchies but, on the contrary, a relocation of hegemonies.

Therefore, within the postcolonial discourse the issue of language is of paramount importance in establishing lateral thinking that avoids easy forms of replicating literary canonization and cultural colonization.

MINORITY LITERATURE

> How many people live today in a language which is not their own?
> —Deleuze and Guattari, Kafka, Toward a Minor Literature,
> 1986, p. 19

Deleuze and Guattari's influential essay "What Is a Minor Literature?"[26] (originally published in 1975) offers a valuable strategy for the assessment of the relocations of hegemonies in literature. It provides a way of evaluating the writings of immigrants with respect to the major tradition since they "live today in a language which is not their own" (p. 19). This minor status, which becomes major, is due to their ability to reinvent tradition and to challenge the major groups by inviting them to "become a nomad and an immigrant and a gipsy in relation to (their) own language" (p. 19).

Deleuze and Guattari's conceptualization of minority literature is a powerful tool for the debate on postcolonialism because it positions literature politically. In fact, the term *minority literature* accounts for what Gramsci would define as a political positionality, according to which minority is not 'given' but constructed. Consequently, as Stuart Hall also argues,

> political positionalities are not fixed and do not repeat themselves from one historical situation to the next or from one theatre of antagonism to another, ever 'in place', in an endless iteration. Isn't that the shift from politics as a 'war of manoeuvre' to politics as a 'war of position', which Gramsci long ago, and decisively, charted?[27]

This achieved awareness leads us here to explore the issues of gender and location in a diasporic perspective as an example of Deleuze and Guattari's claim that "minor literature doesn't come from a minor language, it is rather that which a minority constructs within a major language" (p. 16). In this regard postcolonial writers become part of a minor literature, if we consider the British literary canon as major. As a result of different linguistic and colonial policies the emerging

Afro-Italian tradition assumes the role of a minority literature within the context of Anglophone postcolonial literatures and is therefore subversive towards the dominant postcolonial canon.

In order to apply Deleuze and Guattari's conceptualization of minority literature to this postcolonial reappraisal, it is necessary to shift their analysis of Kafka (and his relation to German literature) to Italian migrant writings. Reading Afro-Italian writing within a minority literature framework highlights its double binding relation with respect, first, to the Italian canonical literature and, second, to other postcolonial established literature, such as the Anglo-Indian literature discussed here.

The condition of Italophone writings, in fact, positions itself according to different axes of minority status. As Deleuze has emphasized, "minority" is not an expression of less value but is a figuration for resistance and subversion within the establishment, a position which is inhabited or must be searched for in order to be able to express creativity and innovation.

According to Deleuze and Guattari

> the three characteristics of minor literature are the deterritorialization of language, the connection of the individual to a political immediacy, and the collective assemblage of enunciation. (p. 18)

Deterritorialization refers both to the position of the writers (outside their homeland and using a language not their own) and to their extreme modes of expression (either excessive and inflated, in the manner of James Joyce, or sparse and intensified, in the manner of Franz Kafka). The *emphasis on politics* affirms that in a minor literature individual dramas become political rather than Oedipal as in a great literature. *Collective values* refers to the writer's terrain where utterances reflect a community's usage, rather than being sharply individuated.

> We might as well say that minor no longer designates specific literatures but the revolutionary conditions for every literature within the heart of what is called great (or established) literature. (p. 18)

Deleuze and Guattari based their theory on the study of Kafka, who was a dislocated Jew writing in German and living in Prague. In this sense Kafka is representative of minor literature because his language is "affected by a high coefficient of deterritorialization" (p. 16). The element of deterritorialization for Prague Jews was dictated by the impossibility of their writing other than in German, which marked their distance from their primitive Czech territoriality and from the German mainstream. Furthermore being Jews and writing in German also meant their deterritorialization from Hebrew and from a religious and ethnic belonging. It is in this sense that Prague German "is a deterritorialized language, appropriate for strange and minor use" (p. 17).

For Deleuze and Guattari Kafka constitutes the quintessential example of a minor writer since he positioned himself on the margin of the great tradition of German literature in order to express another consciousness and another sensibility from "within" the German language, a language which even when "major is open to an intensive utilization that makes it take flight along creative lines of escape" (p. 26). Deleuze and Guattari plead, therefore, for a writer who should become a "stranger within his own language" since "There is nothing that is major or revolutionary except the minor" (p. 26). Deleuze and Guattari compare the appropriation of the German language by the Jews with what the blacks in America today are able to do with the English language.

The relocation of postcolonial literatures should be interpreted as being part of a minority literature that is locked in the impossibility of writing otherwise and the necessity of turning English into a deterritorialized language. It is what Deleuze and Guattari envisage as the intense utilization of language such as Joyce did with English and Beckett did with French. While Joyce operated through exhilaration and overdetermination, thereby bringing about all sorts of reterritorialization, Beckett proceeded with dryness and sobriety, pushing deterritorialization to such an extreme that nothing remains but intensities (p. 19). Many postcolonial literatures could be reinscribed along these lines of how excessively or aridly they appropriate English.

However, Deleuze and Guattari's theorization of minor literature falls short. The intricacy of gender-related issues in the appropriation of language and the political accountability of ethnic groups forced to express themselves in the so-called minor language is not a process devoid of pain and alienation. The celebration of all minorities as productive and creative runs the risk of an irresponsible radicalism that homogenizes the differences among them and levels them into a mass of struggling groups of all the same value. Deleuze and Guattari do not glamorize minorities, nor do they reduce the complexity of the concept of minor literature to a static and fixed notion. Minor literature is a dialogic process; it is that element of subversion and uneasiness within language that eventually creates "great literatures," expropriating the mainstream literatures from their throne of canonicity.

It is nonetheless necessary to highlight the relativity within the concept of minor literature because what can be minor in a certain context can become major in another. Some literatures, defined as minor and deterritorialized, can operate as dominant and colonizing towards others: according to Anne McClintock, "While some countries may be 'post-colonial' with respect to their erstwhile European masters, they may not be 'post-colonial' with respect to their new neighbors" (1995: 13). McClintock refers to East Timor, a Portuguese colony which fell straight into the claws of Indonesia after independence and was recognized by the U.N. as an official separate state only in 2002. In her admonition on translating Third World texts Spivak also warns that "what seems resistant in the space of English maybe reactionary in the space of the original language" (1992: 188). The focus here is on the relationship between minorities, with the unstated implication that to be minor is glamorous. As this assumption is not always conscious and visible, it is important to argue for a relocation of cultures and literatures in which certain persisting hierarchies of power are highlighted and assessed.

This privileging of minority status is apparent in the critical acclaim and commercial success that writers in English from the territories of the ex-empire are achieving. They overshadow the traditional British canon to such an extent that Britain has rushed to include writers such as Salman Rushdie and Ben Okri as part of the mainstream of British literature. The effect is to deny them the element of subversion and competition that they would have if they were seen as minor or postcolonials. Making them part of the canon can only bring to light the emergence of other subaltern groups who are called upon to fulfill the role of minority. If certain writers are recognized as British, they have undergone not only a process of canonization but also of normalization. It is in this light that other postcolonial literatures, which are part of Deleuze and Guattari's concept of minor literatures, will be here addressed. Postcolonial literatures in Italian, for example, show the process of reterritorializing the Italian language from a position as outsider. The revolutionary impact of these writers from the ex-colonies is just beginning to show its mark.

What should have been an equal position of minority, on the basis of the experience of colonization, of migration towards the country of the colonizer, and of appropriation of language, becomes instead a highly dissymmetrical field. The hegemony of English as a vehicular language makes a dominant relation that makes the writing from the Italian colonies both dispossessed and deterritorialized: first, towards the Italian language and literature that these authors have adopted in their migration and second, towards English which is the language to be tackled and the literature to be referred to when aspiring to a wider international audience.

This layering of minority status in literature can be brought into perspective by the gender issues that cut across differences of colonialism, language, and literature. Even though sharing the same gender does not make women equal, there are still some vital elements that connect women across nationalities. This is especially evident when women try to articulate their experience of migration from former colonies towards new Western cosmopolitan centers. The differences are due to their individual diversity and to their rather different backgrounds and histories. However, issues related to writing as a postcolonial dislocated woman, their being "out-of-country and out-of-language," as Rushdie would phrase it (1981: 4), link their diverse local and personal experiences through a universal anxiety that transcends individual differences.

Following Deleuze and Guattari's definitions of minor literatures, it emerges that Afro-Italian literatures, or new immigrants' literatures, are only in the primordial stage of minority, whereas the Anglo-Indian tradition has strongly redeemed itself from the status of minority asserting itself against the British tradition as it has gained worldwide attention. Their security in the use of the English language, their mastery of the different literary genres, their access to various expatriate communities that can guarantee them quick integration and contact with publishing houses, and their extreme productivity (one thousand million citizens, not all literate, but even the élite of a quarter of the earth is more than the population of the Eritrean state) has made the Indian postcolonial literature an international success that is able to replicate its appeal due to its established familiarity.

The very fact that these writings have become major in English implies the emergence of other minor literatures once neglected and doubly marginalized, such as writings by women and other ethnicities different from those just mentioned, or writings expressed in minor ex-imperial languages such as Italian. This hierarchical motion demonstrates that the old imperial system is still at work, and that the minority discourse is a pluralistic terrain with internal differences that are neither symmetric nor equally represented.

THE POLITICS OF LOCATION

It is by now very clear that postcolonial rearticulations have not removed colonialism's inherent hierarchy. On the contrary, it has been replaced with more subtle systems of subordination and subjugation. In a multilingual global world, some postcolonialists perpetuate their hegemony and create power structures between languages. However, this hegemonic relationship is neither fixed nor stable and varies according to geopolitical factors. In diaspora, that reason, should unite writers of different origins under the postnational space of migration. It instead heightens these dissymmetries and the axes of gender, ethnicity, class, cast, age, and sexual preference need more careful articulation in order to be assessed in their specificity.

That the women writers here under scrutiny are all diasporic does not mean that they are diasporic in the same ways. A very complex filigree of national and international affiliations must be established in order to analyze each in her own right and not just as part of a cluster under the comprehensive term of diaspora. It is necessary to heed Spivak's warning that

Sometimes Indian women writings mean American women writing or British women writing, except for national *origin*. There is an ethnocultural agenda, an obliteration of Third World specificity as well as a denial of cultural citizenship, in calling them merely "Indian."[28]

Consequently, the condition of migrancy sharply emphasizes many of the paradoxes that are implicit in the assumed notion of what a gendered identity should be. In many of the works by female writers of the African and Indian diaspora, the issue of old and new home recurs frequently. The hyphenated identity created by a "mobilization of home," an expression that captures the issue of rooted dislocation, has equipped these authors with particular linguistic tools, ranging from the traditional to the experimental.

As a result we get a sense that the stories most capable of unraveling new global realities are from people from the fringes, as if experiences of marginalization, economic exploitation, and cultural expropriation could better express the implications of rapid transformation. As Homi Bhabha writes,

> A range of contemporary cultural theories suggest that it is from those who have suffered the sentence of history—subjugation, domination, diaspora, displacement—that we learn our most enduring lessons for living and thinking. There is even a growing conviction that the effective experience of social marginality—as it emerges in non-canonical cultural forms—transforms our critical strategies. It forces us to confront the concept of culture outside objects d'art or beyond the canonization of the 'idea' of aesthetics, to engage with culture as an uneven, incomplete production of meaning and value, often composed of incommensurable demands and practices, produced in the act of social survival.[29]

According to Bhabha the experience of social marginalization, which often accompanies the process of diasporization, makes the difficulty of writing as a woman, and of writing as a postcolonial woman in an era of cultural transition, all the more acute.

However, we should be wary of too facile a celebration of uprootedness and multiplicity of margins. Such celebrations have been criticized for leading to the conclusion that we are all decentered, marginalized, *métisse*, mestiza, and diasporic in comparable ways. In this regard, feminist critics have called for a "politics of location" that assumes that we talk from our own situated point of view, which is bound, as Chandra Talpade Mohanty wrote,

> to the historical, geographic, cultural, psychic and imaginative boundaries which provide the ground for definition and self-definition . . . [L]ocation forces enable specific modes of reading and knowing the dominant.[30]

The politics of location therefore assumes a different set of values within recent feminist discourses. For example, Adrienne Rich struck a chord when she wrote that "my whiteness is a point of location for which I needed to take responsibility," or "a place on the map is also a place in history" (Rich, 1986: 219, 212). The location is not only spatial but also ideological. To avoid recreating a hegemonize position, women must specify the material and geopolitical condition from which they speak.

A materialized standpoint means being accountable for one own's vision, as described by Donna Haraway in her concept of situated knowledge. The problem is how to account for other people's experiences while remaining situated in our own vision. The problem becomes more complex in conditions of transnationalism where different realities intersect and enter into conflict, and the question of standpoint becomes more contradictory not only in relation to others but to the self:

> We would argue that the notion of the "post-colonial" is best understood in the context of a rigorous politics of location, of a rigorous conjuncturalism. There are, then, moments and spaces in which subjects are "driven to grasp" their positioning and subjecthood as "post-colonial"; yet there are other contexts in which to use the term as the organizing principle of one's analysis is precisely to "fail to grasp the specificity" of the location or the moment.[31]

The comparative approach presented here endorses a specific politics of location and affiliations. Each author is interpreted as being connected both to broader issues related to diaspora and transnationalism but also to local specific and situated realities.

This approach, therefore, does not presume a "collectivism" of differences, but on the contrary an "explosion" of multiplying differences. Despite falling under the cohesive label of the Indian or African diaspora, these authors resent any affiliation with such a cluster, since it limits them to the "competent representation" of their Indian or African backgrounds without accounting for the free open spaces that each author traces for her/himself and that exceed nation, allegation, and restriction. The strict specificity and individuality of each oeuvre must be respected and the autonomy and original achievements recognized within the vaster connections and aspirations.

Thus in order to locate the different discourses on comparative postcolonial female literature, this approach considers each itinerary as personal and embodied. Each of these writers employs and deploys strategies of home and homeliness to sketch her own literary odyssey which can be entangled or disentangled from the notion of Indianness, Africanness, or postcoloniality. They use and abuse different standpoints and sources, connect to and disconnect from the various discourses of feminism and postmodernity. They are thus writers in interaction with multiple locations and multiple subjectivities.

A NEW COMPARATIVISM?

In order to account for different historical dynamics, postcolonialism demands theoretical flexibility and an innovative approach. It is important therefore to exploit the interdisciplinary character of postcolonialism to the fullest by confronting it with disparate cultural and economic practices. As Prakash has written,

> Even as the three worlds collapse into one, this process does not mean erosion of difference but its rearticulation. . . . Clearly the internationalization of capital proceeds through these instances of differentiation and produces new global forms of unevenness, inequality, difference, and discrimination. The very same process, however, also renders capitalism open to subaltern pressures, to the pressure exerted by the forms and forces it subordinates.[32]

The comparative character of this book aims at establishing new frameworks that can account for different kinds of colonial contacts and for postcolonial multifariousness, but as Ania Loomba states, "this is not enough. We must also think about the relationships between hierarchies, between different forces and discourses" (Loomba, 1998: 240). Therefore, an explanation for the differences between the Afro-Italian and the Indian literatures is provided, thus extending Jameson's interrelation between postmodernism and late capitalism to postcolonialism.

To assess these divergences, it is necessary to explore how language, diaspora, and gender interact in the hegemonic relocations of culture. By accounting for these reformed hierarchies, postcolonialism becomes more than just a new academic badge. What is put forward here is not a discourse of non-European texts that contrast with or are a critical of European literature, but rather an interminority discourse in which texts coming from different margins enter into dialogue with each other. This is particularly vital from the point of view of transnational feminism because new coalition politics must be established which can guarantee solidarity and the respect of difference at the same time. As Teresa de Lauretis states,

> What is emerging in feminist writings is . . . the concept of multiple, shifting, and often self-contradictory identity . . . an identity made up of heterogeneous and heteronomous representations of gender, race and class, and often indeed across languages and cultures; an identity that one decides to reclaim from a history of multiple assimilations, and that one insists on as a strategy.[33]

To establish this terrain of conjuncturalist feminist writings a new form of comparativism will be tested here where different disciplinary fields, such as postcolonial theories, gender studies, and literary analysis are applied to very dissimilar backgrounds.

Due to the dissimilar backgrounds it is obvious that postcolonial literature in Italian (meaning the writings of African writers in Italian coming from the former Italian colonial territories in the Horn of Africa, Ethiopia, Eritrea and Somalia) is not comparable to the avalanche of literary production coming from India. Yet, this dissymmetry is not only necessary for a new comparative approach to postcolonialism but also essential for the epistemological reinterpretation of its precepts. In a way, analyzing the emerging postcolonial literature in Italian helps to retrace the whole postcolonial trajectory, to analyze the sources that have produced such a successful discipline, and to reframe it in its multiple histories. Since the colonial hangover is not homogeneously reflected in newly independent countries, postcolonialism cannot boast a holistic and exhaustive élan that can account for the complex geopolitical realities in the periphery, which are now at the center due to migration, exile, and diaspora. For example, the short-lived experience of the Italian colonial adventure in the Horn of Africa has left a far less coherent and analyzable condition of postcoloniality in the regions of interest than that left by the British in their colonies. Furthermore, the countermovement from the Italian colonies towards the center was a very belated one (for reasons that are discussed in chapter 6). The changing face of the Italian major cities due to immigration from the colonies became significant and visible only at the end of the twentieth-century, whereas metropolises such as London or Paris experienced the explosion of racial problems at the beginning of the 1960s.

This translateral approach to comparative literature has been defined as "anxiogenic" since it empowers comparatists to navigate through different expertise and disciplines, but at the same time provides no firm ground and no stable theory for its practice and delimitations. There is the anxiety, as Peter Brook fears, that seeing literature in the context of cultural studies will be a mistake if thereby the specificity of the aesthetic domain is lost. There is also the anxiety of identity politics: Where should the comparatist position him/herself? Is it enough to merely compare literatures without accounting for the eventual hegemonic relationship that exists among them? Is it correct to substitute a canon of European masterpiece with another canon of non-European works?

These works, moreover, may well be representative only of the dominant traditions in cultures that are themselves hegemonic in their geopolitical contexts. And isn't the entire multiculturalist model flawed by its tendency to essentialize those cultures, attributing to them far more unity, regularity and stability than they actually have? . . . A literary work can never authentically mirror a culture not only because that culture is not at one with itself but also because the work is a *literary* representation and hence not a transparent medium but a formal structure. Furthermore, the criterion of authenticity tends to equalize all cultures in a relativist haze and thereby destroys any possibility of differential judgments and comparison.[34]

Anxiety arises when comparative literature meets multicultural studies because the inherently pluralistic and comparative aspect of multiculturalism often approaches essentialist politics. As Henry Louis Gates phrased it, "the culturalist model normally imagines its constituent elements as cultural bubbles that may collide but that could, in principle, exist in splendid isolation from one another."[35] The anxiety of comparatists who intervene to break down this isolation concerns the problem of entitlement. Questions such as: "Do I have the right to speak about these cultures to which I don't belong?" arise especially for white people dealing with foreign or ethnic texts. As Gates says, "it seems that it is no longer enough for comparativists to speak different tongues: maybe they have to put on different skins as well."[36]

> The more literature you try to compare the more like a colonizing imperialist you may seem. If you stress what these literatures have in common—thematically, morally, politically—you may be accused of imposing a universalist model that suppresses particular differences. . . . If, on the other hand, you stress differences, then the basis of comparison becomes problematic, and your respect for the uniqueness of particular cultural formations may suggest the impossibility of any meaningful relation between cultures.[37]

This is, in short, Bernheimer's formulation of the problems in facing this comparative task. However, this danger is not only amply addressed but also made positive in this comparison. If we do not act as tourists in "alter/native cultures" but opt for a rigorous politics of location in which we are responsible for our visions, to recall Donna Haraway, then we can employ comparativism despite its contradictions and drawbacks, without the risk of becoming free-floating and disengaged.

By accounting for the aesthetic achievements of these texts—in terms of genre, voice, and style—in interaction with their cultural implications—questions of ideology, interpretation, and reception—this specific comparative endeavor undermines the rather canonical and stifling tradition that is based on a classical definition of literary aesthetic values and puts forward a new global aesthetics that supersedes national straight jackets.

Given these premises, Afro-Italian literature should not be dealt with as a "new literary etiquette," but used to build a provisional definition that can help to visualize the particularities of these dissymetrical literary projects. These texts may be unorthodox or experimental, but this approach is a groundbreaking move towards highlighting their interconnectedness, their position as integrated in a postcolonial tradition. Attempting a strategic dialogue along lines of marginalities that would at first glance not be naturally connected eliminates one of the interferences operated by dominant systems at the expense of more fragile expressions:

> Unable to sustain a seamless, autonomous selfhood of Otherness, some margins embarked on internal critiques of their own homogenization (Rutherford, 1990: 23–24). The center/margin dichotomy was undermined, and spaces opened up between center and margins. Due to the multiplicity of specific histories of oppression, several processes of center/margin dissolution could occur in various combinations. Some margins moved to the center. Some margins began to communicate with each other, without the center as interlocutor between them (Mohanty, 1991:11).[38]

This analysis establishes a dialogue among different margins, which share commonalities of issues such as gender, ethnicity and diasporicity. How these problems intersect with issues of nation, globalization and relocation of cultures is the center of the argumentation. Each author offers a personal negotiation of identity and cultural positioning within these intersections.

WRITING ACROSS WORLDS

This book compares authors of different nationalities, literary traditions, and linguistic backgrounds. Experiencing similar, though distinct postcolonial conditions, these female authors share the common experience of diaspora and the difficulty of negotiating new identities in a rapidly changing global world. The common space of diaspora is meant to show the areas of hybridization and cross-fertilization that lead to a possible interminority discourse and not to the recreation of colonial hierarchies.

The purpose of this comparative approach, therefore, is to juxtapose theoretical issues and narrative moods, more than to symmetrically oppose contents. It highlights a multiplicity of voices even as it shows a similarity of discourse among them. The contrasting yet intertwined theoretical approach has been broadly described in the previous sections. The necessity that postcolonial discourse be dominated by the English response and therefore destined to recreate cultural hierarchies along the British colonial order has been strongly undermined by showing how postcolonial categories can be used as indicative and not prescriptive. This approach positions postcolonial literature not only according to the metropolitan center/peripheries axis but also in the context of different peripheries, such as the case of Indian versus Afro-Italian diaspora. This does not imply the exclusion of the centers. On the contrary the issues of the diaspora are meant to emphasize how the center can only be envisioned according to multiple reference points that are linked to past colonial legacies and contemporary multicultural realities.

Here some of the comparative thematic issues at stake will be briefly illustrated in order to strengthen the connections within the differences. The selection of these female authors is in fact not a chance one but rather dictated by deep linkages among their experience of diaspora, gender, and interraciality. In order to show the interconnection that motivated the choice of these specific female narrators across geographies, linguistic, and historical background, a few itineraries for comparative readings will be sketched.

Though the book is divided in two parts, that does not mean that the parts stand alone from each other, nor that each individual chapter does not present links and connections to earlier and later chapters in the book. However, each novel is given a close reading in the light of the postcolonial and feminist theories required by its subject matter. This implies that each chapter can be read on its own even as it relies on the bigger context discussed in chapters 1 and 6, which position this study within the postcolonial debate and describe the innovative contribution of the Italian colonial experience to the postcolonial debate and to the Italian literary canon.

Issues of migration and uprooting are central to all the novels analyzed here. However, in Bharati Mukherjee's *Jasmine* (chapter 2), issues of gender and ethnicity become reinscribed in the condition of diaspora. Meena Alexander's *Fault Lines* (chapter 3) deals with the question of language in the condition of expatriation, showing that language must be tattooed on the body in order to present a feminist standpoint. This theme is very much linked to the subject raised by the Eritrean writer Ribka Sibhatu (chapter 8) in which language and writing become the utmost forms of resistance, both towards colonial and patriarchal oppression and towards the new hosting society where the new postcolonial self is the result of many forms of translation, at linguistic, physical, and figurative levels.

Sara Suleri inserts the important question of interraciality (chapter 4), as it undermines yet redefines the concept of nationhood from new subject positions. Very much in line with Maria Abbebù Viarengo's autobiography and Erminia dell'Oro's novel on miscegenation (chapter 7), Suleri explores the split loyalty of women in between races, nations, and languages in her unusual memoir. Diaspora becomes a soothing way of reconciling the split ends brought about by different ethnic heritages that are set in hierarchical relationships by colonial and patriarchal authority. Torn between the evasiveness of her Welsh mother and the hyperdefinition of her father's identity as dictated by Pakistani history, Suleri opts for an oblique positionality that can make her present yet removed from the national history of Pakistan. From her diasporic position that history can be rewritten from the female standpoint. Similarly, Maria Abbebù Viarengo deals with the past legacy of her Oromo mother, which has been denied her with her forced migration to Italy where her Piedmontese father decided she must go for a European education (in line both with the colonial and patriarchal authority). Similarly to Sara Suleri, Maria Viarengo's double self is safeguarded through re-membering and re-writing the self through gaps, ambivalences, and omissions. Her style refuses the closure and straight-jacket definitions of identity in order to portray the postcolonial female in multiple subject positions that exceed the standard styles, genres, and voices offered by national discourse, be it colonial or postcolonial. The diasporic and interracial self therefore becomes reflected in a narrative mood that eludes easy definition and clear- cut positions.

Even Erminia dell'Oro's novel, *L'Abbandono* (chapter 7) shows that the question of interraciality cannot be disengaged from the legacy of colonial politics. Those racial taxonomies created to justify colonial expansion still linger in postcolonial metropolitan societies. Dell'Oro's narration of the tormented destiny of the *métisse* children during Italian colonialism conveys the discrepancies of colonial sexual politics at the height of the European empire.

Sunetra Gupta's *Moonlight into Marzipan* (chapter 5) investigates in a highly poetical language the possibility of reinventing myths according to the Third World perspective. It entails a project of reimagining the postcolonial subject through alternative forms of representation that focus on language and its fleeting quality. Though not logically connected, it relates to the issue of female infibulation *Voices in Pain* (chapter 9) raised, which is such a powerful taboo in the societies where it is still practiced that it acquires mythological dimension. Being shredded into silence, infibulation disappears from language, making the representation of the wounded female body impossible. The text by the Somali writer Sirad Hassan breaks with this conspiracy of silence and unwinds the mythological nature of infibulation by providing a narration that touches upon personal, medical, and historical aspects. The whole feminist debate on who is entitled to speak for whom and to what extent Western feminists should intervene against the practice in the name of human rights remains problematic. In all the chapters the question of standpoint is central to the postcolonial debate highlighting connections and divergences between major theories and developments, especially feminist issues. These authors show that an exclusionary positioning is not only detrimental to understanding the texts and the postcolonial experience in its complexity, but also to recognizing what it means to be a woman in the diaspora negotiating multiple received and invented selves.

The genres used to explore these technologies of selfhood are mostly auto-biographical, though the way each writer uses a genre varies enormously. While Suleri, for example, pushes her memoir towards the erasure of the self, following a highly sophisticated and intriguing postmodern strategy, Maria Abbebù Viarengo offers a rather impressionistic autobiography in which the closeness to the self is instead strongly emphasized. More in line with Meena Alexander's highly inquisitive prose, Viarengo writes in order to keep in touch with herself and to protect the memory of a past shattered by the experience of migration. Another virtuoso example, but this time more within the category of the autobiography, is Gupta's highly orchestrated text *Moonlight into Marzipan*, a novel hidden within the semblance of an autobiography that could not be written otherwise.

More traditional in their literary enterprise are Bharati Mukherjee and Er-minia Dell'Oro. They privilege the structure of the Bildungsroman in order to give consistency to the shift from colonial or patriarchal enclosure towards postcolonial and diasporic consciousness. While Mukherjee opts for an eclec-tic style, Dell'Oro follows a more traditional route that at times overlaps with the historical novel. A more unusual work is Ribka Sibhatu's children book with *testo a fronte* (in Tigrinya and Italian) that introduces complex issues through a deceptively clear and simple narrative that can address both chil-dren and adults of the Italian multicultural society. And finally, Sirad Hassan has chosen the form of an essay novel, which narrates the direct testimony of two expatriate Somali girls. The different layers of confessional moods are in-terspersed with political, medical, and historical evaluations of the destiny of Somalia, of the cultural impact of emigration, and of the psychological con-sequences of infibulation.

Though from a literary point of view the Italian writing seems less sophisti-cated and less developed as a tradition in its own right, it is surprisingly more experimental in its use of literary genres than the work of the Indian history. By exploring different possibilities for wording the migrant experience and ways of searching through language and style the Afro-Italian writers convey the power of minor writing to which Deleuze and Guattari refer. This evaluation evokes, however, not the minor quality of the Italian tradition with respect to the Indian one, but rather the dissymmetrical relationships according to which different postcolonial literary strands merge and clash.

Chapter 2

The Exuberance of Immigration

Bharati Mukherjee, *Jasmine*

POSTCOLONIAL ANXIETY

Bharati Mukherjee is not only the most commercially successful of the women writers of the Indian diaspora, but she is also the most controversial narrator of Indian cultural identity in a multicultural context.

It is no coincidence that her literary model was originally V. S. Naipaul. Like the Caribbean author, she has an Indian Brahmanic background and a way of tackling issues concerning native values and Western ideology that has been said to be provocative by many postcolonial critics. However, Mukherjee's and Naipaul's most important common trait concerns the investigation of the migrant identity.

As noted above, Naipaul belongs to the old form of Indian diaspora, that of indentured labor, and his Caribbean origin is as important as his Indian ancestry. Mukherjee is a free diasporic. She belongs to that group of intellectual migrants who expatriated for a better education and who were backed by solid financial sources; her family owned an important pharmaceutical company in Calcutta. Educated at the best school in Calcutta, the Loreto Convent school for girls, she picked up that distinguished English accent that has survived even her long North American residence. She studied English and Ancient Indian Culture at Calcutta and Baroda University where she obtained a first-class degree. When confronted with a choice between accepting the arranged marriage planned by her father or accepting the grant to enter the Writer's Workshop at the University of Iowa, she chose the latter.

Mukherjee openly declared her affiliation to V. S. Naipaul in her introduction to *Darkness: Days and Nights in Calcutta* (1977), a collection of short stories based on her experiences in Canada, coauthored with her husband Clark Blaise:

> Like V. S. Naipaul, in whom I imagined a model, I tried to explore state-of-the-art expatriation. Like Naipaul, I used a mordant and self-protective irony in describing my characters' pain. Irony promised both detachment from, and superiority over, those well bred post-colonials much like myself, adrift in the new world, wondering if they would ever belong. (p. 2)

The irony mentioned by Mukherjee is inherited by the two authors through the British tradition of satire. The ironic tone in Mukherjee's first works, *The Tiger's Daughter* (1972) and *Wife* (1975), is replaced in her later phase by a more personal style.

Despite her declaration that her poetics are similar to those of Naipaul, she later began to disagree with him about his negative vision of the Third World. She rejects his view of the colonized people as helpless and doomed to failure because of their peripheral location. Mukherjee attempts a narrative and ideological response to Naipaul's view of the postcolonial world by writing a short story entitled "Jasmine," published in her collection *The Middleman and Other Stories* (1988), which sets her female character in the Caribbean:

> I very deliberately set the story in V. S. Naipaul's birthplace because it was my 'in' joke, challenging, if you like, Naipaul's thesis of tragedy being geographical. Naipaul's fiction seems to suggest that if you are born far from the center of the universe you are doomed to an incomplete and worthless little life. You are bound to be, if you are born like a Jasmine, an Indian in the Caribbean, a comic character, you come to nothing. So I wanted to say, "Hey, look at Jasmine. She is smart, and desirous, and ambitious enough to make something of her life."[1]

Mukherjee's inspiration is drawn from a friend's housekeeper, a Caribbean woman of Indian origin whose energy stemmed from her desire to remake herself and the need to improvise morality. Thus Mukherjee creates her model of fighters, women who have to adapt and struggle for their own survival. In this way the writer highlights that the Third World subject in its imbrications of gender, ethnicity, and migration cannot indulge in Naipaul's assumed paralysis, but on the contrary goes through an intense phase of transformation:

> However, as the author likes to underline, assimilation is not a one sided process. I say we haven't come to accommodate or to mimic: we have changed ourselves, but we have also come to change you.[2]

In Mukherjee's stories of the making and imagining of immigrant identities in America, female subjectivity forms the primary site of dislocation. The writer assumes the standpoint from where there is always a celebration of assimilation and little nostalgia for roots and authentic belonging. On this aspect she profoundly differs from Naipaul.

The aim here is to analyze whether or not Mukherjee, in her novel *Jasmine* (1989), has convincingly articulated the exuberance of immigration. Unlike her short story of the same title, the novel is not based on a Caribbean female character but on a migrant Indian one.

Flowers and Other Influences

In order to understand *Jasmine*'s contribution to the postcolonial debate, it is relevant here to briefly discuss V. S. Naipaul's famous essay "Jasmine," a milestone in the development of postcolonial consciousness. "Jasmine" appeared in the *Times Literary Supplement* on 4 June 1964, and was republished in Naipaul's essay collection *The Overcrowded Barracoon* (1972). In this essay the jasmine flower is used as a leading metaphor for the disconnection between the colonial natural world and the possibility of its representation through the English language imposed by the colonizers. Naipaul recalls that when he was young in Trinidad, he was familiar with the scent of the flower without knowing its name. Later in his life while visiting an old lady in British Guyana, he smells the scent of a flower:

> I knew the flower from my childhood; yet I never found out its name. I asked now. "We call it jasmine." Jasmine! So I had known all those years! To me it had been a word in a book, a word to play with, something removed from the dull vegetation I knew. The old lady cut a sprig for me. I stuck it in the top buttonhole of my open shirt. I smelled it as I walked back to the hotel. Jasmine, Jasmine. But the word and the flower had been separate in my mind for too long. They did not come together.[3]

Like other postcolonial writers Naipaul attempts a critique of the imposed colonial language. This critique entails the disconnecting of the signifier from the signified, of the wording of a world and the reality of it, which is culturally and geographically different. This creates anxiety and fear in adopting the language used in such influential literatures as English since, for example, English cannot express the Caribbean atmosphere but conveys, instead, an alien mythology:

> There was, for instance, Wordsworth's notorious poem about the daffodil.
> A pretty little flower, no doubt; but we had never seen it. Could the poem

have any meaning for us? . . . To us, without a mythology, all literatures were foreign. Trinidad was small, remote and unimportant, and we knew we could not hope to read in books of the life we saw about us. Books came from afar; they could offer only fantasy.[4]

Naipaul's often quoted statement is not only based on the postcolonial dissymmetry between language and representation, but also on the strong assumption that a writer's vision could never be individual, nor could he be separated from his own society. Mukherjee distances herself from this assumption. By modifying Naipaul's botanical image, Mukherjee contests the paradigm of origins in the Third World as being a hindrance for success, and instead she uses the word "jasmine" to evoke the flowering of possibilities. First, she disengages the development of Jasmine's identity from any idea of collectivism and traces a clear path of rampant American individualization for her. Second, she disengages herself from any other postcolonial model. She never thinks of herself as being part of a larger school, even though she has claimed affiliation with Naipaul:

> I'm uncomfortable being bracketed with other expatriate Indian writers, like Salman Rushdie and Anita Desai. I'm simply writing about characters whom I know and who interest me. At the same time I think I am a new kind of American writer for whom novels have a big social, historical moral component.[5]

Mukherjee distances herself from her Indian origin because she wants to be defined as an American writer who expands the border of the American canon. This shift of positionality within the literary world was made by Mukherjee when she decided to move from Canada, where she was racially assaulted for being "dark-skinned," to the United States. Here she came to terms with her uprootedness and underwent the transition from the "aloofness of expatriation" to the "exuberance of migration" (Mukherjee, *Darkness*, 1977, p. 3).

In a famous article that appeared in *The New York Times Book Review*, "Immigrant Writing: Give us our Maximalists!" (28 August 1988), Mukherjee accuses American writers of not including in their narration the faces and voices of the immigrants, who color and dominate all American cities, from buses to universities. "I don't think we are on Ellis Island anymore," she states, presenting a view of American society that can no longer afford to exclude new narrative models. If minimalist writings predominate, and this is supposed to be "American" fiction, then we need to revise the literary canon, she argues, because there is a blind spot in American writing. She lists the reasons for the success of minimalism: "clever, mannered, brittle . . . Minimalist techniques seem a healthy response to too much communication, too much manipulation, and too much of everything in a society that promotes its sports, its causes and its candidates in slick sound-bites." Mukherjee reacts against the minimalist short-hand agenda since she sees in it a dangerous white strategy to eschew the exotic, exuberant embrace of the 1960s culture, and with it the multicultural panorama of the 1980s. She invokes the Maximalists, the Expansionists, under which immigrants, expatriates, exiled people can enumerate themselves as part of the new American canon, and a more real one. Maximalism is an attempt to oppose the imposed mainstream, an illusory "majority," and turn the gaze to the "minority" voices, the immigrant voices, the second generation Jews and Italians and Irish and French-Canadians. Immigrants may look a little different, and carry different-sounding names, but "we musn't be seduced by what others term exotic. Don't choose to be an exile out of fear, or out of distaste."

With these concluding lines Mukherjee professes her new philosophy on migration. Fight against the "static ghetto of little India," don't choose the rear position, don't play the victim, you are part of America and America is made out of you. With this revisionary slogan, which the Indian critic Malashri Lal has defined as "the Maximalist Credo,"[6] Mukherjee not only intends to expand America but to change it, adding a minority point of view that is not clear-cut assimilation, but transformation. The transformation affects both sides and it is in this binary but fluid interaction between origin and modernity, traditional values and emancipation, collectivism and individualism, that Mukherjee's female characters develop.

By letting go of her Indianness and her roots, Mukherjee positions herself as a controversial author. She claims, in fact, to have overcome her "indianness":

I have joined imaginative forces with an anonymous, driven underclass of semi-assimilated Indians with sentimental attachments to a distant home-land but no real desire for permanent return. I see my "immigrant" story replicated in a dozen American cities, and instead of seeing my Indianness as a fragile identity to be preserved against obliteration (or worse, a "visible" disfigurement to be hidden), I see it now as a set of fluid identities to be celebrated . . . Indianness is now a metaphor, a particular way of partially comprehending the world.[7]

Whereas Naipaul anxiously searched for his ancestral roots in India, Mukherjee departs from it with great casualness. She makes of her mother country an India of the mind, as in Salman Rushdie's tradition, and it is exactly this aspect that bothers Indian writers and critics who see their cultural heritage used by Mukherjee as a magician's hut from which icons and myths can be picked up and blended in a literary style apt for the Western audiences.

Mukherjee is often accused by her Indian critics of creating fables, tall tales rather than realistic depictions, and of using orientalizing icons to market her books in the West. However, some critics, in particular female Indian academics whose readings of Mukherjee's texts are psychoanalytic,[8] have rightly observed that these recurring images can be read as the unconscious level of Mukherjee's narrative, which shows that her Indianness has not been overcome but returns constantly as a perturbation. This will become more clear in the analysis of *Jasmine*, the novel that launched Mukherjee as an American writer and which contains the embryo of Mukherjee's recurrent themes about gender, migration, and identity. These issues are better controlled and developed in her more recent novels, *The Holder of the World* (1994) and *Leave It to Me* (1997) and *Desirable Daughters* (2002), which, however, lack the freshness of *Jasmine*'s recklessness in terms of both content and literary achievement.

American Dream

Jasmine is a Bildungsroman rewritten around the postcolonial, postmodern, and feminist agenda. The novel focuses on Jasmine, an underage village girl from the Punjab, who ventures as an undocumented widow to the United States, where her fate will be "rewritten."

The *fabula* level of the novel, which is represented by the series of events narrated, does not coincide with the *story*, which is how the events are organized and conveyed. Therefore, the novel unfolds in non-chronological order, creating a rather cinematic effect that makes it hard to follow the shifts in location, focalization and time. The narration is in the first person and is set in Baden, Elsa County, Iowa, when Jasmine is age twenty-four. The fabula, instead, begins in Hasnapur, a village in Punjab when Jasmine is age seven. The bold events that have allowed her transformation from the ill-fated village girl, Jyoti, to the self-assured emancipated American woman, Jane, are told in a narrative reversion.

> I'm twenty-four now, I live in Baden, Elsa County, Iowa, but every time
> I lift a glass of water to my lips, fleetingly I smell it. I know what I don't
> want to become. (p. 5)

The dialectic interplay between the diegesis (past) and the narration (present), separated in time but ideologically intersecting with each other, makes the evaluation of this novel more complicated than it would at first seem. The distance between past and present time also represents the distance between two cultures. But the translation of the past life privileges the language of the present life and therefore becomes an example of what Spivak calls "translation-as-violation" (Spivak, 1986: 234).

The past is therefore constructed through constant flashbacks from the Baden location of narration, which function also as flashforwards if we consider the time and setting of Hasnapur in Punjab where the fabula begins. Jasmine is not Jasmine yet; she is called Jyoti (which means "light") and is a seven-year-old girl, the fifth of a long line of daughters:

> God's cruel, my mother complained, to waste brain on a girl. And God's still more cruel, she said, to make a fifth daughter beautiful instead of the first. By the time my turn to marry came around, there would be no dowry money left to gift me the groom I deserved. (p. 40)

Jyoti is presented as an unlucky child: female, intelligent, and born too late down the line of daughters to use her beauty to her advantage. She was good in Punjabi and Urdu, good at counting and at reading and was the first likely candidate for English instruction. An unhappy fate seems to await her. First, Masterji, the English teacher who supports her education, is killed in a Sikh terrorist attack. Then, as described in the opening page of the novel, a scene under a banyan tree, the astrologer predicts a life of widowhood and exile. Jyoti protests against the old man's craziness determining her future. "Fate is Fate" (p. 4), he tells her. Jyoti reacts to the astrologer's attempt to reduce her to nothingness by falling down and making a star-shaped mark on her forehead, which she interprets as "my third eye." The third eye becomes the figuration for Bhabha's in-betweenness, for that location of hybridization and ambivalence that allows subjugated subjects, in this case a female subaltern, to operate in the vacuum of hegemonic authority and create their own empowerment. Jyoti starts the war "between my fate and my will" (p. 12) by creating her own interspace for individual growth.

If, according to Hindu wisdom, bad luck seems to persecute Jyoti (she loses her father before he can marry her off), a strange logic seems to be at work for her. She will be free, in fact, to marry at the age of fourteen her brother's friend, Prakash, a twenty-four-year-old electronics student whose voice she falls in love with. Jyoti states at this point, "I was a sister without dowry, but I didn't have to be a sister without prospects" (p. 70). Prakash plays the modern enlightened man. The wedding is, in fact, not a religious one, and no dowry is exchanged. He refuses to live with his extended family and moves with Jyoti to Amritsar, the biggest city in Punjab. He renames her "Jasmine," the name that gives title to the book, to remove from her any trace of traditional dutifulness since as he says to her "only in feudal societies is the woman still a vassal" (p. 77). She is not Jyoti, the village girl, anymore but Jasmine, a modern city woman. Prakash wants to be called by his first name, whereas in traditional India women address their husbands formally. He also prohibits her from having children for the time being, and he encourages her to read his manuals to improve herself and to cherish a better future for them both in America, the land of possibility, in order to break away for good from Indian atavism and immutability:

Pygmalion wasn't a play I'd seen or read then, but I realize now how much of Professor Higgins there was in my husband. He wanted to break down the Jyoti I'd been in Hasnapur and made me a new kind of city woman. (p. 77)

The voice narrating the events is that of Jasmine in Iowa at the age of twenty-four. However, the comments and political insights offered come from backstage and betray the narrator's ideological point of view. For example, when we read,

He was basically an old-fashioned Indian patriot, with a lot of Gandhi and a lot of Nehru in him. (p. 88)

we are aware that this cannot be Jasmine's standpoint since her role in the novel is of the naive, but resourceful migrant woman, who tries to survive in America. She is portrayed in the active role, as the woman making sure she has no time for reflection or nostalgia. These cultural and political afterthoughts, therefore, come from an external omniscient voice that sets the whole novel into an ideological and culturally located frame.

There is, in fact, a distance between Jasmine and the authorial center. Jasmine has a limited awareness. The author has the bigger picture that contextualizes *Jasmine* historically and geographically. She was born eighteen years after partition. Her family was from Lahore and had aristocratic connections. However, with the division of the Punjab and their forced migration from Lahore to Hasnapur, they become simple peasants. Jasmine has already inherited a tradition of exile and migration from her family. At the age of sixteen, she is planning to move with her husband, who dreams of his own Vijh & Wife shop, to the United States. It is the period of the Sikh separatist movement, when Sikh terrorists kill Hindu men and women, accusing them of being rapists and whores. The Sikhs want a state of Punjab that is independent from India and protected by Pakistan, and India fears a total disintegration of the nation state that has been based on secular principles. In this novel readers have to keep counting to establish the dates and historical situations of events. For a careful reader these are crucial data, the added layers to the unfolding life story of Jasmine.

We are now at the beginning of the 1990s, a period when several separatist movements take hold in India. Communalism, which had been condemned by Gandhi and Nehru, had retaken possession of the nation after Indira Gandhi's declaration of the Emergency State in 1977, which greatly restricted rights of speech and freedom in order to protect the supreme unity of the Indian nation. Indira Gandhi's paranoia led to imprisonments and repression of public functions and created political unrest and a growing distrust in Indian democracy.

Things came to a head with Operation Blue Star in 1984 when Indira Gandhi sent Indian troops into the Golden temple in Amritsar, which resulted in a bloodbath and the murder of the Sikh leader. Retaliations occurred throughout the country, the most notorious of which was the murder of Indira Gandhi herself four months later at the hands of one of her own Sikh bodyguards.[9]

The novel is set in the years of tension (the early 1980s), preceding the moment of writing, when Sikh terrorists roam the Punjab on scooters, planting bombs. Prakash is murdered for his secularist vision after he tells his Sikh friend Sukhwinder that "There's no Hindu state! There's no Sikh State! India is for everyone." (p. 66). Jasmine is seventeen and widowed as the astrologer had foretold. In her confusion she can only find direction in her old Indian dutifulness. She decides to go to America to commit *sati*, burning herself along with her husband's suit at the site where he would have gone to the university.

But fate has a few surprises in store for Jasmine. She travels by plane to Amsterdam and starts acknowledging her uprooted identity and her minority status in the big airport lounges. Transmigration begins:

> We are the outcasts and deportees, strange pilgrims visiting outlandish shrines, landing at the end of tarmacs, ferried in old army trucks where we are roughly handled and taken to roped-off corners of waiting rooms where surly, barely wakened customs guards await their bribe. We are dressed in shreds of national costumes, out of season, the wilted plumage of intercontinental vagabondage. We ask only one thing: to be allowed to land; to pass through; to continue. (p. 101)

In order to illustrate how Jasmine manages to escape her Indian fate and the deadlock that many immigrants have to face in the States, Mukherjee highlights a series of strategies that makes successful Americanization possible. Her model is based on adaptation to American otherness through a concatenation of permutations while at the same time keeping Indian diversity and mythological tales for strategic purposes. This is rather an "opportunistic" credo that works wonders in the United States of America, the land of opportunity.

This strategy has been criticized in particular by Indian critics as Mukherjee seems to use easy icons of the Hindu mythology only to market them to the West and to illustrate very unlikely passages in her novel. The writer's plan is to develop a female ethnic identity into an assimilated American at all costs. Mukherjee's creation of fables rather than realistic descriptions does not hinder her in her investigation of diasporic imagination. Juggling a bit with Hindu mythology, a bit with the American dream, Mukherjee creates the illusion of a continuum between the oppressive Indian female identity and the new invigorating, multiplying American subjecthood. Jasmine survives innumerable beginnings and ends; she has "hurtled through time tunnels" (p. 240) and cries "through all the lives (she has) given birth to, (cries) for all (her) dead" (p. 241). She steps from the old world ethics of submission, helplessness, and doom to the exciting new ethics of adventure, risk, and transformation.

SHUTTLING BETWEEN IDENTITIES

Feminist Strategies

> Despite our desperate, eternal attempt to separate, contain, and mend, categories always leak.
>
> —Trinh T. Minh-ha, *Woman, Native, Other*, p. 94.

Mukherjee interrogates the narrative of assimilation and feminism by taking into consideration the struggle that subaltern women have to undergo in the First World. However, her claims can be bigger than her results. Mukherjee isolates, in fact, a particular figure from the Indian reality and forges her into the subject she needs to in order to validate her transformative American model. The author does not take into account the communal aspect of Indian identity but selects subjects who are characterized by inherent distinctiveness. In so doing, the quick passage towards individualization is made possible for Jasmine.

Born with aristocratic traits, Jasmine is particularly beautiful, intelligent, and capable of learning the tricks of survival. In America she is recognized and marked as special, distinctive. Lillian Gordon, her first rescuer in the U.S., strikes the chord of her difference: "You're a very special case, my dear. I've written that to my daughter, so don't hesitate to call her" (pp. 134–35).

The authorial voice shifts in position between Jasmine's inherent nobility, which distinguishes her from other immigrants and allows her to escape a future as a cleaner or paid nanny, and her naiveté as a Third World immigrant. These passages make *Jasmine* a rather American novel, and Mukherjee tries very hard to exploit the resources of Asian exoticness to succeed and to verify the American dream.

American prescriptive feminists have labeled *Jasmine* as not emancipatory enough because the character is too effeminate and passive. Mukherjee has called them "imperialists." According to her, Western feminists do not understand the implications for the gendered Indian struggle and instead impose their vision of how an emancipated female subject should act irrespective of her background and ethnicity. Mukherjee's idea of a militant Third World position is more radical than "middle class Ms Gloria Steinem," as she states in an interview with Maya Jaggi in *Harper Bazar*, 1990. Her idea of integration, mongrelization, and fusion conveys the transformation of Jasmine's different identities, none of which can be wiped out, but all of which are contained and metamorphosed in the new other. Therefore, in the constant politics of renaming, which is Mukherjee's leading device for showing the multiplying of identities, an element will remain unchanged and fixed.

From Jyoti the village girl in Hasnapur, to Jasmine the city woman, to Jazzy the undocumented immigrant who Lillian Gordon teaches to learn and walk American, to Jase the sophisticated Manhattan nanny who falls in love with Taylor, to Jane the Iowan woman who marries the banker Bud Ripplemayer and centers the story, the "J" represents the element of continuity within transformation. As Elizabeth Bronfen writes,

> This "J" serves as a signifier for the dialectic of a progressive engendering of identities as these bar any already existing identities, putting them under erasure without consuming them. In so doing, Mukherjee's novel traces the parameters of the narrative discourse available to the muted subaltern woman. Jasmine's dislocated Other speaks out of a self-conscious and self-induced effacement in the voice of a resilient, and incessantly self-refashioning hybridity.[10]

This is the "J," the aspect which will affect American society, all the men and people around her, that will cause their irreversible transformation. America has transformed Jasmine, but she has transformed America too:

> Then there is nothing I can do. Time will tell if I am a tornado, rubble-maker, arising from nowhere and disappearing into a cloud. I am out of the door and in the pothole and rutted driveway, scrambling ahead of Taylor, greedy with wants and reckless from hope. (p. 241)

These closing lines release the tension, which runs like a red thread throughout the novel, between Jasmine's predicted fate and her desire to escape and transform it. Juggling with both her destiny and her attempt at self-determination, she challenges the astrologer's premonition that reappears frequently as a leitmotiv in the novel. On the first page her future will be read as a widow and exile, but on the last page Jasmine says,

> Watch me reposition the stars, I whisper to the astrologer who floats cross-legged above my kitchen stove. (p. 240)

Jasmine's fate does not differ from that predicted by her astrologer—she will indeed be widowed and exiled—but in America these cultural referents assume a completely new function of empowerment and multiplication. The *"porousness of my days"* (p. 211) helps Jasmine towards self-fashioning in an upward movement within American society. However, some critics have been highly unsatisfied with Mukherjee's use and abuse of the rhetoric of migrancy to support Jasmine's class mobility. Her fairy tales are far from being representative. Susan Koshy argues, for example, that

> Mukherjee's celebration of assimilation is an insufficient confrontation to the historical circumstances of ethnicity and race in the United States and of the complexities of diasporic subject-formation.[11]

Mukherjee's protean feminist text overlooks the important categories of class and caste and how these categories interrelate to gender, ethnicity, and age both in India and on the new American frontier. Mukherjee's main characters are middle-class Indian women, but ignoring their class status creates the assumption that every woman is granted the same possibility of upward mobility.

Mukherjee distances herself from mainstream Western liberal feminists since their "tools and rhetoric" cannot be applied "wholesale and intact" to the situation of "some non-white, Asian women."[12] However, while Mukherjee sketches her character as self-fashioning, autonomous and self-determining, "she is deeply complicit with some of the underlying assumptions" (Koshi, 1994: 70) of mainstream feminism.

Though Mukherjee's feminist strategies are not totally convincing, there are some imprecisions in Koshy's statement. As Mukherjee has tried to demonstrate, more or less successfully, the relation between Third World strategies of survival and First World emancipatory declarations is neither separate nor exclusionary. It is in their interpenetration, which can result in paradoxical and conflictual outcomes, that Mukherjee's revisionist discourse should be placed. Asian women use all the tools they have to succeed, and this can be detected from the boldness characteristic of Punjabi communities of emigrants, to feminine devices such as beauty and passive attitudes, to the embrace of Western feminist self-assertion strategies.

However, it is in her indication of positioning within the structure of dominance that Mukherjee's characters are flawed. They remain flat, without introspection or real believable fusion between origin and point of arrival. As such Mukherjee leaves the frontier of arrival open. Often the success and mobility of Jasmine mislead the readers with her agency and assertiveness, whereas the novel often highlights how much she is still a prey of her fate. Taylor decides to move West to California, and Jasmine joins in, but does not plan it herself. As Koshy observes,

> Mukherjee's writing celebrates assimilation or whether this celebration reveals a positive attitude toward immigration. The question is, how is assimilation constructed in her texts?[13]

Chandra Mohanty has criticized Western feminism for constructing a monolithic image of Third World women as "ignorant, poor, uneducated, tradition-bound, domestic, family oriented, victimised etc. . . ." while implying a self-representation of white women as more modern and sexually emancipated. What is created is the Western standard as the norm and referent versus a Third World standard as "Other" (Mohanty, 1991: 51–80).

In this regard Mukherjee's position is highly questionable. Because of her narrative reversions she presents the backwardness of the status of women in Punjab through an identification with Westernized ideas. These stem from her locating the narration, and therefore the language of emancipation, in Iowa, a cross-location which functions as a trope for the transformations that have already taken place.

Mukherjee unconsciously recreates a split between an idea of feminism as applied to Third World conditions and an idea of feminism applied to Third World migrant subjects in a Western society. She therefore reproduces the objectification mentioned by Mohanty by portraying Jasmine's singularity (with the inborn requisites to become a successfully developed emancipated subject in the West) as compared with other anonymous village women, backward and doomed to oblivion. As Koshy writes,

> The celebration of Jasmine's singularity is dependent on flattening out the subjectivities of other nonwhite women whom she encounters and identifies with, but from whom she is carefully distinguished.[14]

Jasmine's exceptionality is developed at the expense of other nonwhite characters who are homogenized as "Other" and objectified as victims:

> all over our district, bad luck dogged dowryless wives, rebellious wives, barren wives. They fell into wells, they got run over by trains, they burned to death heating milk on kerosene stoves. (p. 41)

This discourse constructs the Third World as a monolithically oppressive society where resistance and rebellion is impossible. Mukherjee becomes trapped by the formulation of her own discourse. If there is no escape for Hasnapuri women, Jyoti escapes through extraordinary means, that is, her mission to commit *sati* in front of Prakash's aspired university in Florida. This narrative trick is insufficient to justify Mukherjee's claim of forwarding a situated and historically bound notion of feminism as applied to Asian women. Her fictional imagination takes over and in constructing her mythography of making it in the *tabula rasa* that is America, Mukherjee emphasizes the fabulistic pattern of the romantic heroine rather than carefully identifying the shifts in the development of identity as centered around a well-articulated notion of race, caste, and class.

Jasmine becomes "special" and "exotic" only for Americans who see her as different from other radicalized women. As Lillian Gordon tells her "Jazzy, you don't strike me as a picker or a domestic. . . . You're different from these others" (p. 134). Once Jasmine is set apart from a monolithic alterity, she is distinguished from and destined to a success denied other migrant workers.

Mukherjee operates the transformation of Jasmine's identity according to two main master discourses, the first relative to colonial oppression (against which technology, the mastering of English, and migration are used), and the second relative to patriarchal oppression (which is answered by becoming multiple selves, seductive and transformative). Jasmine uses the various tools provided by her male partners, adapts her identity to the role she is expected to fulfill, then destroys the master's house, moves on, and proceeds with her self-realization by acquiring new master's tools:

> I have had a husband for each of the women I have been. Prakash for Jasmine, Taylor for Jase, Bud for Jane, Half-Face for Kali. (p. 197)

Jasmine's power is apparent in her restlessness to keep changing shapes and houses. The master discourse cannot trap her in any definite and finite location or self. In this transmigratory mythology, the self that is fluid and accumulative can be killed and endlessly reincarnated, and this strategy defies both the patriarchal and the colonial logic.

However, Mukherjee is not transformative in her gendered and ethnicized representation because she uses clichés and stereotypes to create a postmodern text for the West and an improbable mythological tale of an escaping princess from India: she presents rampant individualism with an exotic tinge. What Mukherjee lacks is thinking through difference according to which "neither the totalitarian effacement of difference nor the delirious celebration of a limitless and ever-proliferating 'in-difference'" take place (Pfeil, 1994: 225). With its celebration of postmodern geography and free-floating identity, the novel *Jasmine* plays with the subject who is in a nonposition, everywhere and nowhere at the same time, consuming differences and creating mobile identities.

The most important particularity of Mukherjee's strategies is her use of language. The characters speak in a fancy, hip American slang, fuse registers and styles, and convey the unique voice of American's multiple idioms. However, Mukherjee flattens the category of difference by making most of her characters—with ostensibly different backgrounds, itineraries, and histories—speak all the same "hip, jumped-up, wordjazz" (Pfeil, 1994: 201). Nonetheless, as Pfeil adds, "the tonal and stylistic equivalence of these voices is, paradoxically, their most salient feature" (Pfeil, 1994: 201).

Despite the declaration of discontent, Mukherjee's postcolonial assimilatory manifesto is a text where the emphasis on pleasure and agency (jouissance) challenges the images of fragmentation and victimization that are usually projected on those who are perceived as the other by the hegemonic subject. It is for this that Mukherjee's book must be praised. Despite its pitfalls and limits of essentialism, the novel shows that the road to America is open. This exuberance of immigration makes the text worthwhile despite its controversial aspects.

Multicultural Identity

In order to position Mukherjee's discourse of assimilation within American multiculturalism, it is useful to briefly discuss Peter McLaren's article, "White Terror and Oppositional Agency: Towards a Critical Multiculturalism."[15] In this article McLaren distinguishes three forms of multiculturalism. These refer to the way in which race and ethnicity are mapped out in the cultural construction of difference or sameness.

The first form is defined by McLaren as "Conservative Multiculturalism." It indicates the white groups who do not question their whiteness as an ethnic category but position other ethnicities and minority groups on a lower ladder of civilization. For the purpose of multiculturalism this implies that the integration of different groups by the dominant hegemonic group takes place at the expense of their specificity. The hegemonic group forwards, in fact, a common culture where the colonialist and imperialist ideology still dominates. The various ethnic groups are added ons to the dominant white culture. For example, in the United States the denial of an education in Spanish is detrimental to the Hispanic community, but favors an English and Anglo-Saxon form of integration.

The second form of multiculturalism indicated by McLaren is termed "Liberal Multiculturalism." This vision defends the natural equality existing among white and other communities. However, as McLaren explains, the social and educational opportunities necessary for competing in the capitalist marketplace are not the same. Liberal multiculturalism erodes, therefore, into an ethnocentric and universalizing humanism. The legitimizing norms that govern the substance of citizenship are, in fact, identified most strongly with Anglo-American political communities.

The third form considered is "Left-Liberal Multiculturalism," which emphasizes cultural differences and suggests that the stress on the equality of races only erases the cultural differences between races that are responsible for different behavior and social practices. The backdrop to this approach is the exoticization of "Otherness" and a nativist trend to locate differences in a primeval past of cultural authenticity. This tendency to essentialize difference by ignoring the historical and cultural situatedness of difference runs the risk of requiring a definite identity as a starting point before a dialogue can be undertaken. Therefore, people can be trapped in a constructed identity on the basis of their ethnicity, gender, or class without taking into account how personal experience has developed within the ideological and discursive complexities of its formation.

Identity is constantly being produced through a play of differences which are linked to shifting and conflicting discursive and ideological relations. As Joan Scott writes, "experience is a subject's history. Language is the site of history's enactment" (Scott, 1992: 34). Therefore, identity politics must be qualified by a more complex tracing of relations and influences that are based on hegemonic relations and on nonlocatable yet fixed assumptions of knowledge. Hegemonic Western cultures are usually not perceived as specific to any particular ethnicity, and they are hegemonic precisely because they are able to represent themselves effectively as neutral and universal.

Following this position McLaren moves towards a fourth position, which entails a radical understanding of the concept of difference. With "Critical Multiculturalism" he wants to stress the central task of transforming the social, cultural, and institutional relations in which meanings are produced. If conservative and liberal multiculturalism stress "sameness," and the left-liberals stress difference, they create a false opposition because both perspectives are based on an essentialist logic. In both cases identity is presumed to be autonomous and self-contained. Critical multiculturalism starts from the notion of differences as constructed between and among groups. Critical multiculturalism interrogates the construction of difference and identity in which the operations of power and privilege are analyzed, examining how structures of exclusion are still at work despite the declaration of equality among differences.

If we follow this classification to analyze how Mukherjee represents assimilation in *Jasmine*, then we have to admit that she skips among the different forms of multiculturalism, holding to only one constant pattern, individualization. Mukherjee puts forward a conservative multiculturalism when she depicts Jasmine as a special case, as an elected immigrant who fulfils the right requirements to be assimilated within the dominant white model of American society. Jasmine shows the capacity to transform and to adapt in order to survive and to acquiesce to the "special" role already written for her:

> I wanted to become the person they thought they saw: humorous, intelligent, refined, affectionate. Not illegal, not murderer, not widowed, raped, destitute, fearful. (p. 171)

However, at the Hayes' Jasmine has to adapt to that democratic idea that she is as worthy as they are, as cultivated and articulate. This idea of liberal multiculturalism sees no differences among human beings:

Taylor didn't want to change me. He didn't want to scour and sanitize the foreignness. My being different from Wylie and Kate didn't scare him. I changed because I wanted to. (p. 185)

Jasmine's efforts to improve herself open the question of which standard will prevail and for whom must this improvement be performed. Jasmine says "for herself," expressing that leading concept of Mukherjee: individualism. Only if you detach yourself from your traditional heritage and fixed familiar bonding can you have a chance at success. Individualism, hence, is an illusion that is upheld by projecting cultural specificity exclusively on others. And therefore Jasmine becomes unique, different, and special in order to fulfill her path towards individualization.

She plays her exotic card to conquer the various men, and she uses modesty and naiveté in order not to infuriate the women whose men she steals, but to win them over as well: "Karin, Bud's ex called me a gold digger" (p. 195) or "'Taylor loves you,' Wylie said, 'but you must know that'" (p. 182). With Bud Ripplemeyer there is an evident case of left-liberal multiculturalism since he falls for Jasmine because of her otherness: "Bud courts me because I am alien. I am darkness, mystery, inscrutability. The East plugs me into instant vitality and wisdom. I rejuvenate him simply by being who I am" (p. 200). Differences are necessary for the construction of identity and within the notion of left-liberal multiculturalism, differences are emphasized and fixed into a static notion of alterity. No one investigates what constitutes Jasmine's Indianness. In America, Lillian Gordon tells her, people know only walking and speaking American: if you divert from this assumed majority, then you have to qualify as other-than-American. Lillian Gordon carries out her humanitarian mission under the flag of conservative multiculturalism, inciting Jasmine-Jazzy's rapid integration.

However, Jasmine survives in America and guarantees her own upward mobility not through purely playing by the rules but also by making strategic use of her difference as an Asian in order to acquire maximum visibility and privileges. Mukherjee has been criticized for accepting Left-liberal Multiculturalism, for essentializing both the notion of Indianness and of Americanness into coded and prescriptive categories. India is fate, immobility, oppression; America is a rewriting of destiny, change, and empowerment. Mukherjee assumes in her novel that there is only one way to be American: by asserting one's own individuality and centering others around the self.

We can also identify forms of what McLaren defines as Critical Multiculturalism, since the historical and situated difference of Jasmine's Indianness hinders her from proceeding unencumbered on her path towards self-emancipation. When she sees Sukhwinder, the Sikh terrorist in Central Park, she knows her past has come to reclaim her and that she cannot shake off her previous role despite the promise of Americanness. Therefore, her identity is relational in the sense that only by maintaining her American environment can she assert a certain kind of identity, whereas in other situations her construction will be immediately demolished. Mukherjee does not ignore the exclusionary structures of power that are still at work within swinging discourses of equality. At a certain point Jasmine remarks, "I wish I had known America before it got perverted" (p. 201), implying that the American dream of a happy melting pot had lost its magic and the different immigrant communities were competing with one another, often with fatal consequences. Whether that pure America ever existed is not Mukherjee's concern, as it is in perversion that the imbalances of a power structure are revealed.

The democratic people, the Hayeses, who are so fond of her, are really interested in other cultures and have exquisite collections:

> The apartment was stocked like a museum. Wylie and Taylor weren't simple acquisitors. . . . Some of [the art pieces] seemed offensive to blacks or women or red Indians. There were slave auctions posters from New Orleans in 1850 . . . ; old color prints celebrating the massacre of an entire Indian village down to the last baby; a poster of a naked woman with parts of her body labeled choice, prime, or chuck, as in a butcher shop. (p. 174)

The minor cultures are represented not only as other but they are clearly objectified with violence, exploitation, and commodification. This is part of the making of America, part of the American dream and identity. However, by letting Jasmine-Jase be part of the American dream, the Hayes compensate for the exploitation upon which their prosperity is based and make Jasmine-Jase complicit with the hegemonic group. This intersection of historical responsibility is rendered more apparent when Jasmine visits Wylie's new lover's apartment:

> He had been to India several times as a guest lecturer in Delhi, as a World Bank consultant, as a U.S. government aid officer. He spoke Hindi passably and owned so many Indian paintings and tapestries that his living room looked to me like a shop or an art gallery. His wife was an Africa specialist, so the walls were hung with spears and masks that competed with mirror-work cloths and Moghul miniatures. (p. 184)

There is obviously not only a commodification of the Third World as exotic and interesting, but almost an artificial need to equalize the values of other cultures to those of America, or even to reduce them to a symbolic world, the world of art in which the Third World is reduced to fetishes and token figures. These figures decorate the modern American apartment of "politically correct" people,

Americans who do really care for the rest of the world and who do have humanitarian positions within the capitalist structure of exploitation. Stuart works as an aid officer for the US, covers an international function for the World Bank, and knows enough about other cultures not to be an exploiter but a politically correct treasurer.

In his article "The Post-colonial and the Postmodern" Kwame Anthony Appiah (1992) offers an analysis of the marketing of African art works in American museums. The selection of pieces for a show at the Center for African Art in New York clearly demonstrates through a politics of inclusion and exclusion how "Africa" is made for the American postmodern world. David Rockfeller, the art collector "who would never surely criticize sculptures from other ethnic groups in terms of (his) own traditional criteria" (Appiah: 1992, 222), tries to assimilate the pieces "between considerations of finance, of aesthetics and decor. In these responses, we have surely a microcosm of the site of the American in the contemporary—which is, then, surely to say, postmodern—America" (Appiah, 1992: 223). Appiah's comments on African art within Western collections unveil the hegemonic colonial structures that are still at work despite the postmodern, postcolonial equalization of all cultures. Appiah's long quote here is meant to offer a clear picture of the concept of multiculturalism in its historical shifts:

> The incorporation of these works in the West's world of museum culture and its market has almost nothing, of course, to do with postmodernism. By and large, the ideology through which they are incorporated is modernist: it is the ideology that brought something called "Bali" to Artaud, something called "Africa" to Picasso, and something called "Japan" to Barthes. [This incorporation as an official Other was criticized, of course, from its beginnings: Oscar Wilde once remarked that "the whole Japan is a pure invention. There is no such country, no such people."] What is postmodernist is Vogel's muddled conviction that African Art should not be judged "in terms of (someone else's) traditional criteria." For modernism, primitive art was to be judged by putatively *universal* aesthetic criteria; and by these standards it was finally found possible to value it. . . . For *post*modernisms, by contrast, these works, however they are to be understood, cannot be seen as legitimated by culture—and history—transcending standards. (Appiah, 1992: 239)

If modernism regarded primitive art as part of a universal aesthetic code, postmodernism has erased the hidden relations of power between dominant and dominated cultures through a politics that sees culture disentangled from its historical context, equalizing cultures by abstracting them so as not to deal with notions of difference and otherness but rather by assimilating them into the dominant pattern of commodification.

This is true of Jasmine who functions as an exotic art work to be integrated into an American multicultural pluralism. Like the Hayes' paintings and Stuart's valuable collection, she enters a market place where she can be commodified according to her "financial, aesthetic and decor" applicability in a Western environment. Mukherjee's resistant discourse, however, requires that the Western environment cannot be the same once it has been in touch with Jasmine, that her tornado, rubble-maker nature affects identity construction both ways. It is through this quality to confront and subvert the concept of Americanness that Jasmine has an agency and is empowered. Bud's innate racism leads him to acquire an Asian wife and to adopt a Vietnamese refugee as a son, to be deserted by them both; the undermining of his American dominance and values are symbolized by his becoming crippled and having to live in a wheelchair.

Jasmine has moved progressively away from the conservative multiculturalism of Lillian Gordon ("walk American") to the Liberal multiculturalism of the Hayes ("you don't have to change") to a left-liberal multi-culturalism in which her difference is enhanced in Iowa. The conclusion is an attempt to represent critical multi-culturalism with her decision to move on and to leave everything behind, everything that was destroyed by her tornado.

However, the dissymmetrical power structures are not really explored by Mukherjee, which prevents us from seeing the novel as an act of critical multi-culturalism. She has sketched more general traits, thus opening up the discussion on multiculturalism. With these general traits she has stumbled on essentialisms, not really thinking through difference and identity, and used existing categories that are appealing and comprehensible to the West. She has not created an alternative representation of agency and pleasure, but a representation of the subject's consent to hegemonic representations of transnational and multicultural reality. Mukherjee has explored this consent as a two-sided alteration/infection. Furthermore, by following the path of consent to hegemonic structure, she has made her minority text extremely successful, thus opening the discussion on subaltern migrant identity to a wider audience and stimulating further representations.

Chapter 3

The Shock of Arrival

Meena Alexander, *Fault Lines*

TECHNOLOGIES OF SELFHOOD

The Aloofness of Expatriation

In her memoir *Fault Lines* (1993), Meena Alexander explores the less flamboyant sides of displacement. She writes, in fact, that she is "a woman cracked by multiple migrations" (p. 3). In this memoir her poetic memory investigates transnational identity, womanhood, and ethnicity. By fusing poetry, prose, and critical thinking Alexander conveys the intricacies of being a female postcolonial writer through a genre, the autobiography or memoir, that challenges traditional notions of subjectivity. The ways in which Alexander's text contributes to the revision of this genre from a feminist and postcolonial perspective will be illustrated.

In *Fault Lines* Alexander makes frequent use of two strands of memory: linear and circular. It takes Meena only one paragraph to chronologically present her life, to dispose of her memory in a linear way:

> The first child of my parents, the eldest of three sisters, I was born in 1951 in Allahabad, in the north where my father was working, in a newly independent India. My sister Anna was born in 1956 and my sister Elsa in 1961. Amma returned to her home in Tiruvella each time to give birth.
>
> In 1956 my father, who worked for the Indian government, had been "seconded" abroad to work in the newly independent Republic of the Sudan. My mother and I followed him in February of that year. I turned

five on the Arabian sea, my first ocean crossing. For the next thirteen years my childhood crisscrossed the continents. Amma would return to her home in Tiruvella, sometimes for six months of the year. The other six months we spent in Khartoum. In 1969, when I was eighteen, I graduated from Khartoum University and went to Britain as a student. I lived there for four years while I was completing my studies. In 1973 I returned to India to Delhi and Hyderabad. In 1979, just married, I left for the United States and I lived in New York City ever since. (p. 6)

However, it takes her a lifetime to reorganize the circular aspect of her memory. This process of reorganization is at the basis of her reflection on her postcolonial gendered identity. For example, in *Fault Lines* she recomposes the fragments of her life into an apparently chronological narrative, but she unsettles her linear organization with repetitions, omissions, and disruptions. Her ethnic consciousness criss-crosses the whole text, intersecting with the more chronological narration. The result is a mosaic of open-ended selves, existential moments that the author tries to catch in language but which are instead constantly metamorphosed. This structure is called upon to express the ontological uprootedness experienced by migrant people.

Alexander appropriates the theoretical perspectives inherent in the definition of identity as indicated by Homi K. Bhabha. Bhabha states "we are no longer confronted with an ontological problem of being but with the discursive strategy of the moment of interrogation, a moment in which the demand for identification becomes, primarily, a response to other questions, of signification and desire, culture and politics" (Bhabha, 1994: 49–50).

Alexander's narrator, whose consciousness widens with the widening of her knowledge of the world, is constantly questioning the self. The persistent interrogations of identification and differentiation constellate the whole text. The author reiterates, in fact, her sense of nonidentity: "Who am I? Where am I? When am I?" These questions keep coming back and create a rhythm in the narrative, a refrain of anxiety that finds consolation in its own repetition.

This autobiography therefore becomes a quilt of different textual genres. What is initially presented as a simple memoir or autobiography becomes instead a complex text interspersed with poems by Alexander herself, with literary references, academic evaluations of female models who have inspired her, and philosophical ruminations on what it means to live as a dark migrant woman.

Despite this narratological complexity the text rests upon one clear kernel that can be located in Alexander's memory of her childhood in Kerala and the transformation of that memory for the purpose of art. Kerala is her lost paradise that works as a pivotal center from which to express the pangs of growing up as a dark female body. To represent this profound embodiedness and yet alienation from the self, Alexander has to forge her own lyrical language, which she develops through her career as an academic, poet, and novelist. Her idiosyncratic concepts and images are repeated in her literary criticism (*Women in Romanticism: Mary Wollstonecraft, Dorothy Wordsworth, and Mary Shelley*, 1989); in her poetry (*I Root My Name*, 1977; *House of a Thousand Doors*, 1988; *River and Bridge*, 1995), in her memoir (*Fault Lines*, 1993); in her essay writing (*The Shock of Arrival: Reflections on Post-colonial Experience*, 1996), and in her novels (*Nampally Road*, 1991, and *Manhattan Music*, 1997). It is as if she has tried to pin herself down to a "momentum" in memory and language that keeps shifting and grafting like fractals, the mathematical figure that keeps adding sides, lines, and shapes to a main contour, Alexander's identity keeps reverberating and refracting, but remains basically engrained in the same area. She is in New York because of what she was in her beloved Kerala:

> And sitting here in New York City, at my writing table, in a room filled with dust, I recall my childhood fears about what it might mean to be born into a female body. (p. 42)

In the following paragraphs the themes and strategies recurring in Alexander's confessional mode and compulsive re-membering are illustrated.

Writing as a Shelter

At first glance Alexander's memoir looks like an impromptu, a long single act of reminiscence in the first person. The author situates herself in her early days and begins her account in a more or less chronological order. She organizes her book into thirteen chapters, each of which deals with a thematic aspect of her life. Her third chapter is entitled "Katha," which means the telling of a story. In the following chapters, she tells us many stories that pertain to her life, from her childhood in Kerala, her crossing borders, her Khartoum journal, and her profound relation with language. She concludes with a chapter called "Real Places or How Sense Fragments: Thoughts on Ethnicity and the Writing of Poetry" in which she offers her declaration of poetics.

Within the well-structured sequentiality of events is a subweb of doubts. These untangle the filaments of self and deconstruct identity from an essential Indian core towards a piecemeal self, as the author defines her existence. Splitting herself between a "strategic essentialism," as Spivak would say (1988), and "an ex-centric nomad," as Deleuze and Guattari would say (1987), Alexander intersects the diachronic narrative of the story of an Indian woman writer—looking nostalgically back at her roots—with the synchronic pattern of dislocation, removal, and dispersal. The self that is constructed is thus redefined as heterogeneous and negotiable.

Therefore, the memoir contains many tales within a tale, as if the self was a complex epos, like the Ramayana or the Bible. Offering a continuous perspective of the self, and windows to the world, Alexander plays with the dialogism of inside/outside, past/present, life/fiction, and ethereal/concrete. It is, indeed, the last combination that gives a homogenous structure to the narration, the alternation of imagination that is ethereal and floating, against concrete and harsh descriptions.

The act of writing constitutes a shelter, gives "space to what would otherwise be hidden, crossed out, mutilated,"[1] a space where the dissonant part of the self comes together in bits and pieces, where the pledge of affiliation with her land of origin, Kerala, can cohabit with her present meandering through the streets of Manhattan, the site of her migrant being. From this site she retrieves all past events from her memory's storehouse, from the red soil and paddy fields of Tiruvella, to the pangs of growing up in the dusty deserts of Khartoum, to her experience of being "unwhite" in America where she has been called "You black bitch" (p. 169). "They don't know what to do with us. Exotic, Asian, border-line black" (p. 188).

Writing is a refuge but also a domain where Alexander tackles her internal differences, her internal alterity as a splitting of the self. In this she is in line with Julia Kristeva's *Strangers to Ourself* (1991), a study of cultural configurations of the foreigner in historical and literary discourses. Kristeva politicizes Freud's discovery of the split subject so as to develop a psychogram for the experience of dislocation. While Bhabha's rewriting of Freud's notion of the uncanny (*das Unheimlich*) articulates the cultural liminality of the nation within any narration, Kristeva uses Freud to argue that beyond issues of cultural and gender specificity, the human psyche is never at home. Kristeva's interest in theorizing the "stranger" is useful because it allows a remapping of the concept of the "other." Kristeva's theory destroys the separation between foreigner and stranger by moving the discussion beyond separation based on national boundaries. Her alternative, the exploration of the marginal spaces that cross national borders, challenges the dichotomy between the immigrant and the native and moves towards a definition of the difference/alienation/*Unheimlich* within the self. An experience of cultural foreignness becomes, for her, parallel to an experience of alterity that the unconscious produces within each individual psychic apparatus. The figure of the foreign is a sign for the subversion of individualism, psychoanalysis, and the journey of migration, mutually exchangeable: "Living with the other, with the foreigner, confronts us with the possibility or not *being an other* . . . oneself other for oneself" (Kristeva, 1991: 13). For Kristeva, to understand the situation of the foreigner means to recognize the incoherence, gaps, and internal uncanniness of the subject itself. Experience of cultural and geographical dislocation calls the stability of the category "me" into question and aligns the dislocated person with other figures of the uncanny, each of which is read as an external representation of an internal difference.

In Alexander's narrative the frightening Otherness has to be rescued in order to reconstruct the displaced self. The dark side of emigration is blended with the empowering act of recovering her lost heritage, burning its imperfections and translating its everlasting beauty into the present:

> But when she approaches me, this Other who I am, dressed in her bits-and-pieces clothing, the scraps cobbled together to cover her nakedness, I see quite clearly what I had only guessed at earlier: she has no home, no fixed address, no shelter. Sure everything else looks fine. She has two hands, two feet, a head of long black hair, a belly, breasts. But it is clear she is a nowhere creature. (p. 30)

As Kristeva stated, writing is impossible without some kind of exile. Perception of otherness is therefore a prerequisite for any critical insight. And this perception is highly emphasized in Alexander's writing.

Making up Memory

For postcolonial postmodernist writers the metaphors of space tend to dominate those of time. Movements across countries, cultures, and languages seem to be a better representation of our contemporary lifestyle, whereas metaphors of time are trapped in a notion of history that is no longer linear. These tensions—scattering versus linearity, chaos versus order, and fragmented self versus universal "I"—have all caused a relocation and recodification of metaphors.

Nonetheless, as Bakhtin has already specified with his notion of the chronotope, there is no time without space. Both coordinates are necessary for the establishment of any notion of being. Of course, the diagrams formed by time/space have been subverted. But we should follow Boyarin's suggestion that one should not focus on "Time and space," but rather on "temporalising and spacialising discourses" (Boyarin, 1994), or James Clifford's proposal of creating "a history of location and a location of histories" (Clifford, 1992: 105). To spatialize time and to historicize space is essential to fight against amnesia and a facile celebration of migration.

The registration of memory according to a continuous sense of recorded time (chronos) can be very concise for Alexander, as we have seen. It is her second strand of memory, defined by Deleuze as the molecular time of becoming (aion),[2] that Alexander has to deal with throughout her lifetime. When a friend asks Meena why she came to America, Alexander simply replies, "to make up my memory," which means to reconnect the two strands of memory that constitute her identity: the linear and the existential one, life and art, self and criticism. In order to reconnect memory with language, hence to create the narrative of her identity, Alexander asks herself vital questions whose tentative answers bring her closer to her core self. Everything is metabolized, becoming a revelation of existence. Everything is, in this sense, symbolic.

> Sometimes I am torn apart by two sorts of memories, two opposing ways of being towards the past. The first makes whorls of skin and flesh, coruscating shells glittering in moonlight. A life embedded in a life, and that in another life, another and another. Rooms within rooms, each filled with its own scent. . . . (p. 29)

According to this memory Alexander acknowledges her childhood, her parents in their shapes and scents, and her grandparental house in Tiruvella:

> Another memory invades me: flat, filled with the burning present, cut by existential choices. Composed of bits and pieces of the present it renders the past suspect, cowardly, baseless. (p 30)

This second strand of memory expresses the author's existential anxiety. Aside from her life's events she traces her history as a woman torn by multiple passages, engrained in multiple languages of which English has become the dominant one. Her native Malayalam is the forgotten but subversive language, which still shapes the rhythm of her poetry. Her notion is of a diasporic postcolonial woman, marked as Other in the new country, without fixed address, other than in her memory.

The writer, therefore, not only transforms the complex nature of memory, of re-membering and of transferring memory into language, but also the idea of collision that is created by having multiple selves. It is not just overlapping, intertwining, and fusing different aspects of identity, but jarring, jolting, tossing of mutilated parts: "In Manhattan it is hard to make the bits and pieces hold together. Things are constantly falling apart" (p. 177). Therefore, writing her own autobiography offers not only the relief and satisfaction of spelling out her own identity, but also the chance to construct a space for the ideal form of migrancy: that within the self. It is indeed a journey wherein the author starts inner migrations, her split self starts to migrate towards an inner dimension. Therefore, contrary to the traditional practice of autobiography, which turns the private self into a public subject, Alexander creates a narrative that digs deeper and deeper and renders what was assumed to be public more private. It is no coincidence that she chose the subtitle *A Memoir*, instead of *An Autobiography*, which indicates a more intimate form of concatenation of the self. However, her contribution to this genre must be found in her centralizing the narration around the self, as in an anti-postmodernist trend. Even though she fragments and pluralizes herself, her world is undoubtedly rich in experience and filtered through her diasporic gendered being, and there is no question of added perspectives, layered patterns, or alternative projections. Her "description of the past and present are like edges averting and inverting to form a uniform, singular border,"[3] that of the self. Her philosophical ruminations do not only centralize the self as a geographically dislocated being, but as a condensation of multiple temporalities:

> And because it was, I am whole and entire. I do need to think in order to be. I was a child there, here I am, and though I cannot find the river that brought me here, yet I am because that was. (p. 197)

And it is in Manhattan that Alexander "must make up memory," a memory co-equal to the tensions of a city filled with immigrants. Making up her memory is for Alexander a work in progress, a life project in which mindscapes and outerscapes intermingle. Time assumes corporality in its setting through spaces and locations, the green paddy fields of her childhood in Kerala, the dusty desert experienced during growing up in Sudan, the cold Nottingham days, where blood hides in cherry trees, and the crowded Manhattan subways of adulthood. It is impossible in Alexander to distinguish spatiality from temporality, not to spatialize time and temporalize space, despite her claims of being a de-geographized and de-temporalized migrant soul. Her spellbinding capacity to reinforce the very categories that she so skillfully deconstructs is part of her mesmerizing lyrical prose, a profound reaffirmation of political identity in a time of postcolonial decenteredness and postfeminist disembodiedness. If, in postmodern fiction, metaphors of space predominate over those of time, Alexander emphasizes memory as a metaphor for giving space to the self.

The Autobiographical Genre

> The case of autobiography raises the essential problem in contemporary feminist theory and praxis: the imperative situating of the female subject in spite of the postmodernist campaign against the sovereign self.
> —Brodszki and Schenck, *Life/Lines*, p. 14

The two projects of writing and of making up memory are intertwined in Alexander's text. A memoir implies an even more confessional and obsessive presence of the "I" than an autobiography, where the narration of the self finds volume in a more fictional representation. However, the boundaries between narrative genres have become very blurred and unstable. The autobiography is one of the most targeted genres in feminist literary studies since it concentrates on a subject that is paradoxically reaffirmed and deconstructed at the same time.

The interesting aspect of Alexander's memoir is that it shows the parallel development of the woman and of the writer as untangled and inextricable and yet constantly deconstructed:

> Sometimes I think I have to write myself into being. Write in order not to be erased. (p. 73)

In recent decades autobiography as a literary genre has been at the center of theoretical discussions since it rotates around two categories, art and life, which become inextricable in the process of representation. As Bella Brodzki and Celeste Schenck suggest in their introduction to *Life/Lines* (Brodzki and Schenck, 1988: 1) this relationship between literature and life has, in fact, turned out to be the most problematic.[4] The universalistic centeredness of the masculine "I," which characterizes the history of autobiography from its birth with Saint Augustine's *Confessions*, has been called into question by recent poststructuralist theories. According to the latter, there is no longer a unified, transcendent self that can be read and transposed faithfully into literature:

> All these representative masculine autobiographies rest upon the Western ideal of an essential and inviolable self, which like its fictional equivalent, character, unifies and propels the narrative.[5]

The idea of autobiography representing a reflection of selfhood, as the surface of a mirror could do, implies that between the perception of a life and its autobiography there are no mediations or interferences. One is the reflection of the other. Therefore, since the Renaissance, the period that established the centrality of the human being in the universe, the autobiographical genre has been asked to represent the outstanding life events of important men, and this production in turn became the representation of an era. This linear understanding of the autobiography remained unquestioned until Roland Barthes highlighted the extremely dialogical nature of autobiography, which derives from an ongoing relationship between author and subject, text, and life. The centrality is established not around the subject but around the text since the very practice of writing is the finality of the autobiography and not its claim to be true to life. Only at this stage does the male autobiographer in quest of self-representation see the allure and distortion of the mirror.

Barthes proposes a deliberate undoing of time, continuity, coherence, and selfhood, and this project offers a model of nonrepresentative, dispersed, displaced subjectivity to a feminist reading of the autobiography. There is a parallel between what Barthes is trying to do with autobiography (a subversive attack on the autobiographical genre and on the self) and the strategies used by women dating as far back as the fifteenth century, when it was impossible to capture the self other than in pieces, fragments, and refractions. This very strategy characterizes modernist literature but has always been present in women's writing because it had to express not an aesthetic enterprise but the social, political, and psychic marginalization of women whose selfhood is mediated. The invisibility imposed by the absence of a proper tradition within a male-dominated culture has denied female autobiographers both the sense of individuality and the need to make public those experiences that were exclusively relegated to the private sphere. This absence of speaking to an audience that could listen, plus the fragmented experience of "reality" conceded to women, made this kind of writing inward-looking, intimate, whispered, and associative, composed of fleeting images because such works were not to report an exemplary life but were intended as a dialogue between the multiple selves, or between the self and the Other.[6]

Moreover, this kind of writing, which was never recognized as being female, was undertaken by modernists in an era of growing uncertainties. Modernists perceived the human being as a divided self lacking a teleological foundation, not as a monolithic integrity. This condition had all along been familiar to women and not avantgardist. Since modernism it has became obvious that a life does not exist until it is worded. The result of writing has a life of its own that is quite independent from its sources. Therefore, autobiography as the mirror of a life gives way to the conception of autobiography as the creation of a life.

These concerns, pertinent to post-structuralist literary theory, overlap with the most vexed questions of postcolonial theory. However, the theories diverge on how to tackle the crisis of representation. Postcolonial critics have concentrated on the possibilities of expressing subaltern subjectivities and alternative identities, in which difference is represented and not erased. Difference must be located in time and space and cannot be thought of separately from issues of race, ethnicity, gender, class, caste, age, sexual preference, and ability. All these variables are indispensable for a representation of the postcolonial subject. It is not that post-structuralist theories foreground an apolitical celebration of free-floating multiplicities and pastiche but more that postcolonialism cannot be conceived outside these axes.

Postcolonial thinking enacts the paradoxical condition of promoting new forms of subjectivity (therefore holding to some kind of representation) while deconstructing the representations given by colonial and dominant structures. This paradox is strongly present in the way postcolonial writers appropriate and undermine the use of autobiography as a literary genre for the representation of subjectivity. In her essay "Resisting Autobiography" Caren Kaplan questions whether or not autobiography is recoverable as a feminist writing strategy in the context of transnational affiliation among women. If Western autobiography criticism is itself a form of colonial discourse, does Western feminist autobiography criticism continue postcolonial forms of cultural domination? Are there reading and writing strategies that historicize and deconstruct mythologies of nationalism and individualism?

Her question can be answered in the positive considering how an autobiographical writer such as Alexander appropriates and undermines the genre. The limits of Western literary structures are abundantly obvious in the powerful elisions and experiments that constitute cultural margins, as Alexander tries to show. Caren Kaplan explains, "As counterlaw, or *out-law*, such production often breaks most of the obvious rules of genre. Locating out-law genres enables a deconstruction of the 'master' genres, revealing the power dynamics embedded in literary production, distribution, and reception."[7]

Alexander's contribution to autobiography is, therefore, to be found in her making epistemological categories, such as time, space, and language, self-collide. In this way her out-law autobiographical repertoire becomes a groundbreaking experience.

RHETORIC OF MIGRANCY

Discrepant Cosmopolitans

> Unresolved historical dialogues between continuity and disruption, essence and positionality, homogeneity and difference (cross-cutting 'us' and 'them') characterise diasporic articulations. Such cultures of displacement and transplantation are inseparable from specific, often violent, histories of economic, political, and cultural interaction, histories that generate what might be called discrepant cosmopolitism.
> —James Clifford, "Traveling Cultures," p. 108

Alexander's ontological rootlessness and excruciating fragmentedness can give rise to some perplexities when her social background and actual position as a migrant are taken into consideration. As the daughter of a well-off cosmopolitan family who became an academic and a successful poet in New York, Meena Alexander definitely occupies a privileged position within the realm of dispossessed postcolonials. It might sound sterile to offer a classification of these most marginalized people. But many transversal positions must be accounted for because these reinscribe and recontextualize marginality. For example, it might be more disadvantageous to be a WASP housewife than an Asian migrant university teacher. Not only do race, ethnicity, and gender concur to create a positioning within the social and economic status of a citizen but also class, education, and experience. In Mukherjee's fiction immigrants are portrayed in terms of class expectations. In Alexander's narrative the pivotal center is dislocated ethnic femaleness.

As Nira Yuval-Davies has pointed out, Western feminists often feel entitled to speak for Third World women who are oppressed and illiterate. However, Third World women are often represented by women, such as the Indians included in this study, who come from even more exclusive circles in their societies than those of middle class white feminists:

> In post-colonial societies they often come from the families of the ruling élites. One of the differences between First and Third World feminist women, therefore, that is very rarely pointed out, is that the Third World women come from homes where domestic servants, for instance, are a much more usual practice than in the homes of the Western feminists. At the same time, of course, the practice by Western middle class professionals of hiring au pairs, nannies and housekeepers, who often come from subjugated ethnic and migrant collectivities, is also growing.[9]

As Kevathi Krishnaswamy has written, many authors turns to the metaphors of migrancy too easily to express their artistic and existential quest. This excess of migrant rhetoric robs the "real dispossessed" of their language of pain and suffering. Krishnaswamy calls for a political relocation of such concepts in which the experiences of political exiles, economic refugees, and migrant laborers are used to designate a wide, confused range of cross-cultural phenomena. He asks:

> What part has the "cosmopolitan", "Third World intellectual" played in the manufacture of "Diasporic Consciousness"? How have metropolitan discourses framed contemporary conceptions of hybridity and migrancy? Has the mythology of migrancy provided a productive site for post-colonial resistance or has it become complicit with the hegemonic postmodern theorisation of power and identity? (Krishnaswamy, 1995: 128)

Examples of South Asian cosmopolitans like Salman Rushdie or Vikram Seth strengthen the idea of the ambiguous status of migrant postcolonial intellectuals writing for a predominantly metropolitan readership. The image of the postcolonial writer as a migrant, of course, is central to Salman Rushdie's politico-aesthetic, which regards the experience of multiple dislocation—temporal, spatial and linguistic—to be crucial, even necessary, for artistic development:

> It may be argued that the past is a country from which we have all emigrated, that its loss is part of our common humanity. Which seems to me self-evidently true; but I suggest that the writer who is out-of-country and

even out-of-language may experience this loss in an intensified form. It is made more concrete for him by the physical fact of discontinuity, of his present being in a different place from his past, of his being "elsewhere." This may enable him to speak properly and concretely on a subject of universal significance and appeal.[9]

In this statement it becomes clear that the image of migrancy is a metaphor for a common human experience, but it also privileges the geographically/culturally displaced writer as someone uniquely equipped to reclaim the contours of a specific lost homeland and to speak of things that have a universal significance. According to this formulation the experience of dislocation provides the writer with a sharpened vision since, as Edward Said writes, the migrant is "a counterensemble of interdependent perspectives, identities and political positions, a 'nomad' between histories, cultures and narrations rather than the citizen of a nation" (Said, 1993: 60).

Both Said and Rushdie are in favor of the abstraction of migrancy as a privileged position, a way of straddling two or more cultures, of becoming self-conscious in the process rather than suffering alienation or internal division. However, if we read the frontier as a metaphor for the margin, as Rushdie does when he presents migrancy as a shared existential condition, we should also include "internal exiles," as Krishnaswamy further suggests, "such as women living within patriarchy, minorities living on the margins of hegemonic cultures, or oppressed majorities living under occupation, thereby undermining the migrant's claim to an exclusive uniqueness." (Krishnaswamy, 1995: 137). The advantage of stressing the positivity of migrancy, as Said, Rushdie, and even Mukherjee have done, is that it accentuates the active subjectivity of expatriate writers and subverts the assumption that being postcolonial and unhomely means being the victim of history. However, even though this affirmation might sometimes be the case, it is not the only side of the coin. Celebrating migrancy too easily, as Krishnaswamy has pointed out, not only deprives "really oppressed people" of their language of pain. It also deprives migrant intellectuals of their malaise despite their "smooth passage West."

Does Meena Alexander turn to an easy rhetoric of migrancy? A superficial answer would say yes. However, a more thorough analysis of her writing not only shows her deep philosophical commitment to the issue of migrancy as positioned, but also to migrancy as identity in becoming. In her memoir *Fault Lines*, Alexander confesses that her feeling fragmented is not a status, but the result of constant negotiation and questioning of the self. Unlike Rushdie, who juggles in the supermarket of identity, Alexander does not take the intersection between postmodernism and postcolonialism for granted and she shares the intellectual enterprise with Spivak: "even as we join in the struggle to establish

the institutional study of marginality we must still go on saying 'And yet. . . .'"
(Spivak, 1991a).

Even though Meena Alexander's life experiences and artistic career could
make her a successful cosmopolitan writer with no need for an anchored identity, she reiterates throughout her fiction that she needs to belong. Coping with
fluid, multiple identities is not a choice for Alexander but a strain, no simple
postmodern empowerment, but anxiety. She articulates the complexities and
limits of being a "dark female" who is uprooted and postcolonial:

> How silly to speak as if years, a life, a fragmented ethnicity might be
> arranged as blocks on a parquet floor, or a row of toothbrushes in a tidy
> Upper West Side bathroom. (p. 196)

The author's politics of location is centered on her diasporic femaleness, and on
experiencing the world through her ethnic body, which cannot be triggered, nor
forgotten:

> Or if I write dazzling, brilliant lines filled with the conjuring tricks, all
> the sortilege of postmodernism and forget the body, what would that be
> like? (p. 200)

Alexander's approach to migrancy, or to the troubled sides of migrancy, is definitely different from the exhilarating permanent migrancy that we encounter in
Salman Rushdie, and in a different way, from the perennial status of exile of
V. S. Naipaul, or even from the endless transmutations of Bharathi Mukherjee.
Alexander's writing does not result in a positive view of multiple identities. The
ancestral land is not recollected as a utopian place of origin but as torn flesh, an
absence physically present in the body. Writing does not flow easily but is syncopated, characterized by ruptured lyrical recollections. This style is inspired
both by the English romantic poets, who cherished the sublime, and by the feminist tradition of writing the body (*écriture feminine*), of conferring immanence
and materiality to the perception of knowledge:

> What should I write with? Milk, blood, feces, spittle, stumps or bone,
> torn flesh? Is this mutilation? Surely milk is not torn out of a female
> body, nor blood: each might be a perfect blossoming. Sometimes I think
> I write to evade the names they have given me. (p. 73)

What, with easy postmodern vocabulary, can be described as "empowering,"
"multiplying" is for Meena Alexander first and foremost a *via crucis*. The body
is a cartography of the self, and it has all the borders and marks on it. The recon-
ciliation of opposing forces within the self is worded by Meena Alexander in a

more problematic way than by Homi K. Bhabha, who sees these spaces in-between as interstices, fruitful positions to occupy and places to act. A "fault line" is obviously a sign of deficiency, failing, or imperfection. To be in such a position entails pain and a feeling of incompleteness. How does one turn the negative valence into an empowering condition? It would take a lifetime to heal the pain or simply to learn how to deal with it, to reconcile "one's own alterity."

This great effort of "re-imagination" and "re-writing" keeps Meena Alexander constantly busy trying to put her multiple selves into a language that is never quite fixed, never quite right. The problems of representation for a postcolonial woman are even more pronounced in Sara Suleri's work, the subject of the following chapter, who rewrites personal and national histories through absences.

Chapter 4

Alienation and Narration

Sara Suleri, *Meatless Days*

I have written only what I remember, so if this book is read as a chronicle it could be objected that it is full of gaps. Even though I am dealing with real life, I think it ought to be read as a novel; in other words, without asking either more or less of it than a novel can give.

—Natalia Ginzburg, Lessico Famigliare, p. 5

OMISSIONS

Sara Suleri represents a complex case of nationality. She was born in Pakistan under British rule and grew up in the new nation created through partition (1947). Therefore she cannot be included under the label "Indian writer," nor is the term "Pakistani writer" appropriate. This is not only because she has lived most of her life in the United States, but mainly because she has established her distance from the Pakistani political regime, as this chapter will illustrate. She could be labeled as a writer from the Indian subcontinent, but the term is viewed with hostility because of its nebulousness and political inconsistency. Around such codifying difficulties Suleri has constructed a rather unusual text of un-representation.

Meatless Days (1989) is an intriguing memoir—her only fictional account so far—which is a humorous blend of autobiographical sketches and of feminist reflections on the discursive problem of representing Pakistani women. Organized in nine chapters, the book opens with "Excellent things in women" in which Suleri outlines her feminist standpoint that works as a subweb in the whole text. The following chapters add new aspects to her mosaic, showing the interface between the personal and political experience of nationhood. The following episodes, in fact, concentrate on the puzzling members of her family and eccentric friends in their refraction of their national history: the father's crusade for a Muslim state in "Papa and Pakistan," her beautiful sister in "The immoderation of Ifat," and the evanescent Welsh mother in "What Mamma Knew" and "Mustakori, my Friend: A Study of Perfect Ignorance."

The relevance of Suleri's text is not only due to her strategic formulation of subject positions in condition of migrancy, as I will illustrate later, but also to the re-narration of the national history of Pakistan from the point of view of matrilinear tradition. Focusing on the restrictive space of female domesticity, Suleri filters the political turmoils of the newly born nation. In a span of time that stretches from the trauma of partition, which marks the birth of the nation in 1947,[1] up to the 1970s, when the narrator leaves for the United States, *Meatless Days* describes great and small events of a troubled country through female eyes. Suleri investigates the various happenings of her prediasporic life through the ambiguous location of her citizenship in the United States, thereby creating a fracture between the location of memory and the location of utterance.

To express this discrepancy, Suleri turns to postmodern devices by proposing an oblique positionality as her strategic location between the two cultures and time settings. She finds her model in her mother, a Welsh woman who married a prominent journalist and went to live in the brand new nation of Pakistan as a guest. Many years later Suleri will repeat her mother's itinerary by moving to the United States for her degree. The metaphor of the mother's dislocation is used to illustrate the author's condition as a postcolonial diasporic subject. Suleri constructs a heterogenous space of indeterminacy by disrupting the national discourse constructed by her father with her mother's articulation of migrant positions. By reclaiming her mother's discourse in the unfolding of the Pakistani nation Suleri retrieves a supplementary history that produces an alternative narration of community and affiliations. The investigation of her mother's positioning within the official narrative of the nation through absence, reticence, and silence explains the intentions behind the book:

> I am curious to locate what she knew of the niceties that living in someone else's history must entail, of how she managed to dismantle that other history she was supposed to represent. Furthermore, I am interested to see how far any tale can sustain the name of "mother," or whether such a name will have to signify the severance of story. (p. 164)

Suleri's narrative approaches the difficulty of representing women in Pakistan as a discursive problem. She, therefore, questions Third World female subject positions that can only be established as tangential to official history. Creating spaces of solidarity in the interstices of patriarchal and imperial culture, women transform a vulnerable position into moments of subjecthood. With this stance *Meatless Days* defies both essentialism and postmodern multifariousness. In the opening page of her memoir Sara, the character, writes: "Leaving Pakistan was, of course, tantamount to giving up the company of women" (p. 1). Later on she declares: "Now I live in New Haven and I feel quite happy with my life. I miss, of course, the absence of women . . ." (p. 19). The paradox enticed by "missing an absence" locates Sara Suleri on the shifting ground between the Pakistani collective identity she has left behind and the individual selfhood she has recreated in New Haven. She argues that women's identity in Pakistan is not individualistic but communal, and within the patriarchal system of Pakistani society women are not allowed to exist as subjects but only as social roles: "the concept of woman was not really part of an available vocabulary: we were too busy for that, just living, conducting precise negotiations with what it meant to be a sister, or a wife or a mother or a servant" (p. 1). Therefore, Sara misses "the *absence* of women" in the sense that she has to feel, "now (that she) live(s) in New Haven," happy with her life as a self-supporting woman.

The category of woman is, therefore, reinscribed as an aporia. By representing Pakistani women through their omission from the official history, Suleri reconstructs a whole community of women who were only occasionally aware of themselves as women. To the linear construction of a historical time (that of the nation and of her father), Suleri opposes the cyclical, disruptive, eternal time of her memory and the transversal unofficial versions of the women in her family: mother, sisters, aunts, servants. Therefore, under the appearance of a family romance the unfolding of an Islamic country is delineated in its untold and ironic aspects.

This narrative and discursive perspective offers not the grand narrative of Pakistan but the counterhistory of a nation told through the gathering of private family anecdotes, parables, and gossip. These make of *Meatless Days*, which is beyond the definition of any specific genre—neither autobiography nor novel nor essay—a repository of crucial events that are often dramatic but presented in a very readable and enjoyable narrative, a web of metaphoric relations between discursive practices and the woman's body.

La historia (non) *oficial*

By taking the position of a tourist in her own life, Suleri humorously narrates the turns of events in her family. Her father, Z. A. Suleri to whom the chapter "Papa and Pakistan" is dedicated, functions as a point of intersection between the Pakistani history and the family. Born in Quadina, North India, in 1913, he moved to Karachi in 1941 because of the political changes. He is nicknamed Pip by his family with obvious echoes to Dickens' character in *Great Expectations*. As the magnate of the Pakistani Press, he lived through the creation and folding of many newspapers, from *The Orient Press* to the *Evening Times* to the *Times of Karachi* to the *Pakistani Times*, "as though his life were determined to be as novel as the nation" (p. 117). He had, in fact, been busy all his life with writing the nation: in 1944 he published the book *The Road to Peace and Pakistan* and a year later *My Leader*. He lobbied hard for the formation of Pakistan and in a letter Jinnah, the founder of Pakistan, thanks Pip for keeping such an affectionate corner for him. Sara ironically asks: "'If this is the corner,' I interpolated to Ifat, 'what on earth does the center look like?'" (p. 114). "'This work,' writes Sara, 'was also making Papa feel the need to be historical'" (p. 128). However by using English instead of Urdu, he feels at odds. As a freedom fighter he had heralded the idea of a Pakistan free from India, but India has to be freed from Britain too. He wanted to be a maker of the nation where Muslims would no longer be a minority.[2] However, Pip missed the moment of Partition because in 1947 he was in London. Sara wonders if her father would have been less supportive of Jinnah had he actually been a witness to the traumatic events of Partition:

> Today I often regret that he was not in Pakistan at the time of the Partition, to witness those bewildering streams of people pouring over one brand new border into another, hurtling as they ran. It was extravagant, history's wrenching price: farmers, villagers, living in some other world, one day awoke to find they no longer inhabited familiar homes but that most modern thing, a Muslim or a Hindu nation. There was death and panic in the cities where they rose up to flee, the Muslims traveling in one direction, the Hindus in the other. I wish, today, that Pip had been a witness of it all: surely that would have given him pause and conferred the blessing of doubt? (p. 116)

The splitting and wounding of partition have left a deep impact on the national consciousness. After fifty years of independence the question of whether this could have been avoided is still alive. Pip's dedication to the Pakistani cause was, however, not a matter of religion: "'The genesis of Pakistan was not Islam,' he shouted, as I knew he would, 'It was different—it was Muslim nationhood!'" (p. 127). He started, in fact, very late in his life to pray, as Sara reports. The necessity of a Muslim state was not based on religious ground for Sara's father but on the necessity to be in control of history and to overcome the feeling of marginality that Muslims experienced in India. Therefore, he was always intent in formulating the grand narrative of Pakistan. He was happy to feel at the "hub of himself and of history" (p. 112) and when he talked it was always "of Pakistan" (p. 5). However, his single-minded focus on the drafting of the country's history alienated him from successive Pakistani regimes, which jailed him, and from his children, who left him.

After one year of independence Jinnah dies and all the various political changes follow, including the bloody war for the secession of Bangladesh which ended with the constitution of another separate Muslim state in 1971. It is at this moment that Sara becomes disillusioned with Pakistan and her divergence from her father's ideals increases:

> "I am not talking about the two-nation theory," I wept to my father, "I am talking about blood!" He would not reply, and so we went our separate ways, he mourning for the mutilation of a theory, and I—more literal— for a limb, or a child, or a voice. (p. 122)

After the war with Bangladesh the Ayub empire began to crumble, and Zulfikar Ali Bhutto came to power. Bhutto proposed the modernization of Pakistan but in the end he opted for autocratic rule to repress all opponents of his regime. This was seen by the Suleri's father as "the decline of Muslim nationhood" (p. 58). It is at this historical moment that Sara decides to leave for the United States. For a man who fought all his life against the status of minority, his daughter's decision to migrate must have seemed outrageous:

> For a while he looked at me as though I were telling him that I was not a nation anymore, that I was a minority: then, slowly, his face crossed over into dignity. "If I say no, you still will go," he told me quietly. "Go, child. I have no choice." (p. 123)

Sara's affectionate but also defiant depiction of her father underscores the emphasis that he consistently placed on his "now"—an accentuation that made "him a wonderful consumer of contexts" (p. 110). His journalistic construction of the genesis of Pakistan is reduced in the end to a spasmodic movement of his fingers: "in a room we could not see, a hand was still awake. It sought the secrecy of surface in the dark, and its finger was writing, writing" (p. 130). Since the private realm of the family was completely dominated by the women's sovereignty, Pip requires the presence of at least one female companion for his domestication—hence his adoption of a daughter when all the others have gone, a Shashida (a variation of the name of his son, Shahid). Pip's reliance on history and on women is such that he orchestrates his personal life as he would public history, reducing the catastrophe that was and is Pakistan into a familiar, coherent pattern. This is the unity that is continuously mobilized by the anecdotal retelling of those details, deliberately forgotten and equally deliberately remembered by Sara, a recounting that forges a community of empowering women sharing what Suleri has called in a different context "the community of loss."[3]

A number of these empowering women are no longer alive. Notwithstanding, Suleri undertakes the task of rewriting their lives in her memoir. It is obvious that the female corporal presence provides an antidote to the impersonal father whose repression of personal histories mirrors the repressive state of Pakistan. When her sister Ifat falls in love with Javed, her father sees it as a betrayal of the Pakistan with which he believed he had fed his daughters who had also participated in his cannibalization of history (p. 110). Javed represents the Pakistan of a "polo-playing army man, a spark about the town" (p. 141), the new Pakistan that Pip refused to harbor in his home, "'but what does he know,' papa asked in horror 'about the genesis of Pakistan?'" (p. 121). Ifat, as adamant as her father, enters the heart of this Pakistan, where women are seen as disposable commodities (pp. 141–42), where tremendous value is placed on the "utterance of name" (p. 142), and where "caste and all its subclassifications are recreated every day in the structure of a conversation which knows which names to name" (p. 142). Unfortunately for Ifat her "complete immersion into Pakistan" (p. 140) results in her death, recorded in a police station in Lahore as an unsolved murder from 1980, either ordered by her husband's family, or by the husband himself, or perhaps perpetrated by Ifat's father's political enemies. Sara recalls her with the words "I miss her body" (p. 42).

From a distance, since she lives in New Haven now, Sara gets independently interested in the events of Pakistan and starts to read articles in the newspaper about the fate of Bhutto's empire. To the dynastic approach to history as conveyed by her father, Suleri opposes her matrilineal reading of the unfolding of the nation, deranging the chronological temporality in an attempt to recuperate the loss of her closest family members. First she lost her "ambivalent" mother, who died in 1978, after Sara had already left for the U.S., knocked down by a rickshaw in a dusty road of Lahore, and two years later her beautiful sister Ifat, murdered for unknown reasons. *Meatless Days*, therefore, establishes transversal affiliations to family members and friends that challenge the nation as a primary site for the feeling of community. Suleri evokes the heterogeneity of the subject positions occupied by women within postcolonial history by emphasizing their resistant and political negotiations as much as their precariousness.

The Phantom of Empire

Sara's mother, Mair, is a crucial character in *Meatless Days*, whose tangential position to the Pakistani history highlights the permanent instability of postmodern subjectivities. As a foreigner she had to disentangle herself from the complicated rules of Muslim society by marking or erasing her distinctiveness according to the situation: "she knew there must be many rules and, in compensation, developed the slightly distracted manner of someone who didn't wish to be breaking the rules of which she was ignorant" (p. 163). Pip had married her in 1944 when he was a foreign correspondent in London, even though he was already married to his cousin, Baji, and already had a daughter, Nuz. Sara reports ironically: "How could he do it, be so absentminded as to forget he already had a wife and a daughter? . . . They talked well together, it seems— Mamma at twenty-five must have been a talking thing—but I would hardly have thought it sufficient for him to pick ten years of his life with Baji and just put it in his pocket" (p. 116). Nonetheless, Pip brought Mair Jones back to Pakistan, where she becomes Surraya Suleri for the Muslim community, but just Mairi to him, "Then my mother learned the ironies of nationhood" (p. 164).

From their marriage several sons and daughters were born: Shahid, the eldest son who would end up living in England, away from the patriarchal authority of his father, Sara, who would end up in the States teaching English at Yale and become Ms. Suleri-Goodyear, Tillat who would get married and live in Kuwait, Ifat, the beautiful sister who would be murdered two years after her mother's death, Irfan whose children would not eat, and Farni, the youngest asthmatic son. After his marriage Pip was sent again to London as a foreign correspondent and all the family moved with him. Sara recollects those years in London, when she and her sister Ifat went to school in Chiswick, as her first experience of race discrimination. When her father asked Sara why her sister Ifat had so many friends at school and she had none, Sara, from the innocence of her seven-year-old race consciousness answered:

> "It's because Ifat's white and I am brown," I suggested brightly. I knew that I had given him, essentialized, a scrupulous rendition of schoolground politics, but Papa, the politician was outraged. (p. 160)

The father, proud of his nation, cannot accept the racial explanation. However, he is subconsciously still under the influence of the racial politics of colonization, which he tries to reverse by marrying a British woman, by retaking symbolic possession of what the colonial empire had taken away. Mair, on the other hand, had chosen to marry a Pakistani perhaps to rid herself of the guilt linked to the cultural oppression of her British legacy. The two cross-cultural visions of race clarify the impact of colonialism on the perception of it:

> How literal-minded of her. Did she really think that she could assume the burden of empire, that if she let my father colonize her body and her name she would perform some slight reparation for the race from which she came? Could she not see that his desire had quickened with empire's ghosts, that his need to possess was a clear index of how he was still possessed? (p. 163)

For Pip, in fact, to choose a Welsh woman as his wife was already a sign of the history that had been inflicted on him. As the maker of the new independent

Pakistan he had to avenge himself. Recuperating the experience of colonization was the only way to overcome it. The Welsh wife represented not only revenge against the foreign dominion, but it also implied the fascination and the feeling of superiority that that dominion's class had left. A British wife was indeed a sign of prestige, and some of their children, like Ifat, were so white that they were considered English.

Mair, on the other hand, contemplates the shade of race as something beautiful and almost incomprehensible: "For my mother loved to look at us in race. . . . Sometimes when we ran into a room she would look at the fascination of race in each of us" (p. 160–61). The children are for her an exoticism born from her own body. It is a purely visual and bodily appraisal for her, whereas for her husband the recognition of himself as different from white immediately brings to the surface the legacy of empire and the colonial mark of inferiority. As a politician and as a freedom fighter he cannot deal with race except in antagonistic terms. Instead, Sara, from her early age, experiences her melange of differences and colors as something she cannot get rid of through discourse. Her father's passionate speech about the ancient civilization of Pakistan and inherited genes persuades Sara of the uselessness of talking back to him: "How could I tell him that I was only trying to locate a difference, a fact that shaped my days much as weather did . . . ?" (p. 160). Their positioning in society is far too different in nature. He is fighting the abstract historical cause, and she is experiencing the result of it on her body. The declaration of the independence of Pakistan cannot erase the racial borders still in full sway within the English society of the 1950s.

Sara has to learn how to be politically correct in naming herself, how to quickly learn the political implications of words used to describe elementary knowledge, like that of color. "'Never call colour by its proper name,' I told myself at seven" (p. 160). Sara during her childhood used to swap the names of things: "I would call a marmalade a squirrel, and I'd call a squirrel a marmalade" (p. 155). Now she transfers the pure playful reversion between image and word from semantic confusion into deep political awareness. Words are heavily loaded with the colonial legacy, and they cannot be disconnected from their implicit reference to hierarchical collocation within society according to race, gender, and language:

> Living in language is tantamount to living with other people. Both are postures in equilibrium that attend upon gravity's capacity for floatation, which is a somber way of looking out for the moment when significance can empty into habit. (p. 177)

Therefore, Sara learns to turn the words as if they were coins, in order to release or hide their ambiguous significance. This double binding relation is enhanced and accelerated in the shift to foreign languages. Shifts and changes from one language to the other imply the abrogation or undermining of dominant positions:

> Speaking two languages may seem a relative affluence, but more often it entails the problems of maintaining a second establishment even though your body can be in only one place at a time. When I return to Urdu, I feel shocked of my own neglect of a space so intimate to me: like re-learning the proportions of a once-familiar room, it takes me by surprise to recollect that I need not feel grief, I can eat grief; that I need not to bury my mother but instead can offer her into the earth, for I am in Urdu now. (p. 177)

The doubleness of language and race is reflected in Sara's experience of herself as a person divided between feelings of entireness and diversity. Talking about her years spent in England, Sara remarks that she had got accustomed "to feeling foreign" (p. 94). But going back to Pakistan she realizes that those feelings of foreignness persisted:

> Lahore in June was hot, and in any case we were not the children any-more, that function having being taken over by Tillat and Irfan, the baby: we were somewhere else, and in-between. (p. 95)

Sara embodies, therefore, the condition of post-independence migrants who feel slightly un-homely wherever they go. Often due to their dilution of ethnic traits for example, or the overlapping of professional languages, the trespassing of national boundaries or the interlocking of past and present and of subjective and collective voice, they feel displaced in any location they choose to inhabit. Sara's personal choice is to opt for the location of herself on interstices (Bhabha, 1994: 2). She thereby strategically rejects the notions of center and periphery, and proposes her mother as a model for diasporic "disinterest . . . in belonging" (p. 164). Mair leaves the feelings of commitment and belonging to her husband's domain, learning "the way of walking with tact on other people's land" (p. 164). The shifting of territorial boundaries was indeed experienced by Sara and her sisters at an early age. Within their own land they felt like a minority before Partition, and after the birth of Pakistan they were different because they were light skinned. Their repeated transference from one place to the other within Pakistan, and back and forth to England, made the Suleris feel possessed by an ongoing identity shaped by the enthusiastic and passionate nationalism of the father and the abstract Welshness of the mother. Therefore, the passage to America looks more like a stabilization of home because of its distance from Pakistan, "Where history is synonymous with grief," a place from where you can remember but also try to forget.

Diasporic Syntax

Sara Suleri is the narrator but also the subject of narration since *Meatless Days* is clearly an autobiographical novel. However, she marks her sense of identity through an intentional absence of the "I." She is speaking—or not speaking—for all the women of Pakistan and by reporting their lives in parables, marking their space by pointing out their embodiment, she puts them in the foreground of the Muslim nationhood. This text, therefore, uncovers the maternal lineage of history and displaces the authority of the narrative instance as a single, essential, autonomous voice. It is an amphibious text, which mixes high and low culture, official history and unofficial stories.

This rhetorical strategy used by Suleri is also a response to the impasse generated by being labeled a postcolonial woman marked as different even according to the most radical feminist approaches. She declares her wariness of being othered: "I've lived many years as an otherness machine, had more than my fair share of being other" (p. 105). By claiming in the opening line of her book that "Leaving Pakistan was, of course, tantamount to giving up the company of women" (p. 1), she tries, on the one hand, to reconstruct the community of women and on the other to eliminate the concept of a Pakistani woman. In this way she cannot be fixed as a Third World Pakistani woman, since that concept was not part of an available vocabulary but rather an invention of the West to appropriate its referentiality.

Suleri plays with the indeterminacy of her diasporic representation, constructing a discourse that can represent her through omissions, gaps, and absences. The intermittent identity forged is "locatable as a discourse of convenience" (p. 20). *Meatless Days* focuses more than anything else on the reification of narrative. It is not a coincidence that from the age of two Sara was "interested in sentences" (p. 155) as her mother tells her. And indeed she constructs her life as a very legible text, where the diasporic syntax creates some "unpronounceability of [her] life" (p. 138). By declaring her feeling of belonging to something larger than herself, Suleri conveys an important condition: not of being a migrant but of speaking from a position of migrancy.

This subtly organized postmodern text escapes classification. By interrogating strategies of representation and by problematizing the location of the observing self, *Meatless Days* challenges both the notion of postcolonial gendered identity and the ground of postmodern representation. Suleri does not choose syncretism or fusion of oppositional categories such as the reiterated self/other, history/fiction, or past/present. Instead she emphasizes the state of perennial transmutation, which presupposes the categories given, but instead only disconnects them from originary functions. In *Meatless Days* the word *transmogrification* (pp. 34, 85) is used to express this errant ontological positioning that is based on linguistic fragility and heterogeneity. It is a word she uses to describe her own fictional encounter with history and with her family. But as a concept it represents the radical decentering of the postcolonial subjectivity that becomes represented through the interaction with other people. The grand narrative of Pakistan is transmogrified by focusing on the female genealogy, and the self is transmogrified by emphasizing the intersubjective, interrelational, and situated nature of its existence. Thus, Sara cannot write herself out of national history, just as national history cannot be written outside her and the company of women:

> By disseminating the transformations and partitions of Pakistani history in the transmogrifications of self and family over gaps of time and space, *Meatless Days* reveals the inscription of the national narrative on the personal story.[4]

As Inderpal Grewal has commented, Suleri's work is a powerful critique of the Western unified subject and suggests that postmodern subjectivity is the only viable position possible within a diasporic world. However, Grewal further argues that it does not enable any practice of feminist resistance (Grewal, 1994: 236).

It is possible to disagree with Grewal's conclusion. Suleri's construction of a feminist discourse must not be sought within the realm of a traditional engagement, such as in a positive representation of difference or in the illustration of specific strategies for female emancipation. By putting the category of Third World woman under fire, Suleri develops new discursive approaches to the problem of postcolonial representation, as I illustrate in the next paragraphs.

OBLIQUE POSITIONING

Time-space Lag: Women's Time

One innovative approach is represented by Suleri's rendition of time in relation to women and to the nation. In a way she resembles Alexander in dealing with two strands of memory, one chronological and the other existential. However, Suleri expands the existential notion of time to all her female family members, creating a consciousness of the nation through female stories.

By collapsing her sense of the differentiated identity of history and of herself, Suleri proceeds in "the construction of unreality" (p. 14), not only breaking down her narrative authority but also performing "identity as iteration, the re-creation of the self in the world of travel" (Bhabha, 1994: 225). Instead of conveying a universal order, *Meatless Days* only conveys uncertainties. This is due not only to the postmodern prose that defies traditional narratives and central authorities[5] but also to the impossibility of combining national history and gender without creating collision and discrepancies. By interlacing texts, temporalities, and locations, Suleri creates a fictive space in which the ambivalence between national narrative and personal story, between history and autobiography, is expressed through a nonplenary "I."

In this context it is important to remember Kristeva's influential essay *Women's Time* in which she expresses the idea of female subjectivity as linked both to *cyclical* time (repetition) and to *monumental* time (eternity). Historical time is, instead, characterized as linear, consisting of project, teleology, departure, progression, and arrival. Kristeva distinguishes between generations of feminists who took different positions in relation to the conception of women's time. The first were feminists who demanded equal rights with men and stressed their right to have a place in the linear time. In contrast, second-wave feminists emphasized women's radical difference and, therefore, their right to remain outside the linear time. Kristeva envisages a new generation of women who will have to reconcile maternal, cyclical time with linear political and historical time.

> In return, female subjectivity as it gives itself up to the intuition becomes a problem with respect to a certain conception of time: time as project, teleology, linear and prospective unfolding: time as departure, progression and arrival—in other words, the time of history. It has already been abundantly demonstrated that this kind of temporality is inherent in the logical and ontological values of any given civilization, that this temporality renders explicitly a rupture, an expectation or an anguish which other temporalities work to conceal.[6]

This conception of time as applied to women's subjectivity is useful in reading Suleri's text, which clearly intersperses the cyclical conception of time (pregnancies, eating, injuries, deaths) and the monumental conception of time, a kind of suspended mythological, past-personal and past-national time with the time of linear history, which Pip strenuously tries to fix in printed words. The multiple dimensions of time cannot be separated one from the other. In that sense, Suleri belongs to the new generation of feminists, mentioned by Kristeva, who find a possible convergence between the maternal and the political.

Historical time is relegated to a secondary, yet necessary, position, and it is always reported in combination with family events. When Sara's mother dies, Bhutto is imprisoned, and when six months later Dadi, the grandmother, also dies, Bhutto is hanged. Sara's mother is constantly coming back in the text, despite her announced death, as does Dadi and Ifat, as if their disappearance from the linear time does not influence Sara's archaeology of memory, since she has learned from her mother "that love renders a body into history" (p. 164).

For her father, instead, there is only one dimension, "obsessional time," as Kristeva defines linear time in psychoanalytic terms, "Pip who needed badly to retain his version, as the only form of history" (p. 127). When Sara states that "I knew it was easier to be invaded by a body than by a notion" (p. 67), she makes very clear that it is the symbiotic relationship that links the female memory to the historical experience of nationhood. Borders cannot be located outside the body; neither is it possible to fix them in conventional writings. Suleri escapes not only the problem of essentialism by not giving a definition of the self, but she also dismantles a concept of nation that is based on a chronological notion of time. The nation is made by the recollection of the self and of other women, which can only happen through a situated view in time/space/body. The nation is, therefore, subject to constant re-membering, re-writing, and revision.

M(other)wise: Stabat Mater

Besides conveying her own timing of experience and of the nation, Sara Suleri develops in *Meatless Days* a very complicated viewpoint in order to establish the matrilineal genealogy. Turning to the figure of the mother as a keystone for the feeling of home, *Meatless Days* encounters the paradox of the mothercountry and of the mother tongue as conveyed by a foreigner. Presumably, women are considered homemakers, preservers of tradition and of national values, but Sara's mother, Mair, can only function as an othering mirror, giving back in the role expected from her a deferred, displaced reflection. That is why she is always elusive for her children, ungraspable, represented in a haze of descriptions that focus on her unrepresentability, on her "posture of disinterest" (p. 167), the "location of her inattention" (p. 168), her "practice of distraction" (p. 179), or her "enchanting in abstraction" (p. 179).

Through the study of the mother's elusiveness *Meatless Days* explores the limits of any category. What is history? What is it to be a mother? What is it to be liminal to national tales? *Meatless Days* stages the re-membering of the mother's story as a subversion of the nation's figuration as fatherland. The recovery of the mother's tale also traces the irrelevance of the margin/center dichotomy and challenges the obsession with otherness that marks the current study of colonial discourse. Surray Suleri's absence becomes Sara Suleri's metaphor for transformation and for showing that contamination between colonial and colonized cultures is mutual and that the transactions between cultures are always evasive and uncertain. Her mother's disavowal of familiarity suggests an alternative and creative location that can encompass the contradictions of migrancy and displacement. Mair Suleri passes on to her daughter that study of tangentiality that allows women to survive in alien cultures: "No wonder my mother sought to teach me, with oblique urgency, the necessity of what it means to live beyond affection" (p. 159).

Her mother's subject position is, in fact, ambivalently constructed: it is not fixed, but established as a dialectic between connection and separation. Her position in Pakistan is exclusively identified neither with the marginal nor with the center, but allows her to include difference as well as the possibility of maintaining a distinct identity. Therefore, Mair embodies Sara's model for the representation of a postmodern diasporic subject. Mair's foreignness positions her ambiguously within the nation, since she is obliged to follow the strict rules of Pakistan but at the same time she is granted some "differences" and even more "absences" because she is "a white-legged woman from Inglestan" (p. 3).

In one of her articles Susan Koshy reads *Meatless Days* as a feminized re-narration of the national allegory:

> The experience of displacement connects the mother's story to the daughter's and provides a metaphor for exploring the repressions and exclusions in the official history of the nation. By reclaiming her mother's discourse, Suleri's stories incorporate a poetics of silence that allows her to interrogate and dismantle the concept of agency, and the segregation of public and private on which a masculinist national narrative is founded.[7]

At a certain point the father, who wrote reams of prose for Pakistan, is imprisoned for sedition. The mother, whose production is located elsewhere (in her children, her teaching, her habit of distraction), as Koshy writes, takes charge of the *Times of Karachi*. She decides to publish an empty paper, sheafs of blank newsprint with nothing but the title. As Sara suggests, "Mamma was more political" (p. 168) than her husband with his endless writing. By speaking in silence, "She made them know how angry she was when she turned censorship into sedition!" (p. 118). Mair reinterprets the political activism of her husband and transforms the possibility of his favorite medium, journalism, into blankness: "She did not have to put it into print" (p. 168).

For her children she is always a puzzling element. Also from a linguistic point of view her rendering of the mother tongue is a performance of difference: "Mamma's Urdu was an erratic thing" (p. 41). This displacement from the self must have been very hard, as Sara recalls: "For a woman who liked to speak precisely, she must have hated her sudden linguistic incompetence: languages surrounded her like a living space, insisting that she live in other people's homes" (p. 163). She has to shift between her identity as British into an open-ended, acquired identity as Pakistani. Pakistan is her new home since she is a mother there. However, she was "a guest, then, a guest in her own name,

living in a resistant culture that would not tell her its rules" (p. 163). In order
not to stumble upon "some hidden cultural ritual that she was too polite to dis-
turb" (p. 59), Mair pleads for invisibility: "My mother gave a ravishingly absent
minded smile and disappeared into Welshness" (p. 59). Her mother tries to
erase herself using the excuse of her being foreign. She uses, therefore, the
codes of her British cultural background to construct a subjectivity that enables
her to disappear within the Pakistani society by living with her "dispersed aura"
(p. 156). She constructs her own space which Sara defines as a position of un-
belonging: "She learned to live apart, then—apart from herself—growing into
a curiously powerful disinterest in owning, in belonging" (p. 164).

Consequently, Sara's account of her mother's story is embedded in all the
paradoxes and conflictual positioning that a postcolonial condition entails. By
making Mair the prototype of the postcolonial subject, but inside out, Suleri illustrates the limits and redundancy of current representations of subjectivity.
Postcolonialism, as Suleri demonstrated, concerns not only the Third World, but
the former empire as well.

No Women in the Third World

The strategy developed by Suleri in *Meatless Days* in order to express postcolonial female subjectivity negates the existence of the Third World woman as
such. In her text Suleri states that women in Pakistan do not exist—"the concept of a woman was not really part of an available vocabulary"—but at the
same time her novel/psychobiography is infused with sparkling and buoyant
women who dominate from their confined spaces and who show a conscious
agency despite the restrictions of the Islamic traditions.

From her new position as an academic and as a writer Sara Suleri chooses to
challenge the public invisibility of women in Pakistan through their representation within the private sphere. The writing of history via the memoir can be
done from the margins, from an author whose location in the U.S., as a Pakistani woman and as an academic, prevents her from seeking or obtaining a
dominant or oppositional subject position. The result is indeed an exemplary
text of postmodernism in its rejection of the unitary subject and its delineation
of a diasporic, multiple, incomplete subjectivity. But a postmodern, multiple
subject position is known to be an extremely difficult path to take, unlike the
ease of taking on a group identity through an anti-essentialist belonging. Sara's
friend Mustakori, for example, possesses no stable self (p. 42). Her mother had
to "walk through her new context in the shape of memory erased" (p. 164), representing a "disembodied Englishness" (p. 156).

In *Meatless Days* the relation to feminism is explained in a double binding
position. On the one hand, *Meatless Days* proclaims no affiliations with feminist

strategies of any kind. On the other hand, it investigates the role of women in the Pakistani society with an unequivocal feminist eye. To understand Suleri's approach to feminist issues, part of an important statement made in her text must be quoted. While Suleri was teaching Third World Literature at Yale, she was interrupted by a female student who asked why Third World women writers are not given equal space in the syllabus:

> Against all my own odds I know what I must say. Because, I'll answer slowly, there are no women in the Third World. (p. 20)

Suleri is trying to evade the Western attempt to essentialize the concept of woman. What she means is that women in the Third World are not constructed as full subjects. They are constructed differently according to social categories, such as class and caste, and social roles, such as wives, mothers, sisters, and daughters. She explains then to her class that "The Third World is only locatable as a discourse of convenience" (p. 20), and therefore, Third World women, as constructed by Western feminist notions, do not exist.

Obviously the word *woman* has been part of the Pakistani vocabulary since the beginning of the century, when Pakistan and Bangladesh were still part of India. Many women writers have written in favor of the women's cause, and many women's movements have been active.[8] However, part of the subtlety of Suleri's definition of Third World women, or Pakistani women, cannot be comprehended if the parameter of analysis does not change. She writes more on the wave of Chandra Mohanty's analysis of the tension between white feminism and colonized Other:

> Women are constituted as women through the complex interaction between class, culture, religion, and other ideological institutions and frameworks. They are not "women"—a coherent group—solely on the basis of a particular economic system or policy.[9]

Therefore, Suleri says that Pakistani women do not exist as visible unitary subjects but as socially constructed within specific practices. However, even though Suleri takes this as a point of inspiration for her argument, she also distances herself from Mohanty's position. Mohanty's critique of Western feminists writing about Third World women as a monolithic group with objective status does not propose strategies to avoid this objectification. In this discussion of Third World feminism it is important to also consider Spivak, who rejects certain forms of feminism that take an interest in women of the Third World and Third World Literature, but that unconsciously reproduce imperialist assumptions, such as the defense of feminist individualism outside any historical determination. Spivak also criticizes Mohanty's theoretical position since the counteraction of the Western construction of the Other cannot be done simply by pointing to the sociohistorical specificity of different contexts, all equally labeled "Third World" according to Marxist categories.

> I see no way to avoid insisting that there has to be a simultaneous other focus: not merely who am I? but who is the other woman? How am I naming her? How does she name me? Is this part of the problematic I discuss?[10]

By shifting the question from "who am I?" to "who is the other woman?" Spivak highlights the heterogeneity and discontinuity of women. Even though women might share similar experience as women, each instance of being a woman is historically specific. Spivak's self-reflective move is not only directed at avoiding the homogenization of the Third World woman, but also at avoiding speaking for her, even as a Third World critic.

Suleri points out another aspect that is not investigated by Mohanty, but is covered by Spivak, which is the difficulty of demarcating the line between what is Western and what is Third World. In her article "Woman Skin Deep: Feminism and the Post-colonial Condition," Suleri writes about Mohanty:

> How will the ethnic voice of womanhood counteract the cultural articulation that Mohanty too easily dubs as the exegesis of Western feminism? The claim to authenticity—only a black can speak for a black; only a post-colonial subcontinental feminist can adequately represent the lived experience of that culture—points to the great difficulty posited by the 'authenticity' of female racial voices in the great game that claims to be the first narrative of what the ethnically constructed woman is deemed to want.[11]

In this article Suleri offers a better theoretical argumentation than her implied discourse in *Meatless Days*. In "Woman Skin Deep" the author investigates more extensively the intersection between gender and race as it constructs the subject position within the postcolonial discourse. Suleri rejects Western feminist constructions of the Third World subject but she also criticizes Black feminist theorists who are obsessed with the racial body and try to reconfigure feminism through their personal narratives. Suleri's criticism is especially directed against bell hooks and Trinh Minh-ha for their defense of a radical subjectivity and for their use of personal narrative as a way to counteract the authority of Western feminism. By using their experiences as authentic and not appropriatable, according to Suleri, they make a fetish out of racial difference and betray the will to resuscitate the self. Suleri's anxiety is to read many of these oppositional discourses as falling into the trap of the categories they attempt to dismantle. Her question is, therefore, "If the languages of feminism and ethnicity are to escape an abrasive mutual contestation, what novel idiom can freshly articulate their radical inseparability?"[12] In order to destabilize the iconic status of postcolonial feminism, Suleri investigates the theoretical possibilities of escaping essentialist oppositions.

She admits that to theorize postcolonial femininity and/or feminism is immensely difficult. However, Suleri criticizes the underlying ideological assumptions, and conclusions, of influential works by Mohanty, Minh-ha, and bell hooks for remaining too entangled in the discourses they try to dislodge. She instead advocates a materialist feminist theory which locates the coordinates of postcolonial femininity within the axes of the institutions of the law and state. By offering an analysis of the existing Hudood ordinances within Pakistani law, which were promulgated in 1979,[13] Suleri points out the inherent parochialism and professionalism of the postcolonial and feminist discourse when faced with the overwhelming realism of the law.

Suleri's theoretical intervention shows that the female subject is constructed as a subject through the positions that have been permitted. Therefore, the effort to reconfigure feminism must not be sought in the promulgation of exclusionary politics on the basis of a personal identity politics and autobiography. What is required is not merely to produce counterhistory but to criticize the far reaching implications of the system in which women play a part. Although her ideas are defended well in "Woman Skin Deep," she does not really escape the risks she mentions and proposes no real alternative representations in her narrative work *Meatless Days*. Instead she avoids representation as a tool of contestation. By problematizing subject positions and locating women beyond national appropriation, she succeeds in circumscribing some of the pitfalls of Third World feminists and Western feminism. In not writing about the self, and in writing with a difference, she manages to convey the unstable selfhood of the postcolonial woman and to escape either situated or universal knowledge. Critics like Inderpal Grewal[14] and Sangeeta Ray[15] are, however, not satisfied with her theoretical outcome.

In defense of Suleri's remarkable tour de force of nonrepresentation, postcolonialism has come to signify for her not the historical fact of prior colonization but an abstraction available for figurative deployment in any strategic redefinition of marginality. She states in "Woman Skin Deep" that "as with the decentering of any discourse, however, this re-imagining of the post-colonial closes as many epistemological possibilities as it opens" (Suleri, 1995: 136). Suleri refers to the advantage of the term to enable a vocabulary of cultural migrancy, which has allowed the theoretical articulations as presented by Homi K. Bhabha in *Nation and Narration*. The limitations, on the other hand, are represented by the current metaphorization, which run the risk of rendering postcolonialism "so amorphous as to repudiate any locality for cultural thickness" (Suleri, 1995: 136). Suleri is well aware of her complicity with the categories she tries to avoid. By denying them through silence, absence, or elision, she reimagines epistemological categories as woman, nation, and autobiography. However, Suleri cannot avoid the limits of this reimagining and unwillingly falls back into an insufficient articulation of social roles within their locality and their specificity.

Nonetheless, her affiliation with postmodern heterogeneity and contradictions is a sign of her irreducibility to any ultimate positioning; even theoretically, she grants neither conclusion nor absolution. She is perhaps guilty of having taken the option of postmodern open-endedness to sketch the feminist need to reconcile gender and race. As she has shown for her mother's "disembodied Englishness" (p. 156) and her friend Mustakori's "no stable self" (p. 42), postmodern subject positions can be a rather hard path to take.

ALIENATION AND NARRATION

Female Saga

Suleri's memoir stresses the crisis of representation even more than Meena Alexander's. The most salient characteristic of *Meatless Days* (1989) is the fact that while it could be described as a memoir or as an autobiographical novel, it is neither. The indeterminacy of genre is emphasized along with the instability of the subject positions and the ambivalence of the narrator towards the object of its narration. *Meatless Days* could to a certain extent be seen as an autobiography, but it is not only about Sara, or only about Pakistan. As Natalia Ginzburg suggested in her autobiographical novel *Lessico Famigliare* (1963), any work of fiction, regardless of how faithful to or inspired by real events it might be, should be read as fiction.

There are, in fact, astonishing similarities between these two novels, despite their different historical locations and family backgrounds. *Lessico Famigliare* (Family Sayings) is one of the most intriguing texts by Italy's greatest postwar woman writer, Natalia Ginzburg. It calls into question the conventions of a written autobiography, the reliability of its narrative center, and its underlying assumption that every life has, or indeed is, a story. *Family Sayings* is Ginzburg's account of her Jewish family's experiences during and after the fascist period. It is narrated by the child, Natalia, who filters the history of the Italian nation during one of its most troubled and violent historical moments with family lexicons and anecdotes. The similarities between the two novels include the highly ironical tone that reduces the tragic history of the nation to the comic, intimate sphere of the family and the elision of the authors themselves within the text. Both Sara and Natalia are often absent, omitted within the narration, marginal figures in a colorful fresco of family members and authoritative political persons interspersed with each other without any hierarchical order.

In Ginzburg's text, for example, important political leaders of the Italian resistance such as the communist Filippo Turati, the industrialist Adriano Olivetti, the writer Cesare Pavese, and many others are given as much relevance as school friends, students, and other people passing though the busy Levi house. Natalia was part of this household before her marriage to Leone Ginzburg, a Jewish intellectual who fled from Russia and who died in Rome as a consequence of his Nazi imprisonment. As in Suleri's texts these main national figures are not narrated in their role as public persons but through the private sphere perceived by the little girl Natalia through incidents, little events, and jokes. The description of the father, Giuseppe Levi, as a tyrannical and maniacal figure helps the family members to distract themselves from a greater outside menace, that of the rise of fascism and the first persecution of the Jews.

Suleri's father, Pip, is also a maniac addicted to power, his authority being so often reiterated in his construction of Pakistan that he is erased within his family, where he is completely marginal despite his vociferations. Both authors skillfully omit details and create gaps in history not only to convey a narrative that is personal and nonauthoritative, but also to write themselves out of the text in order to keep part of their memory private.[16] They negotiate the collective public space of narration as a *chiaro scuro* between truth and fiction, self and collectivity, nation and narration. The critic Judith Woolf writes about *Family Sayings*:

> The book operates, to some extent, by exploiting the ironic distance between events as an historian might relate them, with hindsight and from the outside, and the private, inner narrative of memory, which foregrounds the apparently comic and trivial in order to tell its own symbolic and personal story.[17]

Both in Suleri and Ginzburg we get a clear vision of the surface of history and of the family, and we, as readers, get the message that only by studying the surface, the irrational and peculiar behaviors or the unusual modality of the private lexicon and jokes of family members, can we understand how the family and, as a kaleidoscope of that, the nation works.

Whereas *Meatless Days* is a highly postmodernist text, playing with the tricks of postcolonial and feminist representation, *Family Sayings* is a landmark of Italian literature written after the war, even though it wasn't published until 1963. *Family Sayings*, reflects the vocabulary of the neorealist novel, which used essential and bleak language to express the "disillusionment with all rhetoric, the tyrannical bombast of the Fascist regime under which they had grown up, the utopian propaganda of the divided left for whose resistance many of them had fought" (Woolf, 1997: 205). This language, reduced to the essence, is paralleled with the enterprise of turning the grandeur and disaster of history into small incidents and human figures. Ginzburg has thus reversed the scope of the autobiography; instead of making exemplary private stories into illustrious public ones, she mixes private and public into a continuum of fictional breath:

> The task of the autobiographer is often to make a public version of what has hitherto been private, known only to an intimate circle. Ginzburg, on the contrary, gives us a private and deheroized version of events that have become part of twentieth-century European history.[18]

The impact of post-colonialism and third-wave feminism is evident in *Meatless Days* as it also dismantles the expectations of an autobiographical narration. At the center of the narration is not only the Suleri family, who mirror the events of Pakistan's public life, but more specifically the women, those subjects twice silenced, by the colonial empire and by patriarchal oppression in their own country, especially in Muslim Pakistan. This time the style chosen to reverse roles and subvert subject positions is not expressed in neorealist vocabulary but in quizzical, ambiguous postmodern jargon. However, both texts subvert the history of pain and suppression by returning to the comic private language of childhood, omitting the self, or presenting the self as constructed through others. This makes of *Family Sayings* a superlative text ahead of its time and of *Meatless Days* a redrafting and recontextualization of many possible autobiographical accounts in the light of a new postcolonial gendered consciousness.

Engendering the Nation

> Outside the whale is the unceasing storm, the continual quarrel, the dialectic of history. . . . Outside the whale we see that we are all irradiated by history, we are radioactive with history and politics; we see that it can be as false to create a politics-free fictional universe as to create one in which nobody needs to work or eat or hate or love or sleep.
> —Salman Rushdie in Edward Said "Intelleutuals in the Post-colonial World," 1986: 51–52

Suleri's interpretation of the concept of the nation in the light of gender and postcolonialist thought is particularly innovative. As Leela Gandhi writes, "the encounter with feminism urges post-colonialism to produce a more critical and self-reflective account of cultural nationalism" (1998: 102). This is the enterprise embraced by Suleri, whose concepts of history and nation are, in fact, used ironically and deconstructed.

Consequently, *Meatless Days* offers no linear binding between history and narration but only acts of derangement from each other. This allows Suleri to connect the nation to issues of cultural migrancy since "the migrant moment of dislocation is far more formative, far more emplotting, than the subsequent acquisition of either post-colonial nation or colonial territory" (Suleri, 1992: 5). *Meatless Days* is not only an exercise in postcolonial partition, but the exegesis of the autobiographical self as it is split into two mother tongues (Urdu and English), moving among Pakistan, Britain, and the United States, at home with cultural and racial differences.

Suleri's rendering of the discourse of the nation differs from that of previous male theorists, not only from those who have ignored gender relations (Gellner, 1983; Hobsbawm, 1990) but also from those more sophisticated and post-structuralist theorists of the nation, such as Benedict Anderson (1983), Franz Fanon (1961), Homi K. Bhabha (1994), and Fredric Jameson (1986).

Benedict Anderson points out in his book *Imagined Communities* that

> nationality . . . nation-ness as well as nationalism, are cultural artifacts of a particular kind. To understand them properly we need to consider carefully how they have come into historical being, in what ways their meanings have changed over time, and why, today, they command such profound emotional legitimacy.[19]

The nation is, according to Anderson, an imagined political community, since even in the smallest country no one knows most of their fellow members, but still each lives in the image of their own community: "In fact, all communities larger than primordial villages . . . are imagined."[20] Therefore nations, in the modern concept of Anderson, were only possible with the advent of "print capitalism" when reading spread from the élites to other classes who started to read mass publications in their own languages, thus establishing linguistic national "imagined communities." Anderson's influential thesis on the relation between print textuality and nationalism hides an Enlightenment prejudice. As Peter Van der Veer has pointed out, "Anderson's theory does not deal with what is of at least equal importance in the nationalisms in colonized Asia, namely collective action in public arenas and the oral performance of sacred texts" (Van der Veer, 1994: 254). The marginality of the written word, the nonprivileged connection between scripture and nationalism and the reality of illiteracy especially among women in the Third World, is emphasized in Suleri's gendering of the nation when Surreya Suleri decides to publish a blank page to express her participation in and protest against political events.

However, as emphasized by Anderson the shared community has enabled postcolonial societies to reinvent their social imaginary in order to liberate themselves from the colonial aftermath. Long before Anderson, Fanon had recognized the imaginary component of national community. Franz Fanon understood colonialism to be a form of domestication of the colony, disrupting the patriarchal power of colonized men. His insight consisted in associating the dynamics of the colonial power, even though not the whole aspect of it, with the dynamics of gender. The gender metaphor was used by the colonizers to emasculate or feminize the colonized and the colony representing them as the territorium penetrated by the conquerors. With the movements for independence the colonized replied to this dialectics and, therefore, colonized women were called into question as the makers of national homogeneity. The colonized male is the real Other while women become the site to articulate both the politics of colonization and of decolonization. The main interference of the colonizers was in fact to alter the treatment of women in the colonies, by forbidding unlawful and inhuman practices such as infibulation or sati. However, the colonized women stood for the traditional values undermined by the colonizers in an attempt to destabilize male colonial authority. As a consequence the female colonized subject was subjected to vigilant discipline, with the intensively emotive politics of dress, which saw the return of the veil for women in Algeria and the wearing of the sari for Bengali women. Fanon's brilliant insight into the role of gender in the making of the Third World nation is unfortunately not developed further in the study of female agency and so the militant woman remains a man's "arsenal" to penetrate the body of the enemy during the Algerian war.[21]

Using Fanon's approach to understanding Algerian colonialism, Partha Chatterjee has carefully analyzed the new politics of Indian nationalism that glorified India's past and tended to defend everything traditional and assumedly precolonial. The nationalist project was based on learning superior Western techniques of organizing material life, but this had to be countered by the promotion of a distinct self-identity of national culture, which was done by imitating the West only in the material aspect of life and in treasuring the spiritual domain of the East as superior to the West. In this distinctive, spiritual culture the East had remained the undominated, uncolonized master of its own fate. The material/spiritual dichotomy, to which terms like "world" and "home" corresponded, came to put the women in the role of the treasurers of spiritual values. As Chatterjee writes:

> The home was the principal site for expressing the spiritual quality of the national culture, and women must take the main responsibility of protecting and nurturing this quality. No matter what the changes in the external conditions of life for women might be, they must not lose their

> essentially spiritual (i.e. feminine) virtues; they must not in other words, become *essentially* westernized. (Chatterjee, 1989: 243)

Once the patriarchal authority was restated in this differentiation between the sexes, in which the woman was the recipient of spirituality and femininity (based on mythological female models), women could move freely outside the home. The image of a woman as a goddess or mother served to erase her sexuality outside the home and therefore the woman could go into the world under conditions that would not threaten her femininity and spirituality, nor the politics of insurgency from colonial oppression. Women could therefore be concerned with female issues as long as these didn't clash with what Kristeva has defined in other contexts, using a term by Montesquieu, as the "esprit général" (Kristeva, 1993: 12).

While Fanon and Chatterjee tried to define the symbolic process through which the social imaginary—nation, culture, or gender—becomes the subject of discourse and the object of psychic identification, Homi K. Bhabha retheorizes the nation in his essay "Dissemination: Times, Narrative, and the Margins of the Modern Nation" (1990). Here in the light of the interconnectedness between nation and narration, one term informs the other. Following Bhabha's reasoning, nationalism is coterminous with the most dominant modern literary form—at least in European countries or countries influenced by Europe—the novel. Therefore, as Timothy Brennan says, the ties between literature and nation evoke a sense of the "fictive quality of the political concept itself."[22]

Reading the nation as narrative construction, Bhabha draws attention to issues of language and rhetoric. According to Bhabha the reading of poststructuralist theories of narrative analysis (pertaining to textuality, discourse, and enunciation) evoke the ambivalent margin of the nation-space. To reveal this position of marginality serves to contest the positions of supremacy coming not only from old imperialist nations but also from within the "new independent nations." In this way he advocates an alterity present within the nation itself, a split, a hybridity that allows the national boundaries to always be trespassed. Bhabha coined a theoretical category for these hybrid positions: in-between spaces or interstices. These are sites of incomplete signification where cultural and political authority is negotiated:

> It is in the emergence of the interstices—the overlap and displacement of domains of difference—that the intersubjective and collective experience of *nationness*, community interest or cultural values are negotiated.[23]

With his concept of in-betweeness Bhabha points to the emerging counternarratives created by those cultural "hybrids" who have lived, because of migration and exile, in more than one culture. Those hybrids, writes Nira-Yuval Davies, "both evoke and erase the totalizing boundaries of the nation" (1992a).

In *Meatless Days* the nation as a discourse is redefined from the margins, from those cultural hybrids represented by feminist identification. Making women the foci of a nation's narration, Suleri criss-crosses all the theoretical position illustrated above. In line with Benedict Anderson's *Imagined Communities*, Suleri also understands the nation to be a bonding beyond appropriation: "In an age when it is so common for progressive cosmopolitan intellectuals . . . to insist on the near-pathological character of nationalism, its roots in fear and hatred of the Other, and its affinities with racism, it is useful to remind ourselves that nations inspire love, and often profoundly self-sacrificing love" (Suleri, 1992: 4). Therefore she uses Anderson's emphasis on the concept of nation as being motivated by passion, which is different from rational and civil interests, and which can explain the attachment of people to the nation as a modern concept.

However, the nation is not a gender-neutral construction. As Nira Yuval-Davies points out, "it is women—and not (just?) the bureaucracy and the intelligentsia—who reproduce nations, biologically, culturally and symbolically. Why then are women usually 'hidden' in the various theorizations of the nationalist phenomena?"[24] Carole Pateman (1988) answers that this is due to civil theories that divide society into public and private domains. According to this compartmentalization, women and families belong to the private sphere and, therefore, are politically irrelevant. However, this concept of the nation rests on a paradox since, as Anne McClintock notes, the family trope is important for nationalism: "the family as a *metaphor* offered a single genesis narrative for national history while, at the same time, the family as an *institution* became void of history and excluded from national power. The family became, at one and the same time, both the *organizing* figure for national history and its *antithesis*."[25]

Feminists have, therefore, challenged the validity of the public/private divide. Third World critics such as Kumari Jayawarderna (1987) and Partha Chatterjee (1986) have shown that the line that divides public/private is a completely inadequate way of analyzing civil societies in postcolonial nations. Jayawarderna's important book *Feminism and Nationalism in the Third World* also signals a possible way out from the deadlock between feminists and nationalists. The loyalty of Third World feminists to nationalist movements does not mean that they have not been active within their societies to improve the position of women.

These dichotomies that are relevant for the concept of the nation (feminism/Third World; public/private; gender/nation; world/home) clarify the theoretical difficulties around which Sara Suleri has tried to construct her discourse on the nation. She is aware of the muddled terrain among the discourses on the nation. In her preface to the *Rhetoric to English India*, Suleri highlights how impossible it is to produce an idea of the nation that belongs neither to the colonizer nor the colonized. Consequently, she illustrates the guilty transactions and mutual interferences within the dynamic of imperial intimacy. Suleri explores the condition of transnationality that necessitates a narrative of the nation that must be reinvented through complex radical strategies of subject position. In this way *Meatless Days* avoids the nativist construction of a community in favor of an awareness of the complex formation of national, gendered, and diasporic consciousness. Using the Suleri's household as one of the narratives of the nation, *Meatless Days* is built upon an ambivalence of the private and public that cannot be told separately. And if the concept of nation is an artifact, only women can act as an element of continuity and transnationality since "men live in homes and women live in bodies" (p. 143), meaning that men cannot be thought of outside of their patriarchal civil society. By saying that men live in homes, instead of in nations, Suleri infers the dependency of men on the female presence, as the example of "Pip's tyrannical dependence on history and on women" (p. 101). This view of gender will make Shahid, the first son, detach himself from the repressive authority of his patriarchal father, which he had to endure more than his sisters, since he had no "female community" to find respite in. He clashes with his father "over history and over womankind" (p. 101) and finally decides to leave Pakistan, unable to connect his view of gender and nation within Pakistan.

The concept of the nation is not a moment of recognition in *Meatless Days* but of alienation and estrangement since, to quote Bhabha once more,

> The subject is graspable only in the passage between telling/told, between "here" and "somewhere else," and in this double scene the very condition of cultural knowledge is the alienation of the subject.[26]

However, Suleri does not offer a pure free floating postmodernist subject, disembodied and nationless. As already illustrated, she attempts to forge a possible transversal positionality that enables her to regenerate both the discourse on the Third World woman and on the nation.

Transversal positionality comes to signify a coalition politics in which differences among women are recognized and voiced from subject positions that are rooted in the personal experience (of nation, ethnicity, age and ability) and in the collective experience. This allows to show solidarity among women of different rooting and live in other women's experiences without becoming decentered. As Kristeva has written, "Women have the luck and the responsibility of being boundary-subject: body and thought, biology and language, personal identity and dissemination during childhood, origin and judgement, nation and world—more dramatically so than men are" (Kristeva, 1993: 35).

Therefore, their "strangeness within" enables women to define the contour of the modern nation not as a bordering and hierarchical domain, but as a map for getting lost, for establishing a horizontal solidarity within or for connecting outwards. As Sara Suleri has fictionalized in *Meatless Days*, "Third World is only locatable as a discourse of convenience. Trying to find it is like pretending that history or home is real and not located precisely where you are sitting" (p. 20). Trying to locate the interests that are behind those discourses of convenience is a task left outside the text, an inquiry which Suleri has decided not to explore. These absences are nonetheless resounding.

Floating Myths

Sunetra Gupta, *Moonlight into Marzipan*

Seek and learn to recognize who and what, in the midst of the inferno, are not inferno, then make them endure, give them space.
—Italo Calvino, *Invisible Cities*, p. 127

MIGRATING INFERNO

Sunetra Gupta, born in 1965, spent her formative years moving between her native Calcutta and Africa. After studying biology at Princeton University, she moved to England where she obtained her Ph.D. at London's Imperial College and subsequently went to live in Oxford to do research on infectious diseases. From this picture we gather that Sunetra Gupta is principally a scientist. However, despite her youth and restricted time for literature, she has already published four acclaimed novels, *Memories of Rain* (1992), *The Glassblower's Breath* (1993), *Moonlight into Marzipan* (1995) and *A Sin of Colour* (1999).[1] An analysis of *Moonlight into Marzipan* will show how Gupta reverses Western mythology from a postcolonial perspective through her innovative use of language and interculturality.

Western critics have defined Gupta as the new Virginia Woolf from Calcutta. Even though the comparison may be pertinent, since Gupta's psychological narration often deals with voyages within and often has recoursed to a stream of consciousness, the labeling privileges Eurocentric feminism and assumes British literature as the canon. Because of her virtuosity in language, which covers very thin plots, Gupta has also been criticized for "having no skull under the skin."[2] However these judgments, both positive and negative, do not do justice to Gupta's highly poetical language and to her enterprise of rewriting myths and tales. It would be more relevant to highlight Sunetra Gupta's debt to oral storytelling and to her Bengali background, to which her poetic language owes its inspiration.

Sunetra Gupta's originality consists in her innovative use of the English language and her deconstruction of Western myths from a postcolonial and feminist point of view. Myths have always represented women in demonizing and derogatory ways, hence the efforts of feminist writers and critics such as Angela Carter, Teresa de Lauretis, Hélèn Cixous, Luce Irigaray, Marina Warner, Mahasweta Devi, and Suniti Namjoshi to rewrite and repossess myths in order to develop new ways of representing women.

Myth is one of the elements that characterizes the ideology of the Third World/postcolonial novel. This analysis of Gupta's novel is organized around the points sketched by Viney Kirpal in her very interesting article "What is the Third World Novel?" (Kirpal, 1988: 144–56). In this article Kirpal focuses on the exploration of the ideology of the Third World novel. She identifies at least five features that make the Third World novel different from the Western one: 1) the loose, circular, episodic, loop-like narrative technique; 2) the plotlessness of these novels from the Western point of view; 3) the use of language that is regional, ritualistic, proverbial, metaphoric, and therefore quite distinct from language in the English novel, for example; 4) the use of myths by Third World novelists not just as structuring devices, but as "value-endowed paradigms" of reality; 5) "illustrational" or "archetypal" rather than "representational" characterization (Kirpal, 1988: 150–152).

Even though Gupta has denied belonging to any literary enclave, including that of postcolonialism, her novel can be explained by applying some of the strategies endorsed by postcolonial ways of reading. For example, she revisits and re-narrates many Western mythological quest stories and well-known fairy tales (point 4), managing to insert a postcolonial perspective in them in which the fate of the female characters is rethought in the light of a new conception of female agency. The English language she uses for this purpose is highly visual and rich with dense metaphors (point 3) that refer to the material world. Furthermore, the narrative center is fragmented through the multiplication of the narrative instances (point 1) and an overlap of different literary genres. By promoting a nonhierarchical cross-fertilization among different languages, realities, and literary expressions (point 2), Gupta proposes an alternative to cultural and linguistic hegemony through the fictionalization of reimagined conventional heroes/heroines (point 5).

Moonlight into Marzipan: A Study of Loss

Moonlight into Marzipan (1995) is a very complex and arduous novel that does not follow a regular chronological order of events but shifts back and forth in time and space, leaving the task of reassembling the puzzle of an open-ended story to the readers. The major device used by Gupta is to deprive the narration of its dutiful narrator and from the opening pages we, as readers, have to struggle to detect the central character(s) and the perspective from which these character(s) are viewed.

The novel opens in medias res with Esha proclaiming "that was a month of salt," a sentence that will give to the whole book a tone of fatalism and impending tragedy. It also conveys the sterility of salt out of which life should be created while instead death will prevail. Many narrative manipulations transform the fabula into a story. At the end of the novel we find, in fact, the plot summarized as a fairy tale, which corresponds to the fabula level. It is told by Anya, the presumed narrator's daughter, to her own child:

> There was once a magician, she tells the child as her bedtime story the following evening, there once was a magician, who wanted nothing more than to grow enough food to feed the world. And so he worked hard with his magic in his small dungeon (for he was a poor magician) until he made a small seed, which was like no other seed, but could fill a field with corn in an hour, fill the sea with fish in a day, fill the air with delicious fowl in a matter of minutes. He was about to creep off and try this wonderful seed in the quiet of the night, when his wife, who was a beautiful and very ambitious woman, caught him by the sleeve, and told him that if he did it all at night then in the morning no one would believe that it was all the magician's work—and we will be as poor as ever, complained his wife. And so reluctantly the magician agreed to wait until daytime, while word was sent that such a deed was to be performed, and the crowds gathered in thousands, the king himself, all waiting to see the miracle. But when the time came for the magician to demonstrate the worth of this little seed, it was nowhere to be found, neither in the little casket where the magician had kept it all along, nor in the many folds of his clothes, nor within the strand of his magnificent hair, it was lost forever to mankind, the little seed that might have saved them all from hunger, was lost forever to this world. (pp. 146–47)

If the fabula is rather accessible in its mythological form, the story is organized in a very intricate way and responds to Kirpal's definition of "loose, circular, episodic, loop like narrative technique." The chronological order of the character's life experiences is constantly interrupted, fragmented, repeated, delayed, or anticipated. The narratological devices of flashforward (anticipation) and flashbacks (anaphora), supported by the use of ellipses, through which entire passages are skipped, create a special rhythm. Furthermore, *Moonlight into Marzipan* is not one text, but consists of many texts overlapping one another. If by "text" we mean a finite, structured whole composed of language signs (Bal,

1986), then we have texts within the text that create a choral effect of different cultures and characters that silence each other instead of interacting.

It is only by bravely proceeding with the reading that the novel's organization becomes clearer and the picture of the story of a marriage and its betrayal emerges. The backdrop is the present-day scientific world pivoting around the axis of London/Calcutta. Promothesh, the husband and the scientist, is trying to recompose the story of his life through the writing of his own autobiography. But very quickly we discover that this autobiography was meant to be written for him by Alexandra Vorobyova, a Russian expatriate writer. When Alexandra Vorobyova goes away and abandons the text, Promothesh is left with pieces of his life scribbled down in notes, the result of his long conversations and confessions with the dismissive narrator. The novel therefore takes the form of a dialogue between Promothesh and the missing narrator, and it plays with the ambiguity and confusion between the subject and the object of narration, between the narrator and the narratee. The personal pronouns "I" and "You" are thrown around in the text in the attempt to reconstruct the trajectory of Promothesh's life, which remains unaccomplished and never fully told. The novel that should have been about Third World male ingenuity reinscribing the Western capitalistic world takes the form of an auto/biography never written and ends up being about women without whose collaboration no story of success can be achieved but only stories of failure and damnation.

If we want to reconstruct a linear thread of events (following the indication of the bedtime story as the fabula level), then we have to say that *Moonlight into Marzipan* is about an Indian couple, Promothesh and Esha, two promising scientists who meet each other at the University of Calcutta, where they both studied. After their passionate romance marriage follows, which introduces a hierarchy in their relationship, a hierarchy which is in keeping with Indian cultural expectations. Esha turns into a dedicated, submissive wife who rolls chapattis all day and relegates her thesis to a dusty drawer. Promothesh becomes her priority; his research and his studies are more important than her own aspirations. But Promothesh collapses under her dedication. He feels too unworthy to be at the center of her world and feels incapable of living up to her grand expectations. He will nonetheless resume his research in their Calcuttan garage, which has been converted into a laboratory. Promothesh achieves world celebrity when Esha's copper ear stud accidentally falls into the experiment's solution and provides vital catalysis. The unexpected reaction of the elements brings Promothesh close to the scientific miracle of turning light into food. Grass is made out of gold, and this metaphor recurs throughout the whole book.

This kind of miracle is what the Third World has been waiting for. Through the discovery of a seed that can turn dried fields into highly fertile soil, the whole subcontinent can be rescued from poverty and famine. At the dawn of postcolonial civilization we find an Indianized Greek titan who tries to steal knowledge from the Gods to help mankind. The West is the postmodern Olympus from where an oligarchy of capitalistic gods control their know-how. The novel can be read as an allegory of Western multinationals that exploit Third World countries to make money, the modern form of gold, without sharing their results. Promothesh attempts to counteract Western mythology (read "transnational capitalism") by privileging the spiritual world over the materialist one. His experiments aim to turn gold into grass, the total opposite of King Midas' destiny, who had been condemned by Apollo for his greedy desire to turn everything he touched into gold.

Promothesh's experiment is therefore a strategy of resistance against the Western world of paper money. The wearing of gold is reversed into the resisting politics of grass, which represents a more elementary and essential life. Promothesh attempts to recreate a Paradise on earth that had been destroyed through human cunning. The paradox lies in the Western sponsoring that he gets from Sir Percival, who gives him a five-year position to repeat his experiment in London:

> "It was the sin of knowledge that got us thrown out of Eden," said Percival Partridge, "and it is knowledge that will lead us back in." (p. 32)

It is a typical postcolonial strategy to respond to Western modernism with a sort of countermodernism. This strategy originated at the time of India's independence with Gandhi, who rejected English manufactured products and emphasized the return to superior Indian spiritual values, of which, as Partha Chatterjee (1986) discussed in his study, women were the treasurers.

It is no coincidence that the accidental catalyst is provoked by Esha's will to pursue life through inorganic elements. Her adding a piece of her earstud, a metonym for her body, to the free play of numbers symbolizes a femininization of science. Turning science into nature means that nature has the task of rescuing underdeveloped countries from international monopolistic exploitation. The notoriety unexpectedly achieved by Promothesh's experiment leads him and his wife to move to London and to be sponsored by an eccentric and wealthy patron, Sir Percival Partridge.

However, for Esha and Promothesh, the passage to England also signifies a crack in their relationship that was poised on a very fragile equilibrium of devotion and infused ambition. The second stage of their relationship is, in fact, characterized by Promothesh's infidelity and Esha's consequent suicide. The new character who causes the explosion of elements is Alexandra Vorobyova, the Russian Jewish expatriate who was in charge of helping Promothesh with his autobiography. But while Promothesh is trying to translate himself into narrative for Alexandra, he loses himself to her. Life and fiction, narrator and narratee, get confused and death overwhelms them, with Esha's suicide and the impossibility of repeating the experiment.

This condition of transnationality, fictionalized in the passage to England, is not only a translation in space but also an allegorical voyage that, instead of bringing enlightenment (as in the Bildungsroman) or perfectibility, symbolizes dispersion and the vanishing of purposes. It is literally a migration to the Inferno. Promothesh's journey to Europe confronts him with death, inside and outside himself.

THE POINT OF MYTHOLOGY

Promothesh Bound and Capitalism

Gupta's text is an endless chain of mythological and literary references. This play on intertextuality enriches the text with several layers of interpretation. As Kirpal (1988) has pointed out, "the use of myths by Third World novelists is not just a structuring device by a value-endowed paradigm." The main allegory suggested by Gupta consists in recreating the figure of Promothesh around that of a postcolonial Prometheus, but she then adds onto that allusion other different Western male creators in order to disrupt them in one stroke. She therefore uses characters, to quote Kirpal once more, that are "illustrational" or "archetypal" rather than "representational."

Gupta's engagement with mythology does not have a redemptive and rehabilitative function but is, on the contrary, a process of further demolition. As Georges Gusdorf writes,

> Post-colonial writers have had to invent mythologies of their own, stories and allegories of "self" and "other" that can translate this complex heritage and perhaps make a difference by helping to transform the mentality of the oppressed as well as their self-perception.[3]

In the recreation of this mythology of one's own, Gupta concentrates on one of the most persistent enterprises of human beings: the desire to discover the secret of life. By inventing a story of scientific discovery the writer retraces the stages of human history, but this time she takes care that women and the subaltern are part of this revisitation. She therefore links the thirst for knowledge with the female symbolism of containing the secret of life. The result is a complex narrative on desire and disillusion.

The mythological hero is, in fact, errant and lost without his female "creators." However, he is still a creature who has turned against his makers, since both Esha and Alexandra will be erased from the text. Here there are echoes of

Mary Shelley's *Frankenstein*. Through the power of her pen Shelley creates a monster that defies mortality. But the monster loses control and turns against its male creator, destroying him because he did not give the monster humanity. Esha shapes Promothesh as a creature beyond the failing of humanity. She exerts her power through him, a man, because in traditional Indian society she is not allowed to have a leading role; therefore she hovers in the wings. Promothesh is a god who has to remain above human weakness and who is not expected to fail like other mortal beings. Promothesh rebels against his maker by using the treacherous weapons of humanity: deceit and betrayal. By doing so, he relegates Esha to a tormented, repentant maker. Yuri Sen, Promothesh's alter ego, confronts her with her monstrosity. As a consequence of this humiliation she commits suicide for having failed to control her creation:

> But, my dear, said Yuri Sen, you created him, you had fashioned his biography long before it had been lived. Can you deny, my dear, that in him you set to create the man of your dreams, knowing that none would be your match, unless you made him so? (p. 97)

Contrary to what his name may evoke, Promothesh wanted to remain unheroic in the drift of life. He wanted to be left to the atavism that Westerners have always associated with India, in other words, to be prey to an ancestral passivity dictated by the Hindu dogma of Karma, according to which things go as fate has planned them. But the fate of Promothesh is to fall in love with Esha, the female demiurge, the Eve who would defy God's secret of life. It is the peculiarity of the experiment characterized by magic and casuality that preoccupies the West. Promothesh is, in fact, introduced to Sir Percival as a magician, as someone who can perform miracles. The idea is quite threatening because it challenges the basic assumption of Western power, that results can be controlled and monopolized. Promothesh thus represents the Western fear of itself, the repressed element of irrationality that could also overwhelm and destroy those who live in the West.

The autobiography requested by Sir Percival is a way to get to know and control Promothesh's existence, a way to control his chaotic, dangerous potentiality that represents a challenge to rational faith in truth and science. In a way Promothesh's inability to repeat the experiment represents the rejection of the successful reformation of the precapitalist subject into a bourgeois individual. Moving to the West to make the discovery known to the rest of the world (as if India was not part of the world according to Esha's parable) symbolizes the corruption of intentions and complicity with global capitalism. As Madhava Prasad appropriately writes,

> The moment of revelation shatters the illusion of self-possession and exposes the fragility of the post-colonial subject's assumption of sovereignty.

In response, the subject compensates for this disillusionment by projecting a lost sovereignty onto the (re)discovered past. "Post-coloniality" thus
is signalled by the historic moment in which the coveted private "realm"
is created as the zone of non "interference"; that is off-limits to the "public." The public realm, in this case, is the *inter*national sphere, a neutral
space, real or hypothetical.[4]

Promothesh is a Third World representative ("Third World" here refers to countries that have shared a history of imperialism, colonialism, development projects and experimentalism in bourgeois democracy, and all forms of
nation-statehood). But just as there is not one form of capitalism but several
distinct capitalist social formations, so there is not one Third World. Gupta's es-
sentialization of this oppositional pattern with the construction of a mythological quest story that rotates around the axis of Calcutta-London symbolizes the
existence of many versions of this structural colonial opposition, which can be
reduced to an originary myth that underlies all other stories. The issue of myths
and postcolonialism will be explored in the next section.

Undoing Myths

Moonlight into Marzipan attempts a deconstruction of Western mythologies,
from the story of creation of Adam and Eve, to the Greek world of Prometheus or Pandora, to the medieval quest of the Holy Grail with Parzifal, to the
conquest of knowledge by Faust, up to more modern creations like Frankenstein. Using Yuri Sen, who is the "reason" in the text, as a witness to the vanity of mythologies of any kind, *Moonlight into Marzipan* proposes an unusual
reversion of the binary oppositions established between Western myths and
peripheral appropriation. Promothesh offers the West an image of itself that
is deformed through the ahistorical overlapping of myths and genres belonging to other eras or other locations. Time and space merge into an aporia that
is a powerful metaphor through which Gupta explores not only the problems
of language but also of accessibility, representation, and articulation of
female subjectivity.
It is important to concentrate for a moment on the function of myths in literature and on the way Gupta reinterprets Western mythological quest stories
for the purpose of postcolonial representation. Usually the concept of myth implies a truth beyond concrete demonstration that is shared by everybody because it is eternal, therefore ahistorical and valid through ages and cultures. As
Mieke Bal writes, "in myth-criticism as in the poststructuralist study of myth, a
myth is a myth because, under the layers of dust of historically changing signifiers, it remains the same signifier-independent signified, a universal story. The

relationship between myth thus viewed and the concept of collective unconscious is more or less taken for granted" (Bal, 1987: 59).

Various theorists on myth have concentrated either on the eternal, ahistorical character of myths, like Roland Barthes, or on the existence of different versions that create various stories from and interpretations of the same myth, therefore emphasizing the self-constructive, structualist aspects of myth, like anthropologist Lévi-Strauss and later feminist myth critics. For the first option Barthes writes in *Mythologies* that "Myth deprives the object of which it speaks of all history" (1972: 152) because myth has the goal to immobilize the world. However, for Lévi-Strauss "a myth consists of all its versions" (Lévi-Strauss, 1963). This perspective allows us to rehistoricize myths and to recontextualize them in specific social situations.

As Teresa de Lauretis has shown, the negative connotation of representing a masculine quest where women are obstacles is always attributed to myths. She analyzes, for example, the Greek myth of Oedipus and highlights the position that women assume within oedipal plots and she concludes that:

> The hero must be male, regardless of the gender of the [character or] a text-image, because the obstacle [of the hero's quest] whatever its personification, is morphologically female and indeed, simply, her womb. . . . The hero, the mythical subject, is constructed as sexual being and as male. . . . Female . . . is an element of plot-space, a topos, a resistance, matrix and matter.[5]

Many feminist reinterpretations of myths (by Warner, Irigaray, Cixous, Toni Morrison, Bal, and others) have concentrated not only on rewriting myths from a gendered perspective, but also seeing myths in terms of Barthes' interpretation. They are not static and eternal but rather part of a historical process, and therefore changeable according to context and narration. For Mieke Bal myths are not stable and fixed but come into existence with every "mythological version." According to Bal, "there is no myth underneath these versions, there is no myth other than each version" (Bal, 1987: 62). No myth exists outside the interpretation and reading of its producer and interpreter.

This argument must be further stretched in order to analyze the use of myths as "value-endowed paradigms" within the postcolonial discourse, as suggested by Viney Kirpal, and to relate the postcolonial project with the feminist enterprise of rereading or rewriting myths, freeing them from their patriarchal and colonial prejudices.

Within the mythological quest story Promothesh is the male hero whose attempts to recreate Eden on Earth challenge the West on two accounts. First, by choosing grass over gold, he reverses the relevance of Western capitalism by encouraging a return to spiritual and essential life; second, by recognizing women not as the obstacle, but as the nurturer of any possible quest, he acknowledges that without whom only failure can be achieved. With his mission Promothesh unties the linearity, objectivity, universality, and masculinity of the Western mythological quest. Therefore, as Marianne Hirsch writes, "masculine plotting has to be rethought from the perspective of the feminine" (Hirsch, 1989: 5). In Gupta's mythological quest, women are still not officially included but have to play their role underground, showing an agency that is only rendered in the text with a subweb of secondary narratives that tell different versions of the fabula in the forms of fairy tales, the devil's reflection (in italics), and monologues. They function as the supposedly secondary term that accompanies the male quest.

In this rewriting of the mythological quest story Gupta intersects many contradictory elements that do not offer a straightforward clarification of where agency and empowerment are. It is difficult to detect a form of agency in women who commit suicide, which is how Esha decides to end her life, or are crushed mysteriously by a rock in an abyss, which is how Alexandra dies. It is difficult to state that these female figures are subversive and capable of reinscribing the patriarchal and imperial system. However, the terrain where a form of agency can be theoretically explored is in the return of the repressed elements. Women are pushed aside from the texts in Gupta's novel. They die in the most apocalyptic way, but are not defeated since they come into the text in the form of vacuum, of silence, of perturbation. In this way Gupta attempts a representation of the unrepresentable or unintelligible. It is a disruptive absence that keeps the text from having coherence and forces the male counterparts to face their failures now that there are no more scapegoats. With the disappearance of women, and therefore of Promothesh, the West is also deprived of its chance "to restore Eden to earth, reverse the Fall" (p. 32). The morality in the story tells us about the vanity, and therefore sin, of searching for the source and secret of life, a mystery is beyond unveiling, in the East or West, by male or female, present or past.

Gupta enacts the mimicry of the West through the appropriation of its founding myths. By reinterpreting and rewriting the myth of Prometheus, she not only creates a new version that is historicized in the postcolonial reality of the Third World and situated in the gender perspective offered by women in this tale, but she offers a new vision of myth criticism. As Bal concludes in her article, "the relation between a mythical unit and its so-called versions is not a relation of interpretation but a relation of transference. Such relation is dynamic, historically specific and discursive" (Bal, 1987: 79). In her polyphonic text Gupta enacts the illusion of Western faith in rational scientific knowledge and in the universal, centralizing idea of the male ingenuity as the hero of this quest. The mythical discourse that demonstrates an endless series of open-ended meanings unsettles the myth as a truth beyond appropriation. Putting the different versions in to action empties the original signifier of the myth, an unsettlilng which, as Mieke Bal further writes, "triggers other signifiers, and the mythical discourse comes into being" (Bal, 1987: 81).

To conclude, in Gupta's postcolonial novel myths are revealed as "value endowed paradigms" of reality by making Western myths of male ingenuity ludicrous (Prometheus, Faust, Frankenstein, Percival). Here, the heroes are corrupted by desire for knowledge and the ambition for immortality. Rewriting the myth in the light of postcolonial reality (essentialized and not specifically located in either history or time), Gupta proposes an alternative explanation to the usual male quest story and evokes creation and ambition as pertinent to the female world, which, however, cannot emerge if the patriarchal structures are left unchanged and unchallenged. Like the imperial/periphery interaction (the London-Calcutta axis), both male and female ingenuity are damned if they remain entangled in a binary deadlock, and this is Gupta's response to the limiting schema put forward by Viney Kirpal.

Gupta's novel is a virtuoso attempt to fuse various political and poetic discourses. On the one hand, Gupta traces the postcolonial experience and its struggle to find a voice which is authentic and alternative. On the other, she enacts the female search for writing that is capable of expressing woman's perception of the world, a world of the female body, an *écriture féminine* that Gupta achieves through an eruption of words, a *jouissance* given by the free play of associations. In the novel the two discourses converge, language being the medium for turning poetry into politics. Promothesh's experiment resists the Western world of "paper money." To transform base things into gold was the old colonial enterprise, one of the Western originary myths. Gupta plays out myths that are loaded with an historical and cultural heritage, but that become empty when they are transferred to other geopolitical terrains. The empowerment of the East consists in reappropriating the master's tools and disrupting its purposes by reversing its aim. Gold becomes grass through a demonic catalysis that requires the presence of unknown agents. The elements of casuality that have been erased from Western science since the introduction of modern rational ways of investigation, to the detriment of more intuitive and gambling methods, reenter the scene in Gupta's dialogism between the two worlds.

Even though it is difficult to speak of a canonized postcolonial novel, distinct in its form and ideological orientations, it can be said that many of the features mentioned by Viney Kirpal's article do apply to Sunetra Gupta's novel, who is nonetheless considered in the West to be a Woolfian writer, a highly modernistic tortuous pen. Modernism seems to fuse with postmodernism in Gupta's novel. However, as Brian McHale (1988) points out, we should never speak of an end of modernism and the onset of postmodernism, marked by contrasting characteristics. Instead, we should understand postmodernism as a completion of modernistic intents. Colin Falck offers a brief definition of modernism:

> The technical innovations of modernism—its rendering of the stream of consciousness, its systematic derangement of the senses, its narratological shift of time and of viewpoint, its frequent aggressions against its own medium—are all ways of breaking with the world's appearances and of finding deeper meanings behind the "common sense" spatio-temporal framework of superficial representation.[6]

All these qualities of modernism apply to Gupta's novel; however, there are also elements that trespass upon the project of modernism and enter the terrain of the postmodern, techniques that are, however, bent for the purpose of a postcolonial and gendered representation.

The device of the ever changing roles used in Gupta's novel enacts those new subjectivities, those new identities, that challenge the modernist discourse. It remains nonetheless present within the postmodern and insists on a Self or a Center that needs an Other for its formation. Reversing hegemonic relationships and reterritorializing the space of mythology between East and West and of language between signifier and signified, Gupta succeeds in creating an unusual vision of the postcolonial fin de siècle.

This specifically applies to her creation of an autobiography without a subject, without an authoritative "I," an approach that allows for the decentralized postcolonial person who can only position her/himself at the margins. Gupta creates a postmodern version of the autobiography through the device of different narrative voices, texts, and interpretations of motherhood. She also uses the genre in a postcolonial way, implying with it the destitution of the Western unitary self. Gupta turns the hero into antihero, deprives him of his centrality in the text, and denies him the authorial voice necessary to write an autobiography. She fuses the biography into the autobiography so that all characters are on stage to perform a story that has lost its narrator. Paradoxically, the women's disappearance from the text deprives Promothesh of his symbolic order. He lacks the words, the means to express himself, and he is no longer in control of the logic of the experiment. The language melts, and instead of conveying universal and abstract thoughts or the utter discovery that would have accelerated the rhythms of nature, it conveys fragmentation and immateriality. The characters move closer and closer to hell instead of achieving the secret of eternal life. The result is a layered chronicle of damnation, of an autobiography never written.

Chapter 6

A Short Story about the Italian Empire

From Fascist Propaganda to Postcolonial Representations

The old is dying and the new cannot be born; in this interregnum then arises a great diversity of morbid symptoms.
—Antonio Gramsci, Selections from the *Prison Notebooks*, p. 276

Africa occupies an extremely marginal place within Italian literature compared to its position in both French and English literature. If it is true that its marginality reflects the shorter involvement of Italy with the Black Continent, it also manifests an act of denial. The history of colonialism is, in fact, a forgotten chapter of Italian history. Italy colonized not only Eritrea, Ethiopia, and Somalia (The Horn of Africa, officially named AOI, Africa Orientale Italiana), but also Libya.

It is interesting to note that, despite its aggressive past, Italy still perceives itself more as a colonized country than as a colonizer. Its internal divisions are in fact due to a long history of invasion. Foreigners were always on its territory, including the Greeks, Arabs, Spanish, French, Austrians, and Germans. The others were the guests, while the hosts were subalterns. Furthermore, from the beginning of this century the massive migration of Italians to the Americas and the North of Europe creates a picture of Italy as a land of immigration as an anomaly. And lastly, Italy is a profoundly divided country, characterized by migration from the less developed Southern regions, called Meridione or Mezzogiorno, to the North. Italy has very little symbolism at hand to help imagine itself as a cohesive nation.

VITORIO BOTTEGO
·LX BATTAGLIONE COLONIALE·

That is the reason why, especially during the Fascist regime in the wake of the conquest of Ethiopia, the government set out to create Italy rhetorically, by redefining its relationship both with its past and with its others. Ancient Rome was used as a model for the construction of a virtual Italy. The expansionist drive was meant to remold Italians by infusing them with a colonial consciousness that would replace the national immaturity (Burdett, 2000, 2001). Mussolini's desire was to quickly achieve international prestige and to resolve internal tensions through the annexation of Ethiopia to the Empire. The imperial rhetoric was based on an oppositional discourse in which the empty space of Ethiopia constituted the major object of desire and repulsion. The local population was seen as barbaric and savage and yet exotic and erotic, while the uncharted territory of Ethiopia served as a metaphor for the creation of the nation. The strategy worked as a cohesive device to solicit an imperial expansion of mythological resonance. The actions of the Italian soldiers had to be thoroughly described and reported in order to construct a model for the future by showing how young men going to Africa returned physically and morally strengthened. These images of the fascist offensive, therefore, build on the lineage of the ancient Roman soldier, blackshirts worthy of the empire who, through the metaphor of an Italy beyond the Alps, in uncharted territory set out to construct a miraculous notion of the Italian identity beyond internal problems.

In Italy, in fact, there were major political, economic, and demographic reasons for internal instability. The dangerous combination of high population expansion and low economic growth was reaching explosive proportions. Italy was still a poor country, and industrialization had developed very slowly. The majority of people worked in agriculture. Massive emigration to the Americas was one of the answers to the crisis of the nation. Colonial expansion was, according to Mussolini, a way to guarantee a "place under the sun" for his citizens. It was seen as a form of internal migration within the Empire to insure that Italian citizens were not lost to an alien country.

Even though there were strong internal reasons for expansion, the Italian imperialist enterprise was promoted for pure prestige and for the virtual construction of the Italian nation through a web of discourses based on the opposition between "us," the brave civilized heroes, and "them," the primitive exotic savages. The Other was thus constructed as inferior and aestheticized. Although there were apparently no economic interests at stake, the establishment of l'Africa Orientale Italiana was not only characterized by the astronomical costs of building infrastructures but also by considerable profits, though not in the league of the British, French, Dutch,[1] or Portuguese[2] empires. Despite the fact that leading theories have construed the Italian colonial adventure as a "poor man's imperialism" (*imperialismo straccione*) and that De Vecchi, the quadrumvir in Somalia, was labeled *sciupone l'africano* (the word means "squanderer" and is a pun on the fascist film on the roman figure of "Scipione l'Africano"), the motifs for expansion were not only dictated by noneconomic factors such as prestige, irredentism, revenge, altruism, and fear of revolution but were primarily connected with economic factors: the need to offer a way out to Italian citizens who were facing serious economic difficulties due to unemployment and famine; the need to reactivate industry through the production of weapons for the colonial war; and the need to expand trade and the number of enterprises in Africa.[3]

It is therefore important to analyze the complex political identity of the Horn of Africa, from the colonial period up to the new millenium, in its interrelation to the Italian colonial past and in its intersections with and divergences from other postcolonial conditions. This is necessary in order to explore the process of multiculturalization that is changing the face of Italy from a country of emigration to a site of immigration.

The comparison between British and Italian colonization is not only meant to emphasize the existence of postcolonial histories that are expressed in a language other than English, but also to counterbalance the dominance of the discourse by critics and writers from India with a response from Africa, a continent that remains comparatively neglected. As Robert Young writes, this neglect occurs because of the obvious dominance of India in the field since Said's book *Orientalism* (Young, 1994: 12). India quite clearly retains that central position today, the jewel in the crown of colonial discourse analysis (Young, 1994: 18), a privileging that has lead to a considerable homogenization of the history of colonialism and today's postcolonialism. Clearly the ideology and procedures of French assimilationist colonialism differed from the British policy of indirect rule, or from the policies of the Germans, Portuguese, Dutch, or Italians. And the situation is complicated by current forms of colonization in the world such as those in Palestine, Northern Ireland, and Kosovo. As Young states:

> This heterogeneity points to a correlative problem, namely that of historical difference. Can we assume that colonial discourse operates identically not only across space but also throughout time? In short, can there be a general theoretical matrix that is able to provide an all-encompassing framework for the analysis of each singular colonial instance?[4]

The answer is neither straightforward nor simple. A totalizing matrix is both limiting and distorting, and yet generalizing categories are necessary in order to create contact zones among different discourses, histories, and traditions. The discourse on postcolonialism has, in fact, greatly helped to put differences and alternative narratives under the spotlight, but it also risks homogenizing the complexities in order to address them within a too encompassing and formulaic theory. It is, therefore, important to understand the operations and aftermaths of colonial histories in their historical and geographical particularities.

The reframing of postcolonialism around a new historical and literary background, such as the Afro-Italian case, highlights not only the internal differences within postcolonial discourse but also throws new light on the most recurrent issues at stake. This reframing is necessary because there is, on the one hand, a forced forgetfulness about the Italian colonial deeds, but also, on the other hand, a kind of remembering that romanticizes the Italian colonizers as good brothers of the African people (*italiani brava gente*), as saviors who only brought infrastructures and civilization with no economic exploitation. It is only recently that Italy has started to face and confront its colonial past. Recent anthropological,[5] historical,[6] and cultural studies[7] reveal the other side of Italian colonialism, which was far from being benevolent and benign. The colonial narrative is also being redefined by the returned gaze of African immigrants in Italy who have started writing about their past, their countries, and their encounter with Italy. Parallel to this literary writing back, some of the African women writers scrutinized here have thrown new light on the Italian colonial adventure, offering a gendered perspective to the analysis.

The female writers analyzed in this second part come from the former Italian colonies of Corno d'Africa (Maria Abbebú Viarengo from Ethiopia, Erminia dell'Oro and Ribka Sibhatu from Eritrea, Sirad S. Hassan from Somalia). These writers emerged in the last decade of the twentieth century, and they are shaping an Afro-Italian tradition that questions past legacies and ongoing interracial relations. Often these writers have published only one book, or they write more to keep in touch with themselves than to pursue a literary career. The historical, social, and political background of their countries of origin is very present in their writings. These literatures place an emphasis on politics, according to which individual dreams become political, not Oedipal as in "great literature." In "What Is a Minor Literature?" Deleuze and Guattari call this *deterritorialization*. "Collective values refer to the writer's terrain where utterances reflect a community's usage, rather than being sharply individuated. The text echoes a whole set of preoccupations which are engrained in the social fabric of the community" (Deleuze and Guattari, 1983: 11–13).

A brief introduction to colonial history in the Horn of Africa will make these texts more accessible to those unfamiliar with the Italian period of the Empire, the national history of those countries after independence, and the multicultural situation that stems from the intersection of these two factors. This analysis will shed light on the different postcolonial conditions and cultural developments in the different geographical areas, knowledge that is indispensable for the assessment of different forms of multiculturalization within European countries. While an abundance of theories and studies describes the characteristics and methods of French and British colonialism,[8] little has been said on the forms that other colonizations, such as the Italian, have taken. In order to remove Italian colonial history from the oblivion to which it has been relegated, the focus of this postcolonial discourse analysis will be specifically on Italian colonialism. This means tracing the contour of Italian colonial history but mostly establishing linkages between the colonial racial politics of the 1930s and the contemporary multicultural reality of the new millennium.

ITALY AND FASCIST NOSTALGIA

The Scramble for Africa

The expression *scramble for Africa* refers to the last phase of the European colonial expansion which saw the repartition of the remaining independent African countries to various European States. This action was sealed with the Berlin Conference 1884–1886, the aim of which was to maintain a political equilibrium within Europe among the colonial powers. The region that interested Italy in its belated colonial expansion were those areas in the Horn of Africa (Eastern Africa, the present-day countries of Eritrea, Ethiopia, Somalia) that were uncolonized and were used as a neutral zone between the British (Egypt, Sudan) and the French Empires (Djibouti).

Until the twentieth century the name of the region that includes Eritrea, Tigray, and Amhara was Abyssinia. For over a thousand years, from the decline of the Axum until Amhara domination was established towards the end of the nineteenth century, Abyssinia was a shifting confederation of small kingdoms and principalities. The system was feudal and "rule" often meant no more than nominal submission and the payment of tribute, which was difficult enough to garner in such a mountainous terrain and in the absence of roads. The borders of Abyssinia were never those of present-day Ethiopia. For example, the south of Ethiopia, the home of the Oromo and other people, was never part of the Abyssinian kingdom.

During the first half of the nineteenth century the Horn of Africa was a forgotten region, and Ethiopia was the last region to fall prey to foreign rule. The British Empire concentrated its influence in Sudan, whereas the French Empire established its presence in the Horn of Africa in Djibouti. While Britain was trying to achieve its dream of an Empire from "Cape to Cairo," the French were trying to expand their influence from the Eastern African Djibouti to the French territories on the Atlantic Ocean. They were, however, blocked by the British who started to favor the Italian presence in the Horn in order to limit French expansion. The British dream of colonizing from "Cape to Cairo" was brought to an abrupt halt in 1876 when the Congo was assigned to Leopold II of Belgium. The infamous Berlin Conference 1884–1886 therefore legitimized the European powers in their scramble for Africa.

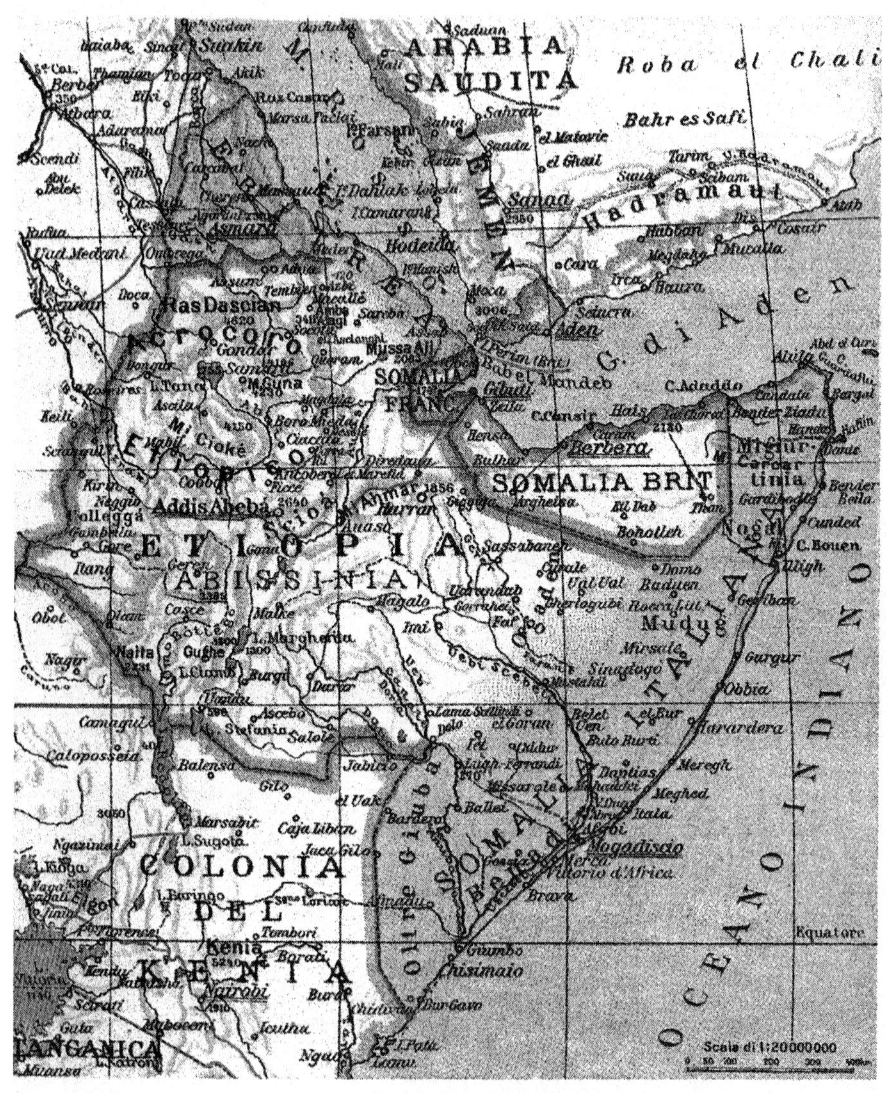

AFRICA ORIENTALE

(In una carta dei primi anni '30)

With the opening of the Suez Canal in 1869,[9] the territories in the Horn of Africa became more interesting to Italy. Italy had searched for supremacy in the Mediterranean and having missed the opportunity to colonize Tunisia (it was snatched by the French) began to consider a base on the Red Sea as an interesting alternative, which, thanks to the Suez Canal, could still grant control of the Mediterranean. The Italian shipping company Rubattino purchased the port of Assab in 1882.

At the time of the expansion in Africa, Italy was far from being a strong nation. It had only been united in 1861 and was facing serious internal problems, both economic and political, as well as serious difficulties in attaining social cohesion. Thus the colonial aggression of Minister Crispi was an attempt to consolidate Italy through a presence in far-off territories. Crispi thought it would give Italy prestige and an international profile. The making of the Italian nation was therefore mirrored by its rise as a colonial power, a process which was brought to its pinnacle during the fascist era.

As Tekeste Negash clearly illustrates in his book *Italian Colonialism in Eritrea, 1882–1941: Policies, Praxis and Impact* (1987), the chronology of the Italian expansion can be divided into three phases. The first began with the treaty of Uccialli (1889), which led to the formation of Eritrea (1890) and ended with the battle of Adwa (1896), a crushing defeat that forced Italy to review its colonial and foreign policies.[10] The defeat at Adwa was deemed a cause for national shame and would be the reason for the strong determination with which Italy would, later under fascism, resume her colonial fighting. The second phase began in 1897 and continued until 1932 and was characterized by colonial settlements and the construction of the initial infrastructure. The third and last phase began with the preparation for the invasion of Ethiopia and lasted until the demise of Italian colonialism in 1941, when during the Second World War the British protectorate took over in these regions.

Various studies have tried to assess the causes and the motives for Italian colonial expansion. Italian colonialism was seen as *lascia fare* (laissez faire). It differed, for example, from other imperialisms such as the British and French.[11] Italian imperialism had no clear policy, but was the hybrid product of different discourses that are addressed in this chapter. As Malvezzi writes in 1933, "The Englishman has against himself the instinctive, physical loathing for the colored man, the Frenchman wants too much to conform the other to his own image, the Italian lives and lets live, he has not fears, nor prejudices, nor fanaticism, nor missionary spirit, nor proselytizing."[12] This statement stereotypically defines the different forms of imperialisms and sketches the popular view of the Italians as good-natured people (*Italiani brava gente*).

This stereotype is also shown in the famous soldiers' song *Faccetta Nera* (Little Black Face), in which the Italians are almost portrayed as good brothers and saviors of the local people, strangely addressed as *faccetta nera* (little black face

Se tu dall'altipiano guardi il mare
moretta che sei schiava fra le schiave,
vedrai come in un sogno tante navi
e un tricolore sventolar per te!

Faccetta nera
bell'abissina
aspetta e spera
che già l'ora si avvicina!
Quando saremo
insieme a te,
noi ti daremo
un'altra legge e un altro re!

La legge nostra è schiavitù d'amore
ma libertà di vita e di pensiero.
Vendicheremo noi camicie nere
gli eroi caduti liberando te!

Faccetta nera
bell'abissina
aspetta e spera
che già l'ora si avvicina!
Quando saremo
insieme a te,
noi ti daremo
un'altra legge e un altro re!

Faccetta nera, piccola abissina,
ti porteremo a Roma liberata;
dal sole nostro tu sarai baciata,
sarai camicia nera pure tu!

Faccetta nera
sarai romana
e per bandiera
tu avrai quella italiana!
Noi marceremo
insieme a te
e sfileremo avanti al Duce e avanti al Re!

or woman), an ambiguity that personifies the colony as a black face while it undeniably identifies the colonized with a female representation. This is in line with Fanon's description of the feminization of the colony in order to reinforce the act of imperial domination through the trope of masculine possession or even rape. The song, initially launched as propaganda, had immediate success. However, it was later prohibited because it responded more to the popular spirit of light-hearted tenderness instead of expressing the spirit of a warring colonizing nation. The song celebrated the friendship with a race that had to be considered inferior.

Se tu dall'altopiano guardi il mare

If from the highlands you glance down towards the sea,

moretta che sei schiava fra le schiave,

little black woman, you slave among slaves,

vedrai come in un sogno tante navi

you will see, as if a dream, so many ships

e un tricolore sventolar per te!

and a tricolored flag will wave for you.

Facetta nera, bell'abissina,
aspetta e spera, che già l'ora s'avvicina!
Quando saremo insieme a te,
noi ti daremo un'altra legge e un altro re!

Black face, beautiful Abyssinian,
wait and hope, for Italy is drawing near!
And when we are together with you,
we will give you another law and another king!

La legge nostra è schiavitù d'amore
ma libertà di vita e di pensiero.
Vendicheremo noi camice nere
gli eroi caduti liberando te!

Our law is the slavery of love,
but freedom to live and think.
We Blackshirts will vindicate
the fallen heroes, and we will liberate you!

Refrain:

Refrain:

Faccetta nera, piccola abissina,
ti porteremo a Roma liberata;
dal sole nostro tu sarai baciata,
sarai camicia nera pure tu!
Faccetta nera,
sarai romana,
e per bandiera
tu avrai quella italiana!
Noi marceremo
insieme a te
e sfileremo avanti al Duce e avanti al Re!

Black face, little Abyssinian,
we will take you to Rome liberated;
by our sun you will be kissed,
and you will become Blackshirts too!
Black face,
you will be Roman,
and you will get
the Italian flag!
We will march
together with you
we will parade in front the Duce and the King!

Micheli e Ruccione, 'La canzone dei legionari'

To understand the feminization of the colony is essential to comprehend the decolonization strategies embraced by African women writers in order to re-narrate their experiences at the intersection of the patriarchal and colonial. Furthermore, a counterfactual discussion on Italian colonialism by non-Italian historians, for example, brings to light other aspects of Italian colonialism that are definitely not as fraternal as promised in *Faccetta Nera*.

The War of Ethiopia

The colonial aggression against the Ethiopia of *negus neghesti*, Hailé Selassié (the king of the kings, as he had crowned himself), was not only belated with respect to other European countries, but also rather shortsighted. It was by no means a shrewd move to covet a country which had become an African model for independence and which, thanks to the charisma of Selassié, a very skilled and cultivated politician, could attract much international sympathy. As Angelo del Boca writes, "Mussolini seized power in 1922 without having elaborated a real foreign policy and having only imprecise and changeable ideas, sometimes contradictory with respect to the colonial policy. He had not, and would not have for several years, an original project of his own to propose, which could set a real turning point to the colonial plan of the liberal democracy" (Del Boca, 1976: 4).[13]

Mussolini had, strenuously opposed the war in Libya (1911) but once in power he found himself entrapped in a paradox. At a time when the era of colonial conquest was ending and the British Empire was declining, Mussolini started to dream about a great Empire in Africa. Paradoxically enough, it was the growth of another form of fascism within Europe, the *Nationalsozialismus* in Germany, which worried Mussolini and pushed him to multiply his actions in Africa in order to oppose, or at least contain, the aggressive hegemony of Germany.[14]

For the fascist regime, therefore, the war against Ethiopia served to acquire international prestige and to quiet internal turmoil. Despite his international support the *negus* of Ethiopia found himself suddenly alone against Italy. Britain was afraid of serious repercussions within Europe if they intervened against Mussolini in Africa, and to the great disappointment of Selassié, even France decided not to align itself with Ethiopia. It was in the end Germany that secretly supported Hailé Selassié with military aid. This was not because Germany considered Italy a strategic enemy but rather because Germany wanted to weaken Italy militarily so that, when the war was over, Italy could be more easily swayed in terms of the Germans' plans for the reconfiguration of Europe (Del Boca, 1976).

The Italian declaration of war against Ethiopia (3 October 1935) caused upheaval among the British, the French, and all the left-wing opposition in Italy

who believed in the principle of national autonomy. However, this outrage at the reactions to the war against Ethiopia was not matched by material and military aid to Hailé Selassié. In the rough regions in the highlands the Italian troops fought against an Ethiopian army whose leaders knew the landscape much better and who quickly transformed the open war into guerilla warfare, which put the Italians at a great disadvantage. Italy had expected to conquer Ethiopia with a blitz war and instead, after three months of heavy fighting, had achieved no major victories. After the victory of Adwa (6 October 1936), which was considered to be revenge for the defeat of 1896, Italian troops hardly advanced. Mussolini was not interested in anything less than victory after victory. He felt this was necessary to keep both international and national interest alive and he promptly replaced General de Bono, an advocate of a cautious and defensive form of warfare, with the ambitious and manipulative General Badoglio. However, not even Badoglio could break Ethiopian resistance, and when in December 1936 it became clear that the blitz war had became a long, drawn-out affair, the Italians began a form of chemical warfare. General Graziani gave the order to use various types of gas (asphyxiating gas, vesicatory gas, tear gas, toxic gas) in order to inflict a decisive defeat on the Ethiopians. As to the effects of the chemical war, there are many witness reports from the Ethiopians, but it is only recently that these facts have been made known to Italian general public. Angelo del Boca's text. *Gli Italiani in Africa Orientale, Vol. 2, La conquista dell'Impero*, is one of the few which offers an extremely detailed and well-documented description of the Ethiopian war, including the chemical warfare. The news of the massacres greatly discouraged the Ethiopians and the emperor Hailé Selassié decided in February 1936 to change his successful military strategy from the guerilla warfare to open, pitched battle (*battaglia campale*). The reasons for this change are not only to be attributed to the chemical war but also to the difficulty of holding the Ethiopian nation (more than twelve different ethnicities, languages, clans, and religious groups) together for much longer against the Italians. This change of tactics, however, proved fatal since the Italian air force and the artillery were superior to those of Ethiopia. On 5 May 1936, the Italians marched into Addis Ababa and annexed Ethiopia to the Empire. Hailé Selassié went into exile.

The strong hostility of France, the United States, and Britain forced Italy to seek support from Germany. In October 1936, Mussolini signed an agreement called the Rome-Berlin Axis by which Italy tolerated many aggressive actions undertaken by Hitler such as the Anschluss (the annexation of Austria to Germany) and the Sudete annexation (the German-speaking region of Czechoslovakia). Italy accepted practices that were extraneous to the Italian culture such as the persecution of the Jews (*leggi razziali* of 1938). The axis was further reinforced on 22 May 1939 with the "pact of steel" (*patto d'acciaio*) in which

Italy and Germany agreed to offer each other help in case one of the countries was dragged into war, be it defensive or offensive.

Hitler did not communicate the invasion of Poland to Mussolini, who consequently felt put out and took a year to actually join the fighting. During the war, Italy quickly lost its colonial territories to the British, who established their own protectorate over Ethiopia, Eritrea, and Somalia in 1941 and put the Emperor Hailé Selassié back in power in Ethiopia. This signed the end of the Italian colonial adventure in the Horn of Africa.

Colonial Sexual Difference

Many of the peasants, merchants, laborers, teachers, and those in search of minerals who left the famished rural regions of Italy did so because the internal economic crisis had reduced many civilians to dejection and extreme poverty. They were able to settle in Eritrea because of new agricultural laws which saw land confiscated from Eritrean peasants and given to incoming Italians. Some went to work on the railways others in the building trade; there were also the wealthier Italians, who went to Africa either to increase their wealth or to work in official representative positions, and finally Italian Jews, who went to Africa to escape the racial laws introduced by Mussolini.

This form of migration to the colonies led to the sexual encounters between single white male colonizers and the local dark women (defined as *Veneri Neri* or sable Venus). These encounters were not considered to be at all unusual, at least not at the beginning of colonialism, as there were no European women available in the far territories of the motherland. There is a vast literature on interracial relationships in the colonies, which in the Italian case went under the label of *madamismo.* These relationships were not only initially tolerated but also encouraged because they were considered to have a stabilizing effect on political order and colonial health. Interracial relationships were initially tolerated even though Martini saw a weakening of colonial prestige in this intimacy as well as a threat to the hegemonic position of the rulers upon the colonized.

Familiarity and affable relationships between rulers and local women did in fact lead to the uncontrolled and almost naturalized practice of concubinage and to its, according to colonial racial politics, nefarious degenerating effect, miscegenation. During the fascist regime these benign interethnic relationships were banned because they were considered to be a serious threat to the superiority of the Italian race and were therefore criminalized through newly introduced racial legislation. With the onslaught of Hitler's racial ideas even Mussolini started to promulgate racial laws to be applied in the territories of his empire in order to avoid the Italian race's deterioration through miscegenation. According to Denis Mack Smith, the first law which set Italy on the course of apartheid was promulgated in

121

April 1937, nearly a year after the creation of the Italian East African Empire. By virtue of this decree, an Italian citizen who maintained conjugal relations with a native woman was liable to imprisonment from one to five years. The half-castes, who until this period had the possibility of acquiring Italian citizenship, were presented as the typical consequence of racial degradation arising from miscegenation. The law of 1937 dealt with cohabitation but, as the Catholic Church pointed out, in theory as well as in practice, an Italian could still lawfully marry a native woman. This was soon remedied by the law of 1938 that declared interracial marriage null and void. In June 1939, the separation of races was made even more distinct through the legislation on penal sanctions aimed at the defense of the prestige of the race vis-à-vis the natives. As Tekeste Negash writes:

> By forbidding inter-racial cohabitation and by closing the possibility for the latter to acquire Italian citizenship, Italy created two polarized communities, namely the rulers and the ruled. This polarization made the implementation of the native policy along 'apartheid' lines considerably easier to handle. The widespread propaganda about the superiority of the Italian and that of the degenerated character of the half-caste was used, on the one hand to mobilize the Italian population against the colonized, and on the other hand, to rationalize colonization as an inevitable policy pursued by superior cultures.[15]

Under fascist rule, Italy tried to create a distinct national identity constructed not so much through the newly introduced legal system but mostly through a meticulous campaign of representation which marked the colonized as irrevocably other and inferior. This major cultural offensive involved all mass media, including press, films, radio programs, advertisements, songs, posters, maps, photography, painting, travel accounts, and reports by explorers and ethnographers. The portrayal of the Italian grandeur as echoing the mythic and majestic role of Ancient Rome was strategically opposed to the portrayal of the natives as closer to nature. This closeness to nature made them unpredictable, irrational, and historyless, and ranked them on the evolutionary scale as inferior. The representations of the native as exotic and alluring served the purpose of instigating the virile and adventurous spirit of the Italian soldiers and workers to venture into the unknown, uncharted, and virgin soil of Africa. The representation of the local women—through photography, postcards, and literary accounts—as *Veneri Neri*, beautiful, docile, but mostly sexually available, corroborated the most important aspect of the rhetoric of empire which used the sexual metaphor as a way of fusing the public discourse with the private one.

In relation to this phenomenon images of the "Black Venus" made by photographers journeyed back home in the forms of postcards or photos published in magazines. The advent of photography was a powerful medium to give visual form to colonial culture and to forge a link between the empire and domestic imagination. It created a space for displaying the imperial spectacle. These representations conveyed the very ambivalent territory between the artistic portrayals of the aestheticized exotic female body and the pornographic look, a blurred, thin line justified by the closeness to nature of the women framed. Their documented nudity was not seen a lack of decency and moral chastity—expected by Western standards—but as a truthful and realistic portrayal of the native women, immortalized in their natural environment, as the extra attention to details concerning costumes, traditional items, and hair style demonstrates. The claim of ethnographic reportage versus voyeuristic gaze distinguishes professional from amateurish photography. However, even the so-called serious ethnographic photographic studies of native rituals, costumes, and anthropological features are nonetheless constructed from a particular Eurocentric perspective though they claim to be empirically informed and to convey only the reality of the image.

There are also many examples in literature of voyeuristic descriptions of the African women as beautiful, proud, and docile. The indigenous people were described as objects, beautiful beasts, or children with no histories or feelings. As Angelo del Boca reports on the descriptions of the Somali women, "in other words [native women] are an extraordinary, wonderful object to lust after and to consume, but nothing more. Ernesto Quadrone denies them a soul, a sensibility and intelligence. He attributes to them only instinct, like animals" (Del Boca, 1976: 90). However, these representations of the local women as seductive but historyless objects were more ambivalent in literary texts by writers who were seduced by Africa and who felt a sense of guilt for the Italian incapacity of understanding the nature and value of the local people. The following passage, for example, is an extract of a novel by the Italian writer Ennio Flaiano in 1947 (*A Time to Kill*, 1992), in which the male character is an Italian soldier in Eritrea at the time of the Italian colonization. The protagonist has lost his way, and while he is wandering, he meets a native woman who is bathing naked in a pond, an encounter that leads to a night of love. In the darkness of the night the soldier shoots what he thinks was a beast and finds out that he had accidentally killed the woman instead. His remorse, and with it the allegory for the Italian guilt in Africa, characterizes the rest of the book, which is considered to be a novel about the Italian side of the colonial experience, which is neither prestigious nor glorious. At this point in the novel (interestingly enough published a decade after the war with Ethiopia, and therefore capable of maintaining more distance), the soldier has not developed his thinking about the colonial Other and instead describes the situation according to racial stereotypes. He feels, nonetheless, the disquieting value of a civilization he cannot penetrate from his Eurocentric point of view. The passage below describes the soldier's thinking at his meeting with the woman:

Why did I not understand these people? They were poor creatures, grown old in a country from which there was no way out; they were great walkers; great experts on short cuts; but ancient and uncultured. None of them shaved listening to the morning news, nor were their breakfasts made more exciting by pages on which the ink was still damp. They could live knowing only a hundred words. On the one side there was the Beautiful and the Good, on the other the Ugly and the Bad. They had forgotten their time of splendour, and only a superstitious faith now gave their souls the power to resist in a world full of surprises. In my eyes there were another two thousand years, and she felt it.[16]

Fifty years passed between colonial representations like this in Italian literature and the first postcolonial accounts in Italian. Despite this huge gap the undoing of this racial colonial legacy is present in many emerging texts by Italian immigrants, which often focus on the colonial sexual encounter and the consequences of it.

The contact between the Italians and local women is, for example, central to Maria Viarengo's and Erminia dell'Oro's novels, as illustrated in the next chapter. *Métissage* is dealt with in both the autobiography of Viarengo and the novel by dell'Oro, *L'abbandono: Una Storia Eritrea*, 1991 (*The Abandonment: An Eritrean Story*). These children of empire, born by the encounter of Italians with native women, are the new voices that express the interlocking of old colonial boundaries with new multicultural realities.

In Erminia dell'Oro's novel, *L'Abbandono,* the Italian protagonist Carlo leaves his life of starvation and hunger in the mountains of Pavia and ends up in Eritrea, as a railway builder. After failing to strike it lucky in America because of the economic recession of 1929, he comes to Eritrea in search of a better future. Also Maria Viarengo describes her father from Piedmont as a great adventurer who migrated to Africa in search of platinum. Africa is therefore represented as the Italian Eldorado, a place waiting to be discovered.

These and many more stories reflect a new sensitivity to the issue of the Italian colonial presence in the Horn of Africa and its aftermath.

ITALIAN MULTICULTURALISM

Immigration Outline

In order to understand the process of multiculturalization and the unitary racial model the Italian nation defends against the cultural modification brought about by the increasing phenomenon of immigration, it is first necessary to review the notion of Italian identity.

At the dawn of the twentieth-first century, the notion of the Italian identity is still a controversial one. Italy, which projects itself to the outside world as the country of "made in Italy" and of political corruption, is not based on a territory of cultural cohesion. The recent movement of Lega Lombarda (Lega Nord), which proposes a federal state in which the north can become separated from the rest of the country, is just the latest expression of a long history of linguistic, political, and economic differentiations.

In order to understand the very construction of the Italian national identity, the gigantic exodus from the nation must be taken into account. During the last century there was an enormous migration of Italian workers, mostly from the Southern regions, towards Northern Europe, the United States, Australia, and Argentina.[17] The symbolic role fulfilled by the Italo-Americans in the United States is very interesting because they constitute one of the minor ethnic groups within the United States that is considered ethnically ambigous.[18]

In his article "The Preclusion of Post-colonial Discourse in Southern Italy" Pasquale Verdicchio remarks how the history of Italian emigration is marked by a form of Italian colonization within the nation, since the greater part of immigrants from Italy come from the Southern regions. This condition of subalternity had already been identified by Antonio Gramsci in his *La Questione Meridionale* (1966), but Verdicchio emphasizes the role of the Southern emigrant as the border citizen (1997). In Italy there is, in fact, a common right-wing comment that "Africa begins south of Rome," a historical construction that links Southern Italians to other colonized people.

This is also narrated in Carlo Levi's novel *Cristo si è Fermato ad Eboli*, 1945 (*Christ Stopped at Eboli*) in which the image of a Southern Italian region, Lucania (Basilicata), which has been forgotten by God, functions as an allegory of the central state that defends the interests and the culture of the center-north, and cares little about the development and improvement of the economic conditions of the South:

Christ did stop at Eboli, where the road and the railway leave the coast of Salerno and turn into the desolate reaches of Lucania. Christ never came this far, nor did time, nor the individual soul, nor hope, nor the relation of cause to effect, nor reason nor history. Christ never came, just as the Romans never came, content to garrison the highways without penetrating the mountains and the forests, nor the Greeks, who flourished besides the Gulf of Taranto. None of the pioneers of Western civilization brought here his sense of the passage of time, his deification of the State or that ceaseless activity which feeds upon itself. No one has come to this land except as an enemy, a conqueror, or a visitor devoid of understanding. . . . But to this shadowy land, that knows neither sin nor redemption from sin, where evil is not moral but is only the pain residing forever in earthly things, Christ did not come. Christ stopped at Eboli.[19]

The massive emigration from Italy precluded any postcolonial discourse within Italy itself, and maybe because of that, the Southern Italian citizen has managed to maintain an identity of his/her own, distinct from the general national model abroad. In the United States the regional origin, with its linguistic and cultural variations (Sicily, Sardinia, Calabria, etc.) is, in fact, more relevant than the declaration of affiliation to a national Italian identity.

To the complexity of the large-scale political realignments within Italy, which have accelerated in pace, we must add the paradox which characterizes Italy: a country among the five most economically powerful countries in the world, the country of fashion, design, and high culture which is at the same time seen within Europe as *piccola Italia*; a nation still struggling with forms of backwardness and civil immaturity, dragged down by public sector debt, organized crime, government corruption, bad administration, economic disparity between north and south, and political instability; a nation entangled in Catholicism and committed to a concept of the nuclear family that undermines faith in the state, or civic trust. The obvious immaturity of the Italian civil state can be further analyzed since it does not correspond to the model of modernization present in other European countries such as Germany, the UK, and France. It is, nonetheless, an economically competitive country with relatively widespread prosperity and is a member of the Euro zone. This makes Italy's "exceptionalism" a model that in a way is closer to other Mediterranean realities.[20]

This anomalous image of modern Italy is further complicated by a new situation generated by the sudden stream of immigrants coming from the former colonial territories and other world regions. The status of these new immigrants resembles the economic and cultural status of past Italian migrants from the South. Revising the concept of Italian history by redefining its margins, these immigrants expect solidarity because they find parallels with the experiences of the Italian emigrants from the South. However, this is not what happens. The process of admitting different races and often different religions is marked by outbursts of discrimination, violence, and social intolerance.

The limited colonial experience in Africa did not generate a great immigration of people towards their ex-colonial country at the time of independence. A few came with the annexation of Eritrea to Ethiopia but they did not acquire the visibility of the more recent forms of immigration. But the recent state of these countries, with civil wars, famine, and political upheaval, has forced much of the population to flee, sometimes towards Italy, which has become the gateway to Fortress Europe for people from other countries in Africa, Asia, and Eastern Europe (the latter due to the dissolution of the communist bloc).

Italy is a latecomer as far as immigration is concerned in comparison to France and Britain, which have a history of immigration from the former colonies that dates back to the 1950s. The immigration policy in Italy is considered anomalous within Europe because it does not have an old tradition of immigration based on a social policy that can manage both the stream of immigrant arrivals and the consolidation of their presence on the territory.

The immigrant reality in France is, for example, characterized by its ethnocentric assimilation, which reflects its colonial model. The assimilationist project is based on the fact that immigrants must abandon their original culture for the French language and customs in order to be positively integrated. This is in accordance with the idea of a French nationhood, which is based on the centralization of the secular state that excludes ethnic minorities. Citizenship is given on the basis that ethnic minorities become perfectly assimilated despite their different cultural needs.

The British also follow an immigration policy that reflects their colonial model. Characterized by a liberal and autonomous strategy, Britain is ready to accept the particularities of the customs, traditions, and habits of ethnic minorities since it is taken for granted that they will never become truly British. In practice ethnic minorities are ghettoized and relegated to a marginal space which is exchanged for freedom but is in reality a form of unequal pluralism. This approach to immigration is a clear consequence of the British colonial past since autonomy was granted to the ruled as long as they recognized the authority and superiority of the rulers, i.e. the British. The flexibility of this system offered a satisfactory solution to the changeable social situation of immigration until a decade ago. However, Britain is now confronted with the second and third generation of immigrants who are well aware of their legal and social rights and their interconnection with their cultural specificity. This generation of immigrants is not willing to accept the subordinate role attributed to them but is equipped to modify the very concept of Britishness, expanding it from within, as Stuart Hall and Homi Bhabha have demonstrated in their critical analysis of "Reinventing Britain"[21] and as Salman Rushdie and Hanif Kureishi have shown in their fictional works.

The situation in Italy is more blurred because of its unclear project during colonization (characterized by the Italian *arte di arrangiarsi*, the art to manage, to get by) and its anomalous form of immigration. Within the changed European panorama the Italian solution is rarely the first choice for the immigrants but rather an alternative to other countries that have closed their borders.

The condition of immigration in Italy is anomalous because it is generated by a complex set of political and economic contexts which are specifically related to the historical and economic conditions of postmodernity. Recent immigration is, in fact, not only connected to Italy's imperial past and its neighboring countries' postcolonial policy, but also to the contemporary reality of the global marketplace. An intersection of factors affect the Italian national identity both within Italy and abroad.

With the exception of immigration from Morocco since the 1960s Italy really entered the immigration picture at the beginning of the 1980s when other European countries toughened their policies on immigration or simply closed their borders. Italy has become a makeshift solution because it has no clear legislation for primary immigration or regulation of immigrants already present. Italy can offer unqualified or semi-skilled job opportunities that for many immigrants are better than the conditions back home. Work is one of the reasons for the immigration from the French-speaking former colonies, such as Senegal. The Senegalese are very often street salesmen on the Italian sidewalks, where they are called *vu' cumprà*, which is a derogatory term for all the street salesmen from Africa. The word mocks the way the Africans mispronounce the Italian phrase *vuoi comprare?* (you wonna buy?).

Another strong association of labor and race in Italy is that of tomato pickers. In the last decade a stream of black illegal immigrants have gone to work in the south of Italy. The local population were not properly prepared for their arrival and there were no adequate facilities for them. The local population responded with racism and violence as shown in the film *Pummarò* (1990) directed by Beniamo Placido, in which a young Ghanaian doctor, Kwaku, goes to Italy in search of his brother, nicknamed Pummarò, who has gone to Campania to pick tomatoes. Pummarò has rebelled against the abuses of the black market of tomato picking. When his salary is cut as punishment for having trade union ideas, he reacts by appropriating a gun and a van from the *camorra* (the local mafia) and flees to the north. In order to find his brother, Kwaku repeats Pummarò's journey from south to north (from Naples to Rome, from Rome to Verona, and from Verona to Frankfurt), experiencing in his doubling act not only the different levels of integration and racism within Italian society but also different forms of solidarity and work opportunities. However, he will arrive too late. He finds his brother murdered in Frankfurt.

Many of the stories of immigration have entered and permeated the realm of cultural representation within Italian society. Immigration is not only addressed as a legal and criminal issue but also as a social and cultural one. The press and media coverage of the past decade has mostly concentrated on demonizing and on blowing out of all proportion the presence and impact of the immigrants within Italian society, depicting the immigrant other from Africa, Albania, or Muslim countries as sources of imbalance and evil.[22] Recent critical, fictional, and artistic renderings of the situation have, however, shown the other side of the Italian racial wall, offering more complex insights into the problems and the possibility of hearing different voices. The voice of women has been slow to be heard but the fictional accounts analyzed in the following chapters bear testimony to a progressive and self-conscious change in which even the weaker parts of the immigration outline, such as women, play an active role, reshaping Italian identity from their own perspective.

Italian Colonial Literature

The recent phenomenon of multiculturalization has reopened interest in the Italian colonial past and its resonance within today's cultural climate. This shift from denial to recognition and conscientization nonetheless still plays a marginal role within Italian culture. As Maria Cutrufelli explains,

> The imperial dream of Italy in the Horn of Africa . . . is a forgotten history, buried in the collective unconscious of the nation. . . . it is a war covered by other wars and maybe because of that it has left few traces in our culture, few influences in the prose of our narrators.[23]

Many connoisseurs and specialists of Italian literature share this opinion. Even in a multicultural approach to literature such as the one offered by the text *Altri Lati del Mondo* (*Other Sides of the World*)[24] edited by Maria Antonietta Saracino in collaboration with other important authors (Isabella Camera D'Affitto, Alessandro Portelli, Vinicio Ongini, Goffredo Fofi, and others), there is a reticence about attributing a role within Italian literature to Africa.

This collection of essays sketches the articulation of the literary, musical, artistic, and cinematographic encounters between far and near worlds. Dealing with different literatures (Afro-American, Anglo-Indian, Anglo-African, Arabic), it confronts the immaturity of Italy in its encounter with the literary other:

> Maybe because of the brevity and the modality of our colonial experience, a significant literary stream based on that event did not have the time to be born, as it has been present in the English literature for more than three centuries.[25]

Maria Antonietta Saracino makes a reference to the classic works of English literature in which the other becomes a familiar presence such as in Shakespeare's *Tempest* (Caliban), Daniel Defoe's *Robinson Crusoe*, Joseph Conrad's *Heart of Darkness*, Rudyard Kipling's *Kim*, or E. M. Forsters' *A Passage to India*. We should not forget the newly resuscitated text *Ooronoko: Or the Royal Slave* by Aphra Ben (1688), the first woman in England to make her living by writing (1640–1689), which tells the story of a black man who begins his life as a prince and ends it as a slave. The book, set in Surinam, is the first modern English novel,[26] written with an autobiographical voice that is explicitly and proudly female, a text that precedes by more than hundred years any other antislavery narratives. The list of literary encounters with the other could be much longer but what is important is the answer to this white encounter, the literature produced by migration, the writing back. In Britain it is the leading literature at the moment, with authors such as Salman Rushdie, Ben Okri, Derek Walcott, Hanif Kureishi, and many others. In France, beside the great literature of Tahar Bell Jelloun, Assia Djebar, and Rachid Boujedra, there are also many ironic stories for children showing an advanced phase of multiculturalism, such as in Didier Daeninckx's *Il Gatto di Tigali* (*Tigali's Cat*) in which a Tunisian cat is murdered for racist motives.

Even though the African presence, assumed by the colonial link, plays a marginal role in Italian literature, that does not mean that it is absent. On the contrary there is a consistent number of literary works dealing with Africa, or better with *mal d'africa* (African malaise). These texts, which are definitely part of Italian colonial literature, deal with the irresistible attraction for the Black continent, the fascination for the African primordial landscape, for its ancient customs, and for its capability of evoking myths. This kind of fascination for Africa was often seen as dangerous and the reason for the *insabbiamento* (muddling) of Italians, which referred to the seductive and frightening allure of the dark continent that made the Italians reluctant to leave.

A considerable number of literary works were produced on Africa by the first explorers and travelers, but literature was also produced by writers and journalists during the consolidation period of the colonial empire.[27] As already mentioned, the rhetoric of the fascist regime clearly linked textual production and colonization. Innumerable accounts of the expansionist deeds were written in order to create that "factory of consensus," as the historian of colonial Italy Angelo Del Boca has stated. In order to produce the discursive rhetoric of imperial propaganda, various literary representations on colonialism prepared for and commented on the Italian expansionist policy. Contrary to what many people may think, there is no shortage of such texts. More recently the literature that we define as postcolonial encompasses both the Italian's image of Africa and the writing back by African authors who have started writing in Italian for reasons of colonialism or immigration.

During the first phase of colonial literature we have the accounts of the explorer Vittorio Bottego, who was an aggressive adventurer very much in favor of de Crispi's colonial policy. Arnaldo Cipolla was considered "the Italian Kipling" for his extensive and vivid accounts of his journeys. He published novels and stories about exotic locations and people. On the eve of the invasion of Ethiopia he published *L'Abissinia in Armi* (Firenze: Bemporad, 1935) which articulates a complex and yet stereotypical view of Ethiopia based on a clear-cut binary opposition between patterns of disavowal and attraction. He mixes the view of Ethiopia both as a sinister, barbarous country and as an exotic, appealing country for tourism. This tension is present in future accounts of the Italian experience in Africa.

In addition to these are the more eerie descriptions left by other travelers and explorers, such as Emilio Cecchi, or accounts by fantasists, such as Emilio Salgari, who wrote about far-off places such as Africa and Malaysia (Sandokan) without ever having been there. Of a different nature is the poetry written by Ungaretti, founder of the hermetic literary movement. He was born in Alexandria in 1888 and uses images of the African desert regions in his later work.

During the fascist expansion fascist virility was celebrated by writers such as Gabriele D'Annunzio, who wrongly appropriates the myth of Nietzsche's superman, for example, in his tragedy *Più che L'Amore*,[28] to elevate the figure of Vittorio Bottego as a pure hero, a superman of the Ulysses' type. In this way D'Annunzio reopens the old myth of Africa as a regenerating land, and he transforms it into the political dream of expansion. Africa is presented as a land to conquer where the infinite personal potentiality can be deployed. To mark the conquest of Ethiopia he wrote "Teneo te Africa. La seconda gesta d'Oltremare."[29] Similarly, in his poetics of action and movement the futurist poet Marinetti contemplates Africa as the land of creativity about which he writes a novel, *Mafarka il Futurista* (Milano: Edizione Futuristiche di "Poesia," 1910) and also "il Poema Africano della Divisione 28 Ottobre" (Milano: Mondadori, 1937). The impact of D'Annunzio and Filippo Tommaso Marinetti and other futurist writers of the avant-garde on fascist ideology can be better assessed in the work by Giovanna Tommasello in *La Letteratura Coloniale Italiana: Dalle Avanguardie al Fascismo* (1984).

In addition to these abstract representations of Africa are the journalist reportages of Orio Vergani, Curzio Malaparte, and Dino Buzzati, all of them correspondents for *Il Corriere della Sera* at the time of the Empire in Africa. Orio Vergani was one of the most authoritative voices in the press at the time, and his journey through Ethiopia, *La Via Nera: Viaggio in Etiopia da Massaua a Mogadiscio*, was published in 1938. However, these journalists fell under the spell of the fascist propaganda and their articles did not have serious portraits of Africa, did not denounce the sordid aspects of colonization, but rather fell back into a process of exoticism with descriptions of nature and people which were in line with Mussolini's requirements. Marie-Hélène Caspar also underlines this aspect of censorship in her introduction to the publication of Buzzati's seventy-four articles written during his time as a foreign correspondent in Africa. Buzzati arrived in Africa in 1939, three years after the annexation of Ethiopia to the Empire. Buzzati's articles are not interesting for their content, which had to be in line with the colonialist propaganda (including narration of the glorious actions of the Italians, construction of enormous infrastructures such as the *strada della Vittoria*, description of the simplicity and primitivity of the native populations, or descriptions of the

African landscape and fauna in its exotic aspects), but they are interesting for the omissions and censorship required both by the director of *Il Corriere* and by the fascist regime, which are brought to visibility again thanks to Caspar's additions in italics.[30]

However, with the end of the colonial adventure and the demise of the bombastic fascist propaganda, dissonant voices started to appear that described the Italian enterprise in Africa in all its unpleasant and dehumanizing aspects. Already in 1923, with his novel *Kif tebbi: Romanzo Africano* (Milano: Treves, 1923), Luciano Zuccoli manifested the desire to eliminate the exotic component in the colonial literature in order to show more interest in the indigenous people. Similarly, other works such as Mario Tobino's *Il deserto della Libia* (1952), Riccardo Bacchelli's *Mal D'Africa. Romanzo Storico* (1934, reprinted in 1990 by Rizzoli), and Enrico Emmanuelli's *Settimana Nera* (Milano: Mondadori, 1966) continue to sketch the "other" face of the Italian colonial literature. The most important work remains Ennio Flaiano's *Tempo di Uccidere*, 1947 (*Time To Kill*, 1992) in which he creates heroes, actually antiheroes, who are petrified by nostalgia or tortured by bad conscience and who know the weakness, malaise, and madness generated by their encounter with Africa.

In the last decade there has been a revival of the myth of Africa with Alberto Moravia's short stories *Passeggiate Africane* (Milano: Bompiani, 1987), *A Quale tribù Appartieni?* (Milano: Bompiani, 1972), *Lettera dal Sahara* (1982), and also his novel *La Donna Leopardo* (Milano: Bompiani, 1991). Pier Paolo Pasolini also tried to film an African Orestiade (*Appunti per un' Orestiade Africana*, 1975). Like Moravia he was in search of the profound explanations for the great existential questions that could be found by visiting Africa. Africa was for Moravia the continent of contradictions and intersections which could offer paradigms for the explanation of the deeper structures of our civilization. Another very recent publication regards the postmodern work of Gianni Celati, *Avventure in Africa* (Milano: Feltrinelli, 1998) in which the life models offered by Africa are seen as the only possible way to escape the daily routine that has been eroded by mass consumption. This Africa is not so much different or primitive, as unspoiled, a place where you can escape if you manage to get off the tourist tracks. The Africa of Celati precedes or ignores the postcolonial world.

In addition to these representations are the representations in postcolonial literature by writers such as Erminia dell'Oro who revisits the colonial past and acknowledges its repercussions for Italy at the end of the twentieth century. Despite her talent at avoiding exoticism and describing the complex nature of Africa, Erminia dell'Oro has a tendency to represent Eritrea as paradise on earth, thus reigniting the old myth of Africa as enchanting and alluring.

To these descriptions, oscillating between crude realism and magic memoir, there is a new response offered by the writers of the Africa-Italian diaspora who narrate their own desire and vision of Africa in their account of immigration to Italy. These accounts often give a positive image of Italy as the land of opportunity and dreams but also acknowledge the reality of racism and intolerance. This friction is described in these texts for the first time from the point of view of the incomers.

As explained earlier, Italy was previously known for its massive emigration, but at the turn of the new millennium it has instead become the destination of a great number of immigrants from African countries and elsewhere. This renewed contact between Africans and Italians, with the flow of migrants going in a historically new direction, presents a new set of issues, problems, and opportunities which have important implications not only for the future of Italian society but for intercultural and interracial relations throughout the world. In an attempt to perceive and understand the diverse dimensions and opportunities inherent in this new encounter between Africa and Italy, it is of the utmost importance to analyze the literary works which have originated from this cross-cultural fertilization, and to provide new frameworks of literary analysis that are adequate for the peculiar brand of multiculturalism that is distinctively Italian.

Postcolonial Literature and Afro-Italian Writings

When one compares the reception of Afro-Italian writings in Italy to the reception of African and Asian writers in the United Kingdom, where they have the backing of successful publishing houses like Longman or Heinemann who often produce special series edition for them, one can see the situation in Italy is far from encouraging. By comparison, the Italian literary market is rather stifling and shows little curiosity towards novelty. Even though no Italian novels of migration can claim such a self-confident opening as that of Kureishi's *Buddha of the Suburbia*, in which he describes his identity as half-Pakistani and half-British, it does not mean that there is not a literature of migration in Italy:

> My name is Kamir Amir, and I am Englishman born and bred, almost. I am often considered to be a funny kind of Englishman, a new breed as it were, having emerged from two old stories. But I don't care—Englishman I am (though not proud of it), from the South London suburbs and going somewhere. Perhaps it is the odd mixture of continents and blood, of here and there, of belonging and not, that makes me restless and easily bored.[31]

Despite some cause for discouragement, there are some signs of an opening of the literary borders. The trend is set and the process is irreversible. The city of Rimini has, for example, established a literary prize (Concorso Letterario Eks&tra) for poetry and short stories by immigrant writers. The Albanian poet

Gezim Hadjari won the Eks&tra prize in 1996 and subsequently won the Premio Montale in 1997. The publishing house Fara has already gathered several collections from this competition; *Le Voci dell'Arcobaleno* (1995), *Mosaici d'Inchiostro* (1996), *Memorie in Valigia* (1997), *Destini sospesi di volti in cammino* (1998), *Parole oltre i confini* (1999), *Anime in Viaggio* (2002), and *Il Doppio Sguardo. Culture allo Specchio* (ANDKronos Libri, 2002). In 1998 the first introduction to Italian migrant literature appeared, Armando Gnisci's *La Letterature Italiana della Migrazione*, which considers both the literature of the Italians who emigrated abroad and the new literature in Italian from the new comers of the 1990s. Furthermore, in Rome the journal *Il Caffè: Per Una Letteratura Multiculturale*, has already published a few issues with migrant texts written in Italian or that have been translated. Even *Effe*, the promotional journal of the Feltrinelli bookshops (Feltrinelli is a large Italian publishing house), has dedicated its second issue to multiculturalism with an article by the Italian journalist Oreste Pivetta, "Multiculturalism, Voci Di razza" ("Multiculturalism, Voices of Race"),[32] in which he states,

> The Pakistanis of *My Beautiful Laundrette*, Hanif Kureishi's famous screenplay, are numerous enough, strong and secure enough, to construct their own language, an English modified on their tradition. I believe that, paradoxically enough, the small number of our immigrants (compared to other European countries and despite the alarmism) hinders the birth of a culture that could be defined as multicultural. It will surely happen because immigration continues, despite even the strictest legislation.[33]

It must be said that the situation has progressed far beyond Pivetta's statement, since the process of immigration to Italy has rather than slow down substantially increased during the last years. The publishing house l'Harmattan, which is based in Paris and has a branch in Turin, has published many texts relevant for the questions of interculturality. The publishing cooperative Sinnos is also editing a series of bilingual texts, *I Mappamondi*, under which Ribka Sibhatu's text *Aulò: Canto e Poesia dell'Eritrea* has appeared.

Tepid statements, such as Pivetta's, about which texts are relevant for questions of interculturality, are also due to the fact that the colonial encounter for the Italians has until now happened elsewhere, i.e., not in Italy. Whereas Britain has experienced a stream of return (*flusso di ritorno*) for the last five decades,[34] Italy had removed its imperial deeds from the national consciousness. But immigrants are now populating the Italian cities and starting to narrate their stories about the country, confronting Italy with its undeniable pluralization.

Italy has not really dealt with the representation of the other since the images created by the fascist propaganda with school books, huge maps, advertisements, posters, songs, and films.[35] These are extremely important for an analysis of the construction of the Italian imagination and representation of the other. However, they are rather dated in their racism and their specific rhetoric of expansion. It is therefore necessary to search for new, less biased representations that can help to assess the new multiculturalization emerging at home. The counter-representation offered by immigrant writers, who through their narratives turn the gaze on the colonizers and write back, re-narrates the Italian nation as they—the others—experience it. The literary works by African immigrants writing in Italian are analyzed here not only for their specific link to Italian colonialism, but also in order to counter that postcolonial totalization according to which India is overrepresented and Africa is neglected.

Many of the texts by Italian immigrants are written in collaboration with an Italian writer or a journalist who in the genuine intention of civil *engagement* give voice to those who do not have it, lending their language to the immigrant narratives, trying to mix the interest for the current Italian multicultural situation with literary intentions. The results shift from a documentary style to a more articulated fictional account, such as in the novel Alessandro Michelletti coauthored with Saidou Moussa Ba, *La Promessa di Hamadi* (*Hamadi's Promise*) (Novara: De Agostini, 1991). Ba is an example of an immigrant who comes from another colonial background, in this case French, but most Africans who write in Italian come from Senegal, Morocco, and Tunisia. Such backgrounds are inscribed in their texts. France and the French language function as go-betweens from Africa to Italy:

> There is a discrepancy between the colonizing culture that dominated part of these new-Italian-African writers' lives and the literary language into which their lives are being transcribed. These hybrid literary creations are based on the accumulation and relative assimilation of different Western cultural traditions filtered through non-Western eyes and languages.[36]

Saidou Moussa Ba, who is Senegalese, is an example of such a writer. Some notes were written by him in French and were used to develop the plot of the novel that was written in Italian in close collaboration between the authors. Saidou Moussa Ba has written another text also in collaboration with Alessandro Micheletti, *La Memoria di A.* (Edizioni Gruppo Abele: 1995). Mohamed Bouchanes is a Moroccan and his book *Chiamatemi Alì* (*Call me Alì*) (Leonardo, 1991) was originally a diary written in French and Arabic by Bouchane himself. The occasion for this work was incidental. While attending Italian classes, he wrote a composition inspired by his own life. The Italian teacher, Carla de Girolamo, suggested that his diary could be published and worked with him to translate his bilingual French/Arabic work into Italian. In his book he recounts the difficulty of preserving his own religion, Islam, within a strongly Catholic Italian society. Bouchane tries to define his identity as a religious one and stresses that integration for a Muslim in Italy is more difficult than for other immigrants. In Italy much of the attention for the immigrants from outside the European Union (*extra-communitari*) came initially from religious institutions and from the Catholic church which offered charity to them but there was the underlining implication that they would try to convert them. Pap Khouma's *Io Venditore di Elefanti* (*I, an Elephant Salesman*) (Milano: Garzanti, 1990), was created in collaboration with the journalist Oreste Pivetta, who also wrote the introduction to the autobiographical text. Khouma is also from Senegal. He emigrated first to Paris, the capital of the empire, but felt rejected both by the French and by the Senegalese community who had lived there for a longer time. He consequently moved to Italy as an alternative country of emigration, where a tradition was not yet established and where he faces equally insurmountable discrimination. "My experience," writes Khouma, "has been obviously followed by many other immigrants like me, people who know as their official language the language of the colonizers, Spanish, French, English or Portuguese."

Salah Methnani, a Tunisian immigrant, recounts his experience in Italy in his book *Immigrato* (Roma: Theoria, 1990), a straightforward, plainly told autobiography that is a harrowing account of his seemingly inevitable descent into marginalization and criminality. Written in collaboration with Mario Fortunato, this, among other texts, conveys that split identity which goes along with questions of split authority. There is a dialogue between immigrant and Italian culture in this text where a process of fruitful but, at times, invasive collaboration takes place.

Princesa (Sensibili alle Foglie, 1994; reprinted by Tropea, 1997) is an autobiographical account by Fernanda Farias de Albuquerque which was originally written in a hybrid of Portuguese/Sardinian/street-Italian language and straightened into publishable Italian by Maurizio Jannelli. It narrates the story of Fernanda, who is legally Fernando, and describes her life as a transsexual prostitute in Brazil, Spain, and Italy. From the confusion of her mixed identity Fernando/Fernanda (Princesa is her professional nickname) passes from her naive hope of saving enough money for her sex operation to the increasing squalor and hardship of prostitution and drug addiction. She catches what in the text is called "the disease" and ends up killing her landlady. She shares the jail with a Sardinian shepherd who adds an extra dialectal color to her autobiography. The editor Maurizio Jannelli, who shared with Fernanda the experience of the prison due to his political involvement in the terrorist group *Brigate Rosse* (Red Brigades), turned Fernanda's mixed language into proper Italian. He got it published by Sensibili alle Foglie, a company located in Rome and founded by Renato Curcio, one of the Red Brigades' historical leaders. This publishing company has played an important role in the diffusion of migrant literature because it publishes texts that other publishing houses would refuse. This surprising testimonial has been turned into a successful film (2000) by Henrique Goldman that was financed by a European coproducer.

Mohsen Melliti has published two texts on his own, *Pantanella: Canto Lungo la Strada* (*Pantanella: Chant Along the Street*) (Roma: Edizioni Lavoro, 1992) and *I Bambini Delle Rose* (*The Roses' Children*) (Roma: Edizioni Lavoro, 1995). The first text on the Pantanella, an abandoned pasta factory in Rome where a large number of immigrants found shelter, deals with the social problems created by the occupation and then forced evacuation by the police. This event is also analyzed by Renato Curcio in *Shiv Mahal* (1991).[37]

On the wave of these first editorial successes new texts surveying questions of gender and immigration have found their way towards a broader readership. Jesus Maria de Lourdes' *Ricordai: Vengo da un'isola di Capo Verde-Sou de Uma Ilha de Cabo Verde*[38] tells in a hybrid language little stories, riddles, recipes, and useful addresses concerning the Cape Verdian world in Italy. Like Ribka Sibhatu's *Aulò: Canto e Poesia Dall'Eritrea*, also published by Sinnos, this text is meant to be a useful tool to understand a culture that is already largely present in Italy.

Salwa Salem's *Con il Vento nei Capelli: Vita di una Donna Palestinese* (Giunti, 1993; reprinted in 2001) book appeared after the death of the author in 1992. During her final stage of her illness Salem managed to narrate her life and her passion to Laura Maritano. This confessional book is the fruit of this collaboration and narrates the itinerary of Salem. Born in Palestina in 1940, after her marriage she moved to Kuwait and Syria and finally to Vienna. In the 1970s she settled in Parma, Italy, with her husband and three children. This auto/bio/graphical text is the fierce accusation of a woman who has been forced to prostitution and murder in order to defend her right to be free against the social and economic oppression of male domination. In the end Salem finds a conciliatory voice that reaffirms the need for dialogue and peace.

These texts are very often pure ego-documents, told in the first person in the form of autobiography. As Maria Saracino puts it, "Autobiography becomes a step, a necessary stage to reach creative fiction. As if you could not give yourself to a story before having said who you are, before having exposed your credentials" (Saracino, 1994: 86). This project of announcing the self and dealing with a new identity in the making produces a literary genre which is still hybrid, balanced between chronicle and novel, between the memory of home and the experience of cultural contamination.

After the exuberant production at the beginning of the 1990s there has been a period of silence. At the beginning of the new millennium new voices have started to reappear again, and often without the collaboration of a journalist or a cultural mediators, a freedom which, however, makes the connection to the publishing world more difficult. Some of the authors have managed to reach major publishing houses, while others have disappeared and reappeared in the nonprofit sector of religious organizations or educational institutions.

Among these new emergent writers are the Albanian Ron Kubati, *Va e Non Torna* (2000) and *M* (2002), both published by Besa Editore in Lecce; Jedelin Mabiala Gangbo from Congo who has published *Verso la Notte di Makonga* (Lupetti, 1999) and *Rometta e Giulieo*, (Feltrinelli, 2002), the Algerian Smari Abdel Malek, *Fiamme in Paradiso* (Il Saggiatore, 2000); Muin Madith Masri from Cisgiordania, *Il Sole D'Inverno* (Lupetti, 1999); the Cameroonian anthropologist Geneviève Makaping, *Traiettorie di Sguardi: E se gli Altri Foste Voi?* (Rubattino, 2001), the Senegalese Mbacke Gadji, *Lo Spirito delle Sabbie Gialle* (Edizioni dell'Arco, 1999), the Syrian Youssef Wakkas, *Fogli Sbarrati: Il Mondo delle Carceri Visto da un Immigrato Carcerato* (Eks&tra, 2002); the Somalian Garane Garane, *Il Latte é Buono* (Kúmá, 2003).

Various foreign writers reside in Italy but refuse the label "migrant writer," because they do not always deal with the issue of immigration. Writers such as Jarmila Ockayova, born in Czechoslovakia, *L'Essenziale è Invisibile agli Occhi* (Baldini e Castoldi, 1997), the German Helena Janeczek, of Polish Jewish origin, *Cibo* (Mondadori, 2002), *Lezioni di Tenebra* (Monadori, 1997), Helga Schneider, also German of Polish origin, *Lasciami Andare, Madre* (Adelphi, 2001*), Porta di Brandeburgo: Storie Berlinesi 1945–1947* (Rizzoli, 1997), the American Alice Oxman, *Una Donna di Più* (Bompiani, 2000), *Prima Donna* (Marsilio, 1990), Julio Monteiro Martins, *Racconti Italiani* (Besa, 2002), and Christiana de Caldas Brito, *Amanda Olina Azzurra e le Altre* (Lilith, 1998) the latter two both from Brazil. These authors consider themselves writers in their own right, since they were writers even before coming to Italy and believe the experience of moving to a new country should not confine them to some literary ghetto.[39]

Recent novels such as *La Straniera* (Milano: Bompiani, 1999) by Younis Tawfik have received wide media coverage and good critical review. The most important aspect of this very new tradition of migrant writing in Italian is that in this text the writer does not coincide with the narrator. Younis Tawfik, an Iraqi poet who has lived in Italy since 1979, has a degree in Italian literature and has already published several novels, *Nelle mani la Luna* (Ananka, 2001), *La Città di Iram* (Bompiani, 2002), and several texts on the Islamic civilization, the Arab language, and the condition of the Kurds. *La Straniera* is set in Turin. A successful and well-integrated architect from the Middle East starts a complex relationship with Amina, a girl from Morocco who, unlike him, lives at the margins of Italian society, is forced into prostitution, and is doomed to die too young. Described as a disquieting multiethnic love story, both touching and bitter, *La Straniera* represents one of the first attempts to narrate the gendered experience of migration from a male point of view. Balancing exoticism and refined prose, Tawfik signals the beginning of a new tradition within Italian literature that moves away from confessional ego-documents towards more sophisticated narratives that reach wider coverage.

Within these different accounts on immigration the whole history of the Italian presence in the Horn of Africa becomes relevant. Many of these texts, though linked to the new global economy, bear a complex relationship with the Italian imperial aftermath. Both readings are necessary in order to comprehend the confused Italian multicultural panorama. The Afro-Italian literature must therefore be placed within a frame of minority literature with respect to other "mainstream" postcolonial literatures, in this case the Anglo-Indian one. The element of continuity between the authors is represented by the common experience of diaspora which is analyzed as a concrete social and economic condition (especially for the Afro-Italian writers), but works also as a trope that connects people of different origins and nationalities and brings various peripheries to the center. This allows different forms of marginality to enter into dialogue with each other and places, for example, South Asian literature in an unprecedented context of postcolonial writing such as the Afro-Italian one. The issue of gender, and the implications of being a woman writer in the condition of diaspora, creates a crucial link between different historical and geographical traditions and questions the utility of recent feminist theories for the retrieval of Third World women's voices. The risk of reigniting processes of recolonization and canonization are in fact the pitfalls of both postcolonial and feminist theory. The second part of this book theoretically and textually articulates many of these pitfalls and proposes alternative frameworks of analyses for understanding an increasingly more complex postcolonial world.

Chapter 7

Daughters of Empire

Métissage and Hyphenated Identities:
Erminia dell'Oro and Maria Abbebù Viarengo

We have to articulate new visions of ourselves, new concepts that allow us to think *otherwise*, to bypass the ancient symmetries and dichotomies that have governed the ground and the very condition of possibility of thought, of "clarity," in all of Western philosophy. *Métissage* is such a concept and a practice: it is the site of undecidability and indeterminacy, where solidarity becomes the fundamental principle of political action against hegemonic languages.

—Françoise Lionnet, *Autobiographical Voices*, p. 6

DAUGHTERS OF EMPIRE

This chapter will deal with two authors who have experienced exile and carry memories of the short-lived Italian empire in the Horn of Africa. The first one, Erminia dell'Oro, is an Italian writer who grew up in Eritrea and currently lives in Milan. The second one is Maria Abbebù Viarengo, an Italian-Ethiopian writer who lives in Turin. Maria Viarengo is a "competent native informant," to use Spivak's definition for someone who can speak for her/his native group to outsiders. As the fruit of an intercultural encounter between her Oromo mother and her Piedmontese father, she bridges the two cultures which are at the center of this postcolonial location. Her still to be published autobiography *Koborò e Violini Io Non Scelgo* functions as an ego-document and as a tribute to her Oromo mother, who has been silenced. The few fragments analyzed here were published in an Italian review *Linea d'Ombra* in 1990, under the title "Andiamo A

Spasso?" and constitute excerpts of her autobiography. In this autobiography she sketches her life as an Afro-Italian woman forced by her father at the age of twenty to leave both Africa and her mother for a European education.

Unlike Maria Viarengo, Erminia Dell'Oro is not the fruit of an intercultural encounter. She was born in Asmara in 1938 of Italian parents who lived all their lives in Eritrea. Her grandfather, who was originally from Lecco, went to Africa at the end of the eighteenth century in search of adventure. Like Karen Blixen (who described Africa as "heart's home" and Denmark as "living death")[1] and Doris Lessing,[2] Erminia dell'Oro felt the need to rework her African life. There is a precedent in Italian literature in the narrative of Fausta Cialente, an Italian from Trieste who lived part of her life in Egypt in the 1930s and published several books in the 1960s and early 1970s.[3] Erminia dell'Oro left Eritrea voluntarily for Milan at the age of twenty to study because there was no future in Eritrea. She declared once in an interview that the Italians who had remained in Africa were old colonizers who had kept a fascist mentality. Moreover, the civil war between Ethiopia and Eritrea worsened conditions for all the inhabitants, and the nationalization of industries and firms by the Ethiopian government drove the Italians out, as did the destruction and confiscation of the *sciftà*.[4]

Dell'Oro went to Italy with the idea of becoming a journalist. However, she worked mainly as a bookseller, got married, had children, and only resumed her dream of becoming a writer in her middle years. In 1988, at the age of fifty, she published her autobiographical account of her life in Eritrea, *Asmara Addio* (1988), which was an immediate success. This African debut was followed by other well received works. Her first novel, *L'Abbandono: Una Storia Eritrea* (Torino: Einaudi, 1991), has been translated into French and Dutch. In 1993 she published a children's story, *Matteo e i Dinosauri*, and in 1994, *Il Fiore di Merara*. In 1995 *La Pianta Magica* appeared and only in her last autobiographical book, *Mamme al Vento*, does she diverge from the African cycles.

The belated appearance of Erminia Dell'Oro on the literary scene is particularly relevant at a time when Italy is facing multiculturalization and is confronted with texts by immigrants from its former colonies. The Italian colonial past is textualized from a different perspective when the colonizer returns the gaze. Erminia Dell'Oro, who deals with her memory in order to come to terms with it, functions, therefore, as a decoder of the Italian experience in Africa, which is revised through the filter of time and of racist awareness. Her fictional subjects are at the heart of the new Italian multicultural scene of the twenty-first century. She has reconstructed an historical thread between the Italian political past in the 1930s and the present multicultural asset of Italy. In her texts she creates the space for social responsibility and for emotional involvement with the immigrant group from Eastern Africa. In this way she not only makes the colonized other visible but she also creates the literary space for recognition and assertion from which other immigrants can also speak, for example those from North Africa, who have experienced parallel forms of colonial aftermath from their French experience. Dell'Oro functions as an in-between author, connecting the accounts of the colonial time by writers like Ennio Flaiano, Mario Tobino, Curzio Malaparte, and Dino Buzzati with the postcolonial encounters offered by new immigrant writers. Dell'Oro, who is an insider/outsider, offers a perfect gendered introduction to this new tradition that will be explored here.

MÉTISSAGE AND COLONIAL POLITICS

Erminia dell'Oro, L'Abbandono

Erminia dell'Oro's book offers a literary representation of the historical panorama of Italian colonialism sketched in the previous chapter. However, unlike the complex narratological devices used by Indian writers, *l'Abbandono* is a rather conventional text with an omniscient narrator and a chronologically developed plot. It is a realistic novel which gives the impression of speaking the truth. The text triggers a reaction in the readers whereby they perceive events as a mirror of the political reality of the time and fictional characters as flesh and blood people. It suggests, therefore, that no interpretative frame is necessary to detect the deviation between reality as it is and its representation through a particularly literary genre, voice, and ideological perspective. However, the time lag between the setting of the events in the 1930s and their literary representation at the end of the twentieth century allows for a reading of the novel within a postcolonial frame of analysis. This makes Dell' Oro's realism but the ghost of a past history which has neither been fixed nor can be fully grasped because of its complexity.

The most interesting aspect of *L'Abbandono* consists in its shifting focus in the first part of the novel from the main character Carlo to Sellass and in the second part to their daughter, Marianna, thereby offering different ideological perspectives on the impact of colonization. In this way Dell'Oro tries to convey both the perspective of the colonizer and the colonized, but she also creates a generational shift, with Marianna bridging the two worlds through her mixed ethnicity but also through her age, which positions her as a daughter of the empire. She becomes the embodiment of the postcolonial citizen, divided between languages, nationalities, and races and yet, precisely because of that division more empowered in the international context of migration. The quality of dell'Oro's narrative, despite its conventionality, consists in her ability to offer a view on the colonial context in its complexities and contradictions and in being able to convincingly convey the view of the other. It is particularly this latter perspective which colors the text with a clear anticolonialist tone, even though the writer herself occupied a rather privileged position within the *società asmerina* of the time.

The story's plot develops as follows: after a brief period of emigration in America, which failed because of the Great Depression, the father, Carlo Cinzi, a Lombard fleeing poverty, ends up in the colony to work for the railways. This double emigration embodies the crossed fate of the Italian national identity in the 1930s which was built upon contemporary migration to the Americas and colonization in Africa. In Massawa, Carlo meets Sellass, who at the age of twelve had also left home, Ada Ugri, in the Eritrean highlands, to escape the drought and famine and to seek a better future. Sellass does not consider herself to be "the servant of a white man but his woman" (p. 43). They have two children, Marianna, the creative and independent girl, and Gianfranco, the beautiful child with blond hair and green eyes. Life in Massawa at the time represents the height of the empire, before the approach of decline:

> During the years that Mussolini was building his colonial empire Massawa was a lively city; Muslims, Jews, Indians, Greeks, everyone was very busy trading, teams of Eritrean workers helped the Italians constructing railways, roads and buildings. (p. 10)

The change of mentality and the growing apartheid imposed on the colonies makes Carlo start to realize the difficulty of a future family life. He plans to flee and prepares Sellass and the children for his departure, promising them that he will return. This is the last moment between Sellass and Carlo. In reality, he leaves his Eritrean family at the outbreak of World War II, and this is the keynote that will give the title to the book. However, before he can escape, the British take over the Italian colonies, and he is made prisoner and shipped to a concentration camp in South Africa. The readers know through the omniscient narrator and the chronological unfolding of the story that a Japanese submarine torpedoed the ship, but Sellass and Marianna never learn why Carlo did not return. With this narrative device Dell'Oro tries to portray the colonial encounter in which the Italian and African worlds did not really meet, or communicate, but only intersected with ensuing considerable damage for the local women who had to carry on with the fruit of the colonial encounter: the *métisse* children.

Marianna is the epitome of the *métisse*, a group which was terribly discriminated against, being despised both by the natives and by the colonizers. Marianna's private and racially mixed identity is made public through her search for a double identity as an Italian and an Eritrean woman. Marianna refuses to become merely a maternal reflection, an Eritrean woman abandoned by a colonizer. She declares her right to also be her father's daughter and therefore uses dynamism, resistance, and language as an antidote to the feelings of defeat imposed on her by her mother. When she is beaten because she expresses herself, she retreats into a world of fantasy that replaces the chaos and violence of the post-imperial phase in Eritrea. Marianna leaves for Italy in order to explore her other "Self" that is part of her identity of in-betweenness, and also to acquire her political rights as an Italian citizen.

It is only after an arduous period of integration in Italy, narrated in the last section of the novel, that Marianna succeeds in retracing the history of her father. Through her investigation she, but also we readers, get to know that Carlo was one of the few people who survived the shipwreck and was sent to a concentration camp in South Africa. In South Africa, where he lived until his death, he had married and had had one boy who died at the age of twenty. Since Carlo Cinzi is dead, the daughter from his wife's former marriage, Oriel Douglas, answers Marianna's letter, and the reunification the daughter yearns for with father is revealed to be impossible.

In the novel Marianna becomes the effigy of two conflicting worlds, a side of the coin which is neither heads nor tails, but which is the tangible evidence of the Eritrean women's exploitation by the whites. But it is the *métisse* children, the glory and the stigma of Empire, who face the most difficult destiny.

Métissage and the Challenge to Racial Divide

> Those positioned peripherally to the dominant group, those claiming and/or assigned marginalized identities find themselves partitioned in their bodies.
>
> —Sidonie Smith, Subjectivity, Identity, and the Body:
> Women's Autobiographical Practices in the
> Twentieth Century, 1993, p. 10

From the first settlements of white people in the colonies the problems of racial encounter became inextricable from sexual relationships. The problem of miscegenation was often associated with the degeneration of the white race and with the inevitable contaminations of cultural purity. As Robert Young writes,

> It has often been suggested that there are intrinsic links between racism and sexuality. What has not been emphasized is that the debates about theories of race in the nineteenth century, by settling on the question of hybridity, focused explicitly on sexuality and the issue of unions between whites and blacks. Theories of race were also covert theories of desire.[5]

The metaphoric vocabulary used to express our period of cultural syncretism is, therefore, inherited from the language of racial discrimination. Words like *negritude* by Senghor in which the despicable term *negro* attributed by the whites to the blacks becomes a process of subjectification and resistance, or *creolization* by Brathwaite to indicate the cultural, racial, and linguistic melting pot of the Caribbean, or Françoise Lionnet's *métissage*, which refers to the racial intersection between French and Algerians and comes to signify an act of trespassing, the term *mongrelization* used by Rushdie to indicate cultural fusion, the *mestiza* figure used by Anzaldua used as a figuration for crossover identities, gender, and nationalities, or even Homi Bhabha's *hybridity* used to express the space occupied in between cultures, at the interface of belonging and alienation. It is a colorful vocabulary, which is called upon to express marginal identities that foster plurality and replace exclusive dichotomies.

To step back into the source of this rhetorical figuration of the new cultural and postcolonial studies, it is necessary to briefly explore the situation since the time of colonization. The sexual encounters between single white male colonizers and the local dark women (defined as *Veneri nere* or sable venus) were considered nothing out of the ordinary, at least at the beginning of colonialism, because there were no European women available in the far-flung territories of the motherland. In a later stage the visible creation of a class of *métisse* children confronted the colonial authority with a menacing form of otherness, closer to them than the colonized black and yet not white enough. The fact that many *métisse* could pass as white created much insecurity about the concept of racial purity, and at the beginning of the twentieth century both the Dutch and the British banned concubinage in the colonies. As Laura Ann Stoler illustrates in her article "Making Empire Respectable" (1990), concubinage (the cohabitation of a white man with a native woman) was at first not only tolerated but encouraged by the authorities because it had a stabilizing effect on colonial health and political order, "a relationship which kept men in their barracks and bungalows, out of brothels and less inclined to perverse liaisons with one another" (Stoler, 1990: 40).

Furthermore, concubinage was economically advantageous as it gave white men access not only to sexual services but also to other domestic ones too they could otherwise not afford. The Dutch East Indies Company (VOC), for example, kept the salaries of the officers low, enrolled only bachelors and almost no women, thus making concubinage the most financially attractive domestic option. This was true of many colonies including the Italian colonies where various forms of cohabitation thrived.

From Stoler, whose perspective on gender and empire in the discourse on "the war of races" builds on her Foucauldian background, we get insight into how the "colonial order of things" was inextricably linked to sexuality.[6] Since the politics of language and race played a constitutive part in the formation of European identities and in European discourses on sexuality, the contact between the white subject and the dark colonized other was a site of constant threat. Whiteness was a problem rather than a fixed identity. In a society where interracial sex was an everyday occurrence, the upstanding bourgeois men fresh from home could not be entirely relied upon when under the spell of "colonial desire."

Stoler's key argument is that colonial authority and racial distinction were fundamentally structured in gendered terms:

> European women in the colonies experienced the cleavages of racial dominance and internal social distinctions very differently than men precisely because of their ambiguous positions, as both subordinates in colonial hierarchies and as active agents of imperial culture in their own right.[7]

European women who arrived in the Empire in a later phase, mostly as the wives of the high officers, came to fulfill the role of bearers of colonial morality, thus sharpening the line between European respectability and degeneration. By becoming the representatives of the home values of the rulers, colonial women were more directly in charge of racial and class politics, a role which increased the tensions of the colonial encounter.

Among the factors creating moral uneasiness were the cases of *métissage*, for whom the Europeans felt responsible and who posed this moral dilemma: recognize the *métisse* children and in so doing save them from the barbaric life of the indigenous or refuse to do so, neglect them, and reject any connection. The *métisse* clearly represented a compromise of racial hierarchy, "Children who straddled the divisions of ruler and ruled and threatened to blur the colonial divide" (Stoler, 1990: 41). As Stoler further writes, "*métissage* (interracial unions generally, and concubinage in particular), represented the paramount danger to racial purity and cultural identity in all its forms" (p. 55) and "concubinage children posed a classificatory problem, impinging on political security and white prestige" (p. 56). "Orphanages for abandoned European and Indo-European children were not new features of the 20th century colonial cultures; however, their importance increased vastly as an even larger number of illegitimate children of mixed parentage populated gray zones along the colonial divide" (p. 57).

The *métisse* children created the problem of community cohesion since they embodied the threat to colonial order of things. By embodying the corrosion of racial boundaries, they represented an unclassifiable category according to which the racial lexicon of empire was displaced and unsettled. Despite being the signs of interracial encounter and, therefore, of disobedience to the law, *métisse* children aroused mixed feelings. They existed not only in between colors but in between civilizations too. They could not enter the society of the whites but they inspired tenderness for their beauty and their crossed fate. They were not completely rejected by the whites, but their sense of semi-affiliation was more painful than any open rejection since they were tolerated but not assimilated.

The term has recently acquired a theoretical valence thanks to Françoise Lionnet who uses the concept of *métisse* in a postcolonial context to talk about the destruction of cultural and racial dichotomies in order to privilege a transcultural, linguistic hybridity: literary *métissage*.[8] Defining *métissage* as an act, rather than a condition, describes the deliberate creation of a space in-between cultures and traditions where the monolithic, monologic, linear, uniform, and totalitarian Eurocentric history and forms of literary representation are in opposition to multiple, intersecting, and discontinuous histories. This double hybridity has been distinguished as a model that can be used to account for the forms of syncretism that characterizes all postcolonial literatures and cultures (Rushdie, 1981: 394).

In the case of African-Italian texts, the final literary creations are based on several acts of *métissage*. The exemplary case of Dell'Oro and Viarengo's narrations of *métissage* will be traced from the destiny as biologically interracial daughters to their transcultural move of braiding cultures and overcoming the paralyzing effects of colonization and canonization. They appropriate and modify the monogenic platform of Italian literature and create cultural terrains in which other perspectives can find space and representation.

Reclaiming Double Identity

This reflection of the concept of *métissage* is necessary to understand the development of Marianna, from half-breed and victimized child into a resistant and multiple subject. Half-way through the novel, in fact, the focus shifts from Sellass and Carlo to Marianna. The narrative thread which has passed from mother to daughter functions as a slow process of redemption from the humiliating feeling of abandonment towards the freedom of self-definition. Marianna refuses the names that identify her as a victim in order to construct for herself an independent identity. She starts her passage into self-knowledge through the exploration of the city, of its limits and infinite possibilities, to the edge of the desert where she often encounters caravans of nomads. While her mother is working as a servant, she constructs a world of her own, an inner space where her duality can find solace. She counts her thoughts and she tells her brother, who is melancholic and depressive, many stories to entertain him.

The narrator focuses on Marianna to portray the image of Africa as paradise on earth. Through the eyes of Marianna, we experience the flora, the fauna, and the sense of mystery that is often associated with the African landscape. In a certain sense Dell'Oro's alter ego is that magic that can only be perceived through the eyes of childhood and that will be later retraced through memory and flashbacks. This resuscitated paradise becomes the intersection between the remembrance of a lost place and of one's own lost innocence. The African nature is Marianna's only element of continuity and trust, whereas human relationships cause her constant distress. After distancing herself from her mother, who punishes her not so much because she is *métisse* but because she refuses to accept her destiny with resignation, Marianna constructs her own private language and representation of the world, a world in which the exuberance of African nature conveys the importance of staying alive.

Without other emotional standpoints Marianna chooses all forms of marginalization to survive her split identity, which is thrown at her as dirty guilt. She starts to migrate within herself to find a space of autonomy, in the elsewhere of the diasporic imaginings (adventure, bush, insects, flowers, dog) of her inner migrations (she tells many stories, she counts her thoughts). She makes friends with a blind stray dog and with Tedlà, a mad, limping tramp whose origins no one knows. She elects *Zubuc*, a bush in front of her house, as her best friend, to give her a sense of belonging to the earth and a resistance against the wind and feelings of uprootedness and drifting. Like her, the bush is withered and struggling for survival, trying to grow, and it becomes Marianna's personification of her existential being, her own epistemology. The image of the bush, *Zubuc*, to which Marianna tells her anguish and stories, works as a symbol for her existence. Like the bush she is withered on the surface, but her roots spread in a rhizomatic way; in Deleuzian terms, she pluralizes her identity by taking advantage of what the community makes her feel as shame.

Also the mother who punishes her for her diversity is placed at a distance and replaced with a symbolic mother. Marianna encounters Elsa, whose real name is Haimanot, an old Eritrean woman who makes *anghera,*[9] and whose child from an Italian man has been taken away from her. Elsa assumes the role of the good mother, someone who can make her children feel special and unique, and also a woman who, unlike Sellass, has decided to treasure instead of repress her past.

For the first time Marianna understands that her in-betweenness can be an advantage and not a curse and she feels at ease with her color. Instead of accepting her mutilated identity of *métisse*, Marianna transforms the binary division between black and white into a site for transformation and development. Eventually through these inner migrations, which help her to know both sides of herself, she becomes a complete subject of her own action, and this is literally represented through Marianna's need to be outdoors, explore space, and expand her territory to Italy.

That conquest of mobility is made possible for Marianna through the appropriation of language. As shown in all these stories, the self cannot be constructed as a subject until it is encoded in language. Marianna's ability to express herself both in the language of the father and of the mother allows her to start to explore and invent that interstitial space as a dimension that can be positively transformed. She wants to create a new identity for herself in which being *métisse* is a privilege. Finally she moves definitely away from her mother—her stay at the *collegio* is her first step towards total removal—then she goes back to work in Addis Ababa and finally sets off for Italy where she will reconcile herself with her other half.

Marianna is depicted as the character who refuses to identify herself with only one nationality and who claims her plurality beyond national belonging. At the end of World War II the Italian government had established that any *métisse* child who was recognized by his/her father could have Italian citizenship. But Sellass denies Marianna Carlo's declaration of his fatherhood. Sellass' obstinate denial obliges Marianna to borrow another Italian man's name, Gianfranco's employer, and to carry the scorn for not having the right to her father's name. Denying Marianna her father's name constitutes Sellass' last vain attempt to erase her past as a woman used by a white man. The fact that Marianna does not hate her father as much as her mother has learned to do, blocks Sellass from any feelings of maternity towards her own daughter. The dissymmetry of the colonial encounter does not allow double affiliation.

The character of Marianna comes to indicate the difficulty of reconciling two worlds and the necessity of choosing a personal syncretic solution. More than a *métisse* identity, she creates a terrain of *métissage* in which different heritages can be claimed at the same time but they do not become limiting or exclusive. By searching for a name of her own, instrumentalizing the patriarchal authority of a man she hardly knows and for whom she refuses to offer any kind of secondary services, she creates a mythical link between herself and Italy and invents a new identity for herself, in accordance with her desire for a different personal history. By reclaiming her Italian side, Marianna enacts a political intervention since she speaks with a difference.

Like Glora Anzaldua's *new mestiza* (1987) Marianna represents the concept of the mixed-race woman as one involving "crossing over" and "perpetual transition," thereby avoiding unitary paradigms and dualistic thoughts. She chooses a space which is a location or a site for contestation and yet defends her right to belong. Through a site for *métissage* she can collide or interchange different cultures, identities, race and geographies.

LANGUAGE AND AUTHORITY

Maria Abbebù Viarengo, Io Non Scelgo

> I was Abbebù. Daughter of Noritù Faissà
> and of the only Italian man who lived in Ghidami.
> An Italian, Oreste Viarengo.
> I became Maria Viarengo.
> I was different from the children who were born in Ghidami.
> I was two . . . Will I always be two?
> —Maria Viarengo, *Andiamo a Spasso?* p. 74

Both Maria Viarengo's self and Dell'Oro's main character, Marianna, are *métisse* daughters, heroines without a stable geography or national space, struggling with ethnic and gender identity. They have a special way of crossing boundaries which is linked to various mythologies, the myth of the lost origin in Eritrea or Ethiopia and the myth of Italy, which is to be later confronted as a racist country.

While Dell'Oro invents stories that speak for others, Viarengo uses her own life story to speak for herself, profiting from her in-betweenness to claim bonds both with Africa and with Italy. The fact that Viarengo searches for her Oromo roots sets her African identity in an even more resistant perspective. The Oromo ethnicity in the South of Ethiopia (often called Galla) is in fact an ancient group of more than twenty million people who from Menelik II's reign in the eighteenth century onwards have been subject to the centralizing power of the Amhara group (around fifteen million).[10]

On the other hand, Viarengo's Piedmontese heritage subtly underlines the economic and political privilege that her father's region (Piedmont) occupied both at the time of the Italian unification and within a more recent history where the gap in prosperity between north and south still remains. During the twentieth century the Italian southerners came to populate the north in order to find work but they were seen as the Other within national borders until today. There is a common saying that "Italy stops at Rome" and whatever lies south of the defined Italian belt is not part of the Italian civilization. And even though Naples is often named with fascination the "doorway to the Orient" or "*Città partenopea*" (Venus City), its economic and political realities are envied less. The history of the Italian south is one of internal colonization carried out by Piedmontese forces in order to unify Italy. The consequent great unrest of the south was one of the reasons for Crispi's action in Africa.

Therefore, Viarengo's reclaiming of her Oromo and Piedmontese identity marks her difference within the homogenous space of the Italian identity, but also sets her duplicitous aspect of subalternity and of supremacy within it. The Italian-Ethiopian writer, Maria Viarengo, opens her yet unpublished autobiography, *Koborò e Violini: Io Non Scelgo* (*Koborò and the Violins: I Do Not Choose*) by addressing the difficulty and the right to remain double, "to be two," across countries cultures and languages. As in many diasporic writings, references are often made to the pain of carrying the past self merged in the new identity. For Maria Viarengo and for daughters of mixed blood, the task is to defend the plurality against the engulfing dominant culture present in the cocktail of being. In this case the dominant culture is in line not only with the patriarchal authority but also with the colonial one. Viarengo's father was, in fact, an Italian man, and the only white in the village, who went to Africa in search of wealth and found it.

Maria Abbebù Viarengo was born in 1949, after the decline of the colonial empire. She used to go to Italy for holidays with her sister Terù, who now lives in London, married to a Caribbean. Viarengo dedicates her autobiography to her. After an idyllic childhood in Africa, as rendered through the filter of her memory, the father forced the daughters to settle permanently in Italy in 1969. In a way her father claimed the white side of his daughters back. When he forced them to leave for Italy for their own good, he behaved as a father and as a colonizer imposing his rule on the locals, and saving his daughters from the risk of possible infibulation. This dubious rescue recalls Spivak's analysis of British imperialists who in 1829 prohibited the practice of *sati* in India with the implication that "white men (were) saving brown women from brown men" (Spivak, 1988: 296–97). The outlawing of *sati* is clearly the obverse of the more usual narrative of legitimation of white men saving white women from brown men. It still prompts the question of whom the brown women are being saved *for* in this act of delicious gallantry by the white men. Doubtless the answer was for the white men themselves.

We can stretch Spivak's interpretation of British gallantry to Oreste Viarengo. The father "is attempting to protect her from the same patriarchal oppression that he embodies" (Parati, 1996: 137). Maria's whiteness is privileged over her savage brownness. She is not allowed to shift between her double identity or encouraged to search for a balance but is obliged to become one, a clear-cut Italian woman. But this had implied not only leaving her African culture behind but also repressing her relationship with her mother. Only later on in her life does Maria Abbebù Viarengo understand her father's coercion as the only way to offer his daughter the future that Erminia dell'Oro herself, and Marianna as a character, could not find anymore in a country torn by civil wars, famine, and political dictatorship.

Viarengo's three pages rotate around the organizing motif of the lost mother. Her presence is less imposing in the rest of the unpublished autobiography which emphasizes the great importance of the father figure and with the impact of multiculturalism in Italy since the 1960s.

However, these few excerpts of her autobiography clearly emphasize the mother, to whom Viarengo's writing is offered as a homage, a homage in Italian to the Oromo mother who had to be forgotten. Only through the patriarchal language is Maria Viarengo able to recognize her mother whom she can no longer reach since she is dead, but it is also a recognition of her mother by the Italian community which until then had ignored Maria's doubleness except for her exterior appearance. Viarengo creates a lyrical and careful reminiscence of her lost maternal side as the crucial source for her female identity. Viarengo's journey from Ethiopia to Italy is therefore replicated by her psychical return to the "mother's world" of her childhood.

LANGUAGE AND AUTHOR/ITY

The fragments of Viarengo's yet unpublished autobiography *Andiamo a Spasso? (Let's Go for a Walk?)* that will serve as a reference to this analysis appeared in an Italian review *Linea D'Ombra* 54 (Nov. 1990, p. 74–76).[11] They will be analyzed as fragments and not as a cohesive text. The author was astonished when the publisher of her autobiography decided to translate the title in Oromo *Scirscir 'n demna* into Italian, erasing once again her mother's heritage. The autobiography was meant as a tribute to her mother, to the culture and the language Maria and her sister had to leave behind. For the author, autobiography was a way to reconcile and retrieve her doubleness and her plurality. Therefore, at least the title, if not the text, was in Oromo, the language of her mother.

This overlapping of languages is another aspect of the dichotomy that Maria has to inscribe on her body as a *métisse*. This duality is often denied her and sometimes imposed according to the context she moves in. This inability to exercise control over her plurality is reinforced by the Italian editor who allows her to publish extracts of her story of diversity as long as it conforms to Italian linguistic assumptions, which means the packaging of her African reminiscences in Italian. The dominance of the Italian language over the Oromo title simply reasserts the priority that Italy has had in the colonial enterprise in Africa, making in this way, Maria Viarengo's story part of the Italian historical collective memory more than a tribute to the Oromo's language literature. Thus, the very terms of publication reveal the impossibility of erasing borders in the attempt to create a real transnational literature. Trying to shift from private memory to public experience Maria Viarengo has to take into account forms of silencing that have already erased her mother and her own African hybridity.

When dealing with the literature currently defined as postcolonial—in this particular instance African-Italian literature—the question of the language adopted for creative writing becomes of paramount importance. As pointed out in the opening chapter, in nineteenth-century Britain, the establishment of the study of English as a privileged academic subject became intimately connected with the growth of cultural imperialism in the colonies. There, the imposition of the English language, together with the teaching of English literature, served as a very powerful ideological tool of control and subordination of the colonized. This was exercised both at a purely utilitarian level, as propaganda for instance, and at a more unconscious level, with the legitimation of constructed values (i.e., civilization, humanity) against their antithesis (i.e., savagery, nativeness, primitivity) for the purpose of bringing conformity and order. As a consequence, the English language and its literary tradition were presented as the privileged norm, the canon, while at the same time they defined the marginality of any native or emergent literary expression. As Ashcroft, Griffiths, and Tiffin explain, "Literature was made as central to the cultural enterprise of Empire as the monarchy was to its political formation" (1989: 3).

With the same ideological implication the Italian language was imposed in a far more restricted territory of influence upon local languages and literatures. Italian was imposed on Maria as her educational language. She was sent to Italian schools, and she had to speak in Italian in front of her father's friends. Oromo was confined to the private sphere, a family language that connoted the "primitive" and "savage" against the more illustrious role of Italian as the language for the public sphere where civilization and humanity were exercised. "Our language was Oromo. At home we spoke Oromo. Everyone in Ghidami spoke Oromo" (p. 75). But this was her mother's language. This shift between the paternal and the maternal tongue invalidates in a way Lacan's theory about the acquisition of language. With the acquisition of a language the symbolic order of the father also gets assimilated and the symbiotic relation with the mother remains in a sphere which is unspoken. But in the symbiotic realm Maria could still keep her Oromo, a special private language between her and her mother.[12]

She remembers the first time her father brought her to school in Asmara, an Italian school which had meant her official entrance into the father's signifying system. She was confronted for the first time with her sinful duality:

> In a big school the woman who spoke to my father asked him if I had been baptized, my father answered that we did what our mother did as far as religion was concerned, the woman looked at me worriedly and said "she is the devil's daughter" holding myself tight to my father's leg I started to scream that he was my daddy. (p. 75)

The separation of her parents and her moving to Khartoum meant the separation of her identity, the splitting, the fragmentation, the pluralization of selfhood.

With the failing of the symbiotic/bodily relationship between mother and daughter, the linguistic bond also starts to vanish. This first separation from the mother and the maternal land is repeated in Maria's life. As a child, she is brought to live with relatives in Khartoum, Sudan. This movement involved a loss of the maternal language as English, Italian, and Arabic "slowly . . . start to overwhelm Oromo" (p. 75). Her sister Terù reacts by silencing herself; Terù only talks to Maria and creates a dialogue in Oromo in order to express her nostalgia for the "mother's warmth and softness" (p. 75). Adopting the new language (English, Arabic, mainly Italian) over the maternal language involves a radical act of separation and mutilation against which Terù reacts by refusing the dominant language imposed on her. She still has a voice in the maternal language, the private language shared with her sister, the link with the past (i.e., Oromo identity) that she is forced to leave behind. Oromo is therefore enclosed in the private sphere of memory and becomes unacceptable as a public language:

> But in Khartoum all things were slowly changing name. Numbers were not tocco, lama, sadì, afour, scian anymore, but became: one, two, three, four, five. Uahed, itnin, talata, harba. Uno, due, tre, quattro. I did not know which language they wanted me to talk, the uncles I was living with spoke Italian, at school they spoke Arabic and English, Teresa and I spoke Oromo. Slowly the other languages were getting the upper hand on Oromo; Vieni, come, tahali, reminded us of cottu!
>
> I reacted to this confusion by speaking all languages together. No one understood me. Teru reacted by not speaking. Only our weeping, our nostalgia, our games, Teru and I confided in each other in Oromo. We missed so much the tepid warmth and the softness of mamma. Mother and father, for the time being, did not speak to each other in any language. (p. 75)

Identification with her father leads to privileges for Maria but also to a fracture as she has to step out of her coloredness, immediacy, and playfulness, and become a learned woman. She has to renounce her mother and her symbiotic world made of perfume and walks (*scirscir*) in order to enter whiteness, language, and religion. These three crosscutting aspects that reinforce her separation from Ethiopia—the abandonment of the mother, the mastering of Piedmontese, and the embrace of Catholicism—signify the complete entrance into the father's symbolic system and the cry for a doubleness, a multiplicity, and a hybridity, all of which she has to reject in order to become one, unicum, essence.

Viarengo creates a discourse on *métissage* and multicultural identities that involves the personal and the theoretical, the autobiographical narrative and public discussions of otherness. Her autobiographical act in Italian becomes the thread to connect the fragments that compose her *métisse* identity, without privileging the paternal inheritance that has dominated her life. By weaving her different selves, she attempts to create a space where the chronological order is destroyed and past and present can be rewritten in a synchronic order. The sense of loss is, however, present and some missing threads to her past leave the weaving of her story with wide gaps that cannot be filled. This discussion is brought back to the question asked at the beginning of her narrative, to the difficulty of remaining "double" without allowing one side to overwhelm the other.

Maria Viarengo's published passages of her autobiography have not been subject to accurate editing. The punctuation is poor, the change of passages often abrupt, the voice almost a soliloquy. The still unpublished parts of her autobiography in a way better succeed in conveying the on and off activity of memory. Without turning to virtuoso narrative devices, by just limiting herself to a clear first person narration and making author coincide with the narrator, Viarengo has created a life document which is not deprived of poetic force. On the contrary, her syncopated sentences, her phrases put on paper, which still need to be chiseled, create an atmosphere of immediacy and liveliness.

With three pages torn from her autobiography we are able to reconstruct the crucial stages of her life, sewing sequences together. The double self of the past reconnects itself with the woman of now who is educated and married to an Italian and who has two children, a woman who can formulate her thoughts to pay homage to her mother: not an absent mother, not a mother manqué, but a mother left behind, in the dust and the smell of a beloved country which the daughter manages to return to only after thirty years. She composes sentences like the following to express its beauty:

> Ghidami is a village like many others in the world. It wakes up with the crowing of the cock, the scent of earth, of eucalyptus and the arrival of the sun on the horizon. The sky in Ghidami is round and full, no building cuts it to squares, rectangles or stripes. The noise is made up of silences broken by machines grinding coffee, the buzz of bees and flies, the bray of asses, at night the loud laugh of the hyenas, sometimes the shouts of a newsboy announcing the death of a citizen. (p. 76)

Passing: Métissage as Disguise

> By colored people I am described as an individual with light complexion, chestnut-color hair and brown eyes; by people devoid of color, as a darkish girl with frizzy air and two black eyes.
> —Viarengo, "Andiamo a Spasso," (1990), p. 74

The division between her father and her mother becomes sharper during Maria's childhood and communication deteriorates between her parents: "they did not speak to each other in any language" (p. 75). Her temporary residence in Sudan functions as a middle passage for Maria. Her hybridity made her transit in both ways between north and south, center and periphery. But her being a *métisse* displaces her within both communities. She is a diverse "privileged" in Ethiopia and she is a diverse "colored" in Italy.

In black studies the concept of *passing* has acquired a larger resonance than the literal understanding as "passing as white," as in Nelly Larsen's novels. The term was originally used in slave narratives to express the possibility of light-skinned blacks or mulattos to be taken for white, to step beyond the line of their social marginalization. However, both the white and the black communities often rejected those who could pass.

Passing has become a trope for disguise, for *métissage*, for the braiding of different identities that can allow multiple cultures to be inhabited at the same time. Passing refers to a passage, a passage to be performed through bodily signs across nationalities and ethnic borders. In an era of growing mobility, switching cultural codes becomes the norm and despite the return of fundamentalism with its defense of "authentic" identity, passing as a process of transformation and hybridization still remains a strategy for survival and for ambivalence.

Homi K. Bhabha uses a similar concept, that of mimicry, according to which the colonized acts as the colonizer in order to pass as the ruler, but renders the very notion of origins problematic. Mimicry, as he explains, is a doubling which alienates the normativity of dominant discourses since it gives back a gaze of otherness, shattering from the margins the unity of the sovereign white man. Within the textuality of colonialism mimicry addresses difference—*almost the same but not quite*. Mimicry becomes like passing, a discourse "uttered between the lines and as such both against the rules and within them" (Bhabha, 1984: 89). It becomes for the dominant groups a threat, since mimicry embodies the return of the repressed, that projection of the self as performed by the minors who appropriate and distort the model proposed as the dominant and, therefore, normative. Passing also becomes a strategy to gain access to the hegemonic group, but it entails its subversion from within since it is *almost the same but not quite*.

Unlike Marianna, who in Eritrea experienced her being *métisse* as a curse, Maria is privileged in her village, since her father was an important person. However, in Italy her privilege comes under fire. Maria Viarengo acquires or loses her color according to the shades she is compared with. White is considered the non-color, the absence of color, while black offers a rainbow of possibility and nuances from totally black to nearly white. She is white for black and black for white, she is in a way denied an identity and an essence of her own, since she is constructed within the context she is inserted in. What strikes her mind already as a child is that she is in a way always special, she is always quite different from the rest, and there are no others like her except for her brothers or other children of *métissage*. She is even different from her mother and from her father. She is left hovering among possibilities but she is also trapped by racist remarks and pigeonholed in categories considered as culturally pejorative. People in Italy are even disappointed when she cannot stand up for her diversity:

People seem to like diversity but at the same time they are afraid of it. My diversity is requested, my name Piedmontese and simple is a disappointment, "I thought you would have a more exotic name," in many cases to be the daughter of someone from Asti takes me up a notch on the approval scale. (p. 74)

The class elements in Viarengo's existence should not be forgotten since she often mentions her father's prosperity, which allowed her and her sister Terù to quickly occupy an advantageous position within the Italy of the 1960s. In that period Italy was not a multicultural society, and her position as a tourist strongly reversed the stereotype of the white as the traveler.

Viarengo writes: "Italy was the land of holidays. My sister and I could not fully understand how this society worked. In Italy we tasted moments of being that we could only have dreamt of in Asmara. Italy, then, was our America" (p. 74). Maria Viarengo's position was even more unusual in the 1960s, and she could use class to erase the disadvantage that her mixed ethnicity represented. She writes further:

During our first stay in Rome, we were surprised by the relationship between white people and the professions that they practiced. At Fiumicino airport the porters were white, in the toilets the attendants were white, in hotels the cleaning maids, the waiters, the shoeshines, the street sweepers were white. How appalling! In Asmara every white lady had at least two black letté (maids). (p. 74)

Maria looks at Italy through her paternal Italian eyes. Despite her being *métisse* the colonial representation of distribution of labor is very strong in Viarengo. In Africa she was used to having black servants, and her position was that of a privileged white. She is surprised to find that in Italy race did not play a role in the hierarchy of labor, but in the sixties Italy had not turned yet into the multicultural place it is today, where a stream of extracommunitarian immigrants, mostly from Albania and Africa, has changed the colors of labor.[13] Back in the 1960s Italy was still profoundly and homogeneously white. Discrimination was something that took place within Italy itself as hierarchies between rich regions and those that were less economically developed, such as the oft-mentioned north/south divide. Class structures provided for the division of labor and wealth.

And even nowadays, after more than twenty years of what with difficulty can be defined as a voluntary or involuntarily permanence in Italy, Viarengo cannot be compared with refugees from Somalia or with the dispossessed from Eritrea or with immigrant workers or sidewalk sellers, the *vù cumprà*. Her hierarchically organized world collapses in her father's land where she sees herself as a white person, but is seen by the Italians as black. Her social and economic status, which allows her to be a tourist and afford an apartment in Turin, does not save her from embodying otherness for Italians:

> I have heard people call me, hanfez, klls, meticcia, mulatta, caffelatte, half-cast, ciuculatin, colored, armusch. I have learned the art of pretence; I have always looked like whomever others wanted me to look like. I have been Indian, Arab, Latin American, and Sicilian. (p. 74)

Even though she has learned to live with her chameleon-like quality, she also has had to learn to live with her extreme visibility in the two societies to which she belongs. She shifts between being considered an extracommunitarian or affectionately an exotic object in Italy and a white, European type among colored people. Her passing is both a doubling and the impossibility of escaping ethnic restrictions.

Vernacular

The passing of Maria is not only expressed through her ability to play with the shade of her skin color but with her ability to camouflage herself in languages, dialects, and slangs. When Viarengo goes to Italy in 1969, she goes to Turin, the city of her Piedmontese father. Her childhood had been, in fact, accompanied by dialectal inflections and expressions of her father's Italian which she only fully understands after moving to Piedmont. Many cultures and sublanguages interfere with the dominant ones. Her father's Piedmontese constituted a specification within the Italian as much as her mother's Oromo was for the Amharic speaking community. "In Turin I was slowly translating the meanings of words and phrases that had accompanied me throughout my life" (p. 74). Going to Italy was therefore for her a way to classify an intimate and secret language.

To understand her father's dialect properly and start to speak it Viarengo needs a green card to Piedmont, and not simply to Italy. This shows how much Italy was politically and culturally divided within itself and how it was only possible to inhabit the localized spaces, the specific margins within a national culture that were never authoritative. Maria learns to link the incomprehensible phrases in Piedmontese that her father used to tell her in her childhood with her actual presence in Piedmont. It is the Piedmontese language that gives her a sense of belonging in Turin, and not the Italian language.

> The language is something which links me very much to the city. — "Oh, madam but you understand Piedmontese, and you speak it as well. You speak it better then our Neapolitans!" (p. 75)

Neapolitans are people from Naples, and they are mostly immigrants from the South of Italy who went to the north as workers. To immigrate to Turin usually meant to go and work for Fiat, in the Italian car industry. In the North of Italy there has always been a form of racism against people coming from the South, almost another culture. They are called *terrun*, a derogatory term, which means people from the Meridione, the south of Italy which is treated as if it were a ghetto, beyond the Italian civilization, as sketched by Carlo Levi in *Christ Stopped at Eboli*. Maria Viarengo is praised as someone who can speak the local language better than the Neapolitans, but she is still different. She is categorized as a person from the south, the world that for people of Piedmont often starts only a little south of Piedmont itself.

Viarengo notices that there is a shift of hierarchy within the category "southerner":

> But today in Turin the "Napuli" are integrated, and it is the turn of the "marocchino" (Moroccan) to put up with it and if before "terrun" was everything from Turin downwards, now it is Moroccan which is everything from white downwards. (p. 74)

Viarengo's intuition about the shift in vision from a multicultural Italy towards a multiracial Italy is made evident by the introduction of the element of skin color. The phenomenon of multiculturalism was already present in Italy in the sense that there were many cultural barriers within the country itself. But the recent immigration from Africa, Asia, and Eastern Europe has changed the content of the word and has put Italy in line with the multiracial demographic composition of other European countries.

Viarengo also uses in her text, without adding any glossary, notes, or translation, words in Oromo which are naturally blended with the Italian language as magically capable of recreating a duality in the sameness. She does the same with entire sentences in Piedmontese which locates her in that community, both bonding her with anyone who is capable of understanding Piedmontese, but also excluding any reader who is not located within that specific culture:

> "Dui puvruun bagnà nt l'öli" is the language initiation for those who come to live in Turin. I often hear people ask "vairi a custa?" in my mind it brings back a sentence written on the arch of a bridge situated on the road which leads to Massawa "ca custa lon ca custa viva l'Aosta" smiling with gritted teeth, today I translate the meaning of that sentence. (p. 74)

"Dui puvruun bagnà nt l'öli" means "Two capsicums soaked in oil," but this expression works as a command since it can be pronounced only by people from Turin. The other sentence which Maria understands with belatedness has a clear political value since Aosta was the royal family who ruled Italy at the time of Mussolini's colonial empire in Africa and *"ca custa lon ca custa viva*

l'Aosta" literally means "whatever it costs, long live Aosta." In the past the saying was a decorative element upon an arch on the road to Massawa. Suddenly the cartography of her infancy is alive again but only now does she understand the implications of that imperialist slogan for the Ethiopian people who were defeated. She had refused to pray at the Italian school she had been sent to in Asmara only for the Italians who had fallen in the battle of Adwa and had defended her right to pray for the Ethiopian soldiers as well. Her hybridity makes her understand in retrospect how much she dealt with the colonizers/father out of ignorance, learning the language with innocent words which were instead clearly loaded with militaristic and cultural inflection. She has to smile now with gritted teeth because it brings back her memories of childhood but also the oppressive implications of the words despite their rhyming slang.

The vernacular of her mother's words in Oromo is of a very different nature. Linked to the familiar sphere, to clothing and daily habits, Oromo is an unthreatening language which refers to a peaceful and warm world:

> (mamma) did not do any housework, she busied herself with us, she combed us, she perfumed us, she took us to *scirscir*, and she prepared us the *faffatò*. . . . Sometimes she dressed in clothes my father brought her from Italy, a skirt and a jacket. I preferred her with the *scisscigò* so wide I could hide and get lost in it. (p. 76)

The mother's presence in her daughter's life is metonymic. Smells, softness, and, warmth convey the idea of the mother and of the matrilineal. The visceral relationship with her mother is interrupted by Maria Viarengo with her border crossing, which means not only the forgetting of her maternal language but also the beginning of her discontinuous identity. She is traveling backwards in history and memory to reestablish her red thread towards maturity. The representation of the mother, through her symbiotic language, serves the double purpose of establishing both filiation and affiliation with Africa. Maria's mother is not only recalled with phrases, as is the case for her father's Piedmontese, but with the physical presence of her warmth:

> Mama was soft, the air lukewarm as her body. She carried me tight on her back; she ran and played in the wide area in front to the house. I abandoned my body on her back; in the run my legs were flabbily vibrating. I laughed and laughed. She said to me "you laugh like a little hyena." (p. 74)

This is a phenomenon of the maternal espoused in a vocabulary of the body—of hair, gestures, and warmth. The mother cannot be replaced, but she can be remembered, and reinvented in the memory and this is the attempt of the autobiography that has never been published, like her dialogue that was never born.

> My mother was dead; she was thirty-six, leaving me with the anger of a dialogue never born at the time when we could have talked to each other as two women and the powerlessness of a forgotten language Oromo Imbecu. (p. 75)

The autobiography becomes the possibility of a different narrative of belonging, inclusion, and kinship and the performative rewriting of the web of multicultural influences that her mother could not pass on to her after her departure.

Through the insertion of the vernacular and of the mother's metonymic body, Viarengo reproduces not only a binarism but she constructs the Italian language as a third space, as an extra territory in which to position herself both as a Piedmontese and as Oromo and more generally to give volume to marginal cultures that are imbedded in the colonial discourse. But the use of vernacular also has another function; it works as a strategy of exclusion against the reader who is made Other as an outsider. With this device Viarengo powerfully reverses the exclusion and ridicule that *vu'cumprà* have to suffer when marginalized from the Italian language.

The vernacular in the text undoes and undermines the binary relation between center and periphery, history and fiction, language and dialect. In other words, the vernacular offers a continual play of resistance. Although it might be clearly marked as "other"—thus leaving itself open to the possibility of cooptation—it can also create tensions and contradictions within the dominant discourse, setting in motion the dynamics of dissent, intervention, and change that can ultimately allow a minority position to resist integration and assimilation, and even to become its own exclusionary system (Lionnet, 1992: 334).

The presence of vernacular Oromo or Piedmontese dialect in the Italian text creates for the non-Oromo/Piedmontese reader an opacity which places Viarengo's text beyond appropriation, demarcating it as radically "other." Hence the opacity has a double subversive function: it does not aim simply to suggest a specific link to a more or less "authentic" cultural past, and it prevents the ideological adoption of a static form of humanism because it stresses the distance between the narrator and reader, between insider and outsider, vernacular speakers and their others, while undermining the reader's belief in the value of clarity.

Viarengo's duality and resistance to being appropriated get reestablished due to her racial, linguistic, and cultural passing. Her need to be manifold is guaranteed by the revitalization of a past, a memory, a mother, a smell of being. Probably because of her own motherhood Viarengo felt the urge to recreate a tie with her own mother in order to reverse the oblivion and restore herself to the role of dutiful mother. By understanding what motherhood meant for her mother, she explores her own motherhood, restoring a chorus of lost female voices for her own child who one day will ask questions about her mother's *métisse* identity. And the story will be in a drawer, if not already in the bookshops, providing historical legitimacy simultaneously to the mother and her daughters.

Chapter 8

Living in Translation

Ribka Sibhatu, *Aulò: Canto-Poesia dall'Eritrea*

TESTO A FRONTE

The title "Living in Translation," used by Parati for analyzing Sibhatu's work,[1] is particularly suitable from both a literary and a cultural point of view. Ribka Sibhatu offers her narrative written in Italian, *Aulò: Canto-Poesia dall'Eritrea* (1993), with a parallel text in Tigrinya,[2] one of the nine Eritrean languages with a vast literature that has hardly been studied or canonized.[3] This style of publishing with the text *a fronte* is characteristic of the new series *I Mappamondi* created by Sinnos in Rome, an alternative publishing house which aims at making cultures other than Italian accessible and yet valued in their specificity, therefore not completely appropriated through pure translation.

Tigrinya literature is very developed in the Horn of Africa and has a very long tradition, both written and oral, of poetry, novels, and stories. Ribka Sibhatu is one of the contributors to this literature of the last decade, but again she marks it with a difference. Sibhatu has chosen to make her text available both in Italian, which is for the Italian publisher the original version, and in her mother tongue Tigrinya, corrected with the help of an Eritrean priest. Paradoxically, Sibhatu's flight from her own country and her further education in Amharic in Addis Ababa, in French while living in Lyon, and in Italian, has shaded her competence in what she considers her mother tongue, Tigrinya. In a game of appropriation and accountability Sibhatu leaves a space open in order to shift between the original self and the translated one. The Italian language on the left side of the book assumes the authoritative space of the privileged text while the Hebrew-looking characters in Tigrinya on the right side acquire the ancillary function of decoration and of "othering" the Western reader. A tacit agreement is established from the beginning between author and reader in which the validity and faithfulness of the translation is agreed upon in order to convey a parallel motion of meanings and images both on the right and left sides of the book.

Wonderfully enough, the intricacy of such a linguistic appeasement makes this children's book the center of cultural negotiations. *Aulò* is, in fact, a children's book which depicts Sibhatu's family and the recent history of Eritrea, torn by war for thirty years. The year of publication of the book also marks the end of the struggle for independence and the declaration of Eritrea as a free, independent state, the fifty-second in Africa. Sibhatu fled from Asmara in Eritrea in 1980 where she was persecuted because she refused to continue her education in the former Soviet Union and expressed her resistance towards Marxist indoctrination, imposed by Mengistu's regime, which at the time was allied to the Soviet Union. After hiding at her aunt's place, she disguised herself as a country woman, braided her hair, and escaped to Ethiopia, where she succeed in completing her high school education in Addis Abeba (in Ahmaric) under a false name and finally found "freedom" in Europe through migration. Sibhatu took great risks in escaping since she moved away from her native country hiding within the boundaries of the enemy's land. This escape was the consequence of the fragmentation brought about by a dividing war, the death of her cousin, killed by Ethiopians, and the death of her aunt during the exodus from Eritrea, an attempt to escape what Sibhatu calls "the extermination of our people carried out by the Ethiopian government" (p. 16).

There are many acts of translation in Sibhatu's life, starting from her dressing up as a country woman in order to pass unnoticed, braiding her hair to pass as someone from a lower class, and smuggling herself across the border. The paradox of this flight lies in the space she goes to inhabit, that of the enemy who had invaded her native land. From the position of being colonized and persecuted in her own country, Sibhatu shifts her position to that of a silent resister within the dominator's boundaries in order to cheat the enemy by taking advantage of his educational system while completing her high school and using the country as a springboard towards freedom. Translation of identity through disguise, migration, and language is the essence of Sibhatu's courageous enterprise, which she dedicates not to adults who cause war and genocide, but to children, who can make the future look different.

Sinnos is a publishing company in Italy that attempts to make Italian children familiar with the idea of a multicultural Italy by introducing them to the life stories and the languages of the immigrants in Italy. A future is thereby opened for children to grow up accustomed to diversity. The readership chosen by Sibhatu is innovative and refreshing both in its message and style.

The book, *con testo a fronte* (with the original), is told in the first person, the narrator coinciding with the figure of Ribka. The text is divided into four parts and presents itself also as a manual. The first part, "Il Paradiso Perduto" ("Paradise Lost"), is about the life of Ribka and of her family intertwined with the cultural identity of her country. The second, "La Mia Abebà" ("My Abebà") is a collection of Eritrean fairy tales, songs, riddles, and proverbs and includes an important poem written for her prison friend sentenced to death, Abebà. The third part, "La Nuova Eritrea" ("The New Eritrea"), deals with the history of Eritrea, its religions, cults, and customs. The fourth part, "Antologia, tentativi di ricette" ("Anthology, an attempt at recipes") offers an excursus on the eating habits and traditions in Eritrea and gives recipes for some of the most typical dishes.

I Have Exiled Myself: Literature as Resistance

Ribka's foreword to the book quickly summarizes her biography and introduces the reader to her resistant position both in her country of emigration and in that of arrival, Italy. The author writes,

> It was Tuesday afternoon, after the Easter of 1980, when I was forced to abandon Asmara. In 1982, under a false identity, I exiled myself at Addis Ababa. (p. 5)

The improper use of the Italian tense "*mi esiliai*" symbolizes Sibhatu's agenda. She uses in fact, not in the regular and grammatically correct passive form "*Mi mandarono in esilio/fui esiliata*" (They sent me in exile/I was exiled), but she turns into the reflexive form "*mi esiliai*" (I exiled myself) which is grammatically incorrect. As Parati writes,

> By "exiling herself", she claims an active role in the construction of her nomadic existence, and refuses the passive role of victim of History, as an oppressive entity which cannot be challenged. Her grammatical transgression, published and made public in the story of her life, also claims her right to hold on to the "accent," to a subjective, culturally marked, "foreign" use of a codified (maybe even overcodified) language. (1996, p. 2)

Sibhatu's reflective act is about negotiating distance by creating a carefully selected public history of her native country and of her private story that details the separation in her exile. It is no coincidence that Sibhatu always brought with her, to accompany her in exile, a copy of Anna Frank's *Diary*, as she tells us in the piece which appeared in *Caffé*,[4] the Italian multicultural journal published in Rome. The parallelism between Sibhatu's life on the run with that of a Jewish girl secluded within the borders of the Dutch nation because of German persecution strongly reflects the idea of writing as a sign of subversion and resistance, but also as an act of exposure. Ribka risked betraying her identity as a cultivated woman by carrying Anna Frank's *Diary* with her while she was trying to escape the enemy within the borders of her nation disguised as a peasant woman and therefore supposedly illiterate:

> It struck me because I found myself in the same situation of hiding. She dies and she communicates with me. I said: "My God, what beautiful writing!" And I also began writing, and since 1980 I have also started writing, writing diaries.[5]

The text also symbolizes the two young women's desire to use writing as a mean of expression under great constraint, writing to remain in touch with the self and with language. Ribka will extend this element of resistance by inserting both in her children's book and in her extract in *Caffè* her chant-poem "La mia Abebà" for her prison friend, who, like Anne Frank, died as a result of political persecution. Here it is important to stress Ribka Sibhatu's narrative as part of what Barbara Harlow has defined as "resistant literature" (Harlow, 1987) literature used in Third World liberation movements for its political subversive impact. The genres used, such as poetry, narrative, and prison memoirs, argues Harlow, are not different from the Western body of writing, but it is the specific historic condition in which they are written and the strategies used that are clearly political. Also writing within the context of a liberation struggle or resistance movement often entails serious consequences for the writer's very person and life. Furthermore, literature is written in a condition of extreme atomization set against the background of ideological propaganda or censorship. Harlow addresses the writer's difficult problems in adopting literary forms often identified with the oppressor's culture. It is often the strong personal experience that gives the writers both their main message and their motive to communicate it despite its inherent contradictions. To quote Bruce Franklin:

> The works of today's prisoners, though predominantly autobiographical, are rarely intended as a display of individual genius. Whereas the literary criteria dominant on campus exalt what is extraordinary or even unique, with "originality" as the key criterion, most current autobiographical writing from prison intends to show the readers that the author's individual experience is not unique or even extraordinary.[6]

It is this intersection between personal experience and global resonance that characterizes resistant literature as both situated in the self and yet reverberating the experience of all freedom fighters. Even though Ribka Sibhatu did not write from prison, she was imprisoned. Her account, written from the safe distance of exile, intends to resonate the experience of many civilians like herself who chose to fight for the freedom of Eritrea. Skillfully introducing her own grammar of migration, Sibhatu resorts to storytelling in order to preserve the link with the abandoned cultural context to which she can now return because today Eritrea is a free independent republic.

Another text by an Eritrean writer which clearly recalls the experience of prison as the main thread of narration illustrates the emphasis on collective experience in resistant literature. The author is Abeba Tesfagiorgis, an Eritrean woman who migrated to the States and who wrote a sober but moving book *A Painful Season and A Stubborn Hope: The Odyssey of an Eritrean Woman* (Trenton, N.J.: Red Sea Press, 1992). In this powerful text she describes her experience as a political detainee in Asmara at the hands of the Ethiopians and the odyssey which followed her escape. Her escape resembles that of Sibhatu since Tesfagiorgis also managed to flee the country with her four daughters by dressing up as peasants with braided hair. Tesfagiorgis's record is not only the remarkable story of one Eritrean woman's experience, but it is also a collective testimony that describes the oppression under the Stalinist dictatorship of Mengistu, who alienated the Eritrean people and created an Eritrean diaspora. Tesfagiorgis' narrative is a clear literature of resistance, and it reveals through a personal experience the collective body of a nation by speaking also in the name of those who suffered the same atrocities but did not have a chance either to express it or even to find their way out of prison. In this context, as Michel Foucault wrote in *Discipline and Punishment* (1977), prison really represents a system in which the discipline of social control becomes an organized project to suppress the subaltern social world.

Abeba Tesfagiorgis has chosen to express her experience in English and in this way to reach a wider audience for the denunciation of Ethiopian crimes and oppression. After Italy lost the colonies, Eritrea remained a British protectorate for ten years (Tesfagiorgis' schooling was in English) and furthermore she belonged to the Eritrean élite who chose migration to the United States. Ribka Sibhatu, instead, has chosen to write in Italian, the language of her hosting country, a factor which has sometimes rendered her text unknown to her fellow countrymen who are exiled in other countries. English is the common language of resistance outside the national borders. Barbara Harlow comments on this point:

Although a considerable amount of the literature of resistance has been written in English (the language of one colonial power) much of it has not and is in French, Portuguese, or Spanish (representing the influence of other colonial powers), or in the native language of the areas, such as Arabic, Gikuyu (Kenya), South American Indian dialects, etc. The very choice of the language in which to compose is itself a political statement on the part of the writer and will need to be considered in each case, from author to author, country to country. The debate on language is crucial to a discussion of resistance literature, involving as it does questions of writer and background as well as issues of readership and audience.[7]

Sibhatu's choice of language is of extreme importance. She targets the Italian audience, from children to adults, in order to make her history and that of her own country known in an attempt to make the Italians aware of a growing condition of multiculturalism. On the other hand, Sibhatu wants to be true and faithful to her country by doubling her text with a version in Tigrinya, a testimony of her continuity with her own language and fellow country people, both within and outside the boundaries of Eritrea. Her trajectory is, therefore, both directed to the future and to the past, Italian for her audience with whom she shares her new existence as a migrant woman and Tigrinya as a sign of resistance within a globalizing world which forces writers to choose a dominant language in order to be marketable. Tigrinya represents her look backward but also her "private national space." Both languages function as elements that mark and erase her difference at the same time, showing her continuity and also her profound discontinuity with both traditions.

RESISTING ENCLOSURE

Memento Mori

The idea that Ribka was born with the war and grew up with the war makes her existential itinerary a rather unusual one. She wants to recollect her country as a paradise lost but this image is in strong contrast with the historical contingency of a military occupation that lasted throughout her lifetime in the country. The pattern of magnifying the country of origin as a perfect place to cherish in the memory is a strategy often deployed by Third World migrants to survive the fragmentation of exile and of living in a foreign country. The country of original belonging and cultural affiliation comes to assume the role of a safe space where harmony and unity dominate over the splitting and the scattering of their present diasporic existence.

Ribka conveys the devastation of her country that brought her to abandon it, disguised as a peasant woman and going into hiding. The enemy made the Eritrean people feel dispossessed within their own country, and Ribka organizes her exile to avoid retaliation. The beloved aunt is her dauntless savior:

I stayed with her when I was organizing my exile. Risking being shot with me. And when her nieces told her: "Do you realize what danger you are putting us in?" she replied: "Listen, if I don't protect her who will?" (p. 40)

Her aunt is portrayed as a Madonna who sacrifices her son to the unnecessary hatred of the enemies. As in the *Pietà* of Michelangelo she is portrayed mourning for the loss of her son's life:

She cried also for the dead Ethiopians, for those who had killed her son! People used to tease her, but she answered: "Can you imagine the pain of their mothers!" And continued her crying. (pp. 39–40)

The exceptionally human figure of her aunt who stands above hatred in the name of motherhood and love is what Ribka searches for again as soon as she is allowed to return to Eritrea, "But my aunt wasn't there" (p. 40). Now that Eritrea is a peaceful country, the absence of the beloved is more marked, a paradise which can only be partly recuperated at the expense of the past which cannot be made to live again.

To exorcise the death created by war, Sibhatu turns to a typical Eritrean genre, the *Aulò* which is a kind of poem-chant as well as a poem-cry. Sibhatu explains that on the Eritrean highlands poems are a popular way of expression and these Aulò are not written nor repeated but left to the memory of the listeners at various occasions like weddings and funerals:

But the *Aulò* is for heroes, or for exceptional people and, therefore, to be emulated; or for an enemy of the people as Mussolini was. (p. 60)

In this book, Ribka dedicates an *Aulò* to Abebà, a woman she had met in prison who was sentenced to death because she was found in possession of *Il pamphlet dei guerriglieri*.[8] In the two weeks preceding her execution, Abebà seemed to inhabit the untouchable sphere of the familiar in order to distance herself from the imminent tragedy: she spent long hours every morning performing the ceremony of preparing Eritrean coffee and weaving a basket in silence. Sibhatu describes her admiration for Abebà's ability to distance herself from tragedy through the daily ritual of coffee making, and for her creation of a tangible memento of her self, the basket, a symbolic legacy of her family:

C'era un'asmarina	Abebà, the daughter of Asmara,
a Haz-haz,[9] sulla collina,	Whose place was in Haz-haz,
Aihmè . . . Abebà[10] la bella,	Indeed . . . Abebà the beautiful,
composta e snella;	composed and slender;
fiore rimava con Abebà,	her name and beauty is the same
come il bistro e l'occhio!	like an eye with the shade!

Perchè il mondo comprendesse,	To make the world understand,
mentre scavavano la sua fossa,	while they were digging her grave,
avvolta dalla morte misteriosa,	wrapped in mysterious death,
intrecciò un'alghelghel[11]	she wove an *alghelghel*
e lo mandò senza hmbascià.[12]	and she sent it without *hmbascià*
In un'intensa notte,	In the middle of the night,
me la rapirono con le manette!	they snatched her away from my side with handcuffs!
....	....
Ogni giorno è assente,	During the day she is absent,
ma nel buio è onnipresente!	but in the dark she comes again and again to haunt my memory!
Poichè non vuole separarsi da me,	Because she resists parting from me,
portatemi l'alghelghel della mia Abebà:	bring me the *alghelghel* of my Abebà:
forse lì è la risposta, la chiave delle sue manette,	maybe the answer is in it, the key to her handcuffs,
che ora stringono me.	which now clench me.
C'è uno scritto solo 'un ricordo ai miei',	'Remembrance to my parents,'
sull'alghelghel della mia Abebà,	is written on the *alghelghel* of my Abebà,
appassito fiore prima di sbocciare,	flower withered before having blossomed,
la mia compagna di prigione.	Abebà, my prison's friend.
	[My translation from the Italian version]

The construction of this act of memory is interestingly analyzed by Parati (1996). She sees in Abebà's daily rituals the resistant signs against the annihilation of personal dignity:

> The connection between Sibhatu's testimony of her experience and holocaust testimonies are evident in this description of the relationship between the familiar and that which "arouses dread and horror," that is, Freud's uncanny.[13] The *heimliche*, the familiar, is used by Abebà as a means to distance herself from her imminent execution, but it also points to the *unheimliche*, the uncanny. For Ribka, the woman who survives, it is the familiar act of "making coffee" that is preserved in her memory as closely linked to the *unheimliche*. In the end *das Heimliche* replaces *das Unheimliche*, because the separation between the familiar and the uncanny has collapsed. In fact, the uncanny is, according to Freud "that class of the frightening that leads back to what is known of old and long familiar."[14]

To extend Parati's analysis a little bit further, it is necessary to add that the *Unheimliche* represents, therefore, traumas and repressed events of our existence which are hidden in our unconscious but which reemerge under another semblance. Rather than this literal application of Freud to Sibhatu's *Aulò*, it is better to rely more on Homi Bhabha's digression on Freud's concept of *das Unheimliche* for the interpretation of Abebà's action. In Freud's study of the uncanny Bhabha attempts to analyze those psychic situations where the subject is confronted with his/her internal difference.

The Unheimliche is that which was once *Heimliche*, familiar, the "un" is the token of repression. While the *Heimliche* can refer either to situations of the familiar and agreeable, the *Unheimliche* emerges both rhetorically and literally as its double, for example as a figure of foreignness that is always already inscribed in the familiar. Bhabha interprets Freud's word *Heimliche* in this literal sense (to expand it to notion of home and nation) only to discover that it develops in the direction of ambivalence, until it finally coincides with its opposite, *Unheimliche.* Bhabha finally forges a new term, *un-homely*, in which the figuration of nomadism overlaps that of settlement. Being un-homely means for Bhabha not homeless, not exiled but simply a bit off center, in those advantageous locations where the familiar is embedded in the foreign, the known in the alien.

Acting from within the boundaries of the enemy, Abebà deploys a strategy of resistance which refuses to acknowledge their threatening role and shows their *Unheimlich* and foreignness. Abebà interiorizes their alterity and transforms it into a familiar, ritualistic gesture linked to her culture, the weaving of *Aghelghel*, the basket with a cone-shaped lid used to preserve *hmbascià*, bread prepared for a special event. It is difficult to envisage a figuration of nomadism in prison but Abebà's refusal to acknowledge the alien, by emphasizing the ritualization of the known, is a challenge against the Ethiopian military extermination. Therefore Abebà's poem must be read within the tradition of resistant literature which, added to the psychoanalytic reading proposed by Parati, has the function of turning a personal and private act into a political statement in which gender and ethnic resistance are expressed. By turning her own death into a feast, Abebà defeats the anxiety imposed by the enemy and also fights the amnesia imposed on her fellow people.

This recalls a strategy used by Primo Levi. He was an Italian Jew, a chemist from Turin,[15] deported to Auschwitz at the end of 1943 because he was active in the antifascist resistance. He was lucky that in 1944 the Germans were running short of labor force and decided to prolong the average life of the prisoners. His chemistry degree made him valuable and he survived. At the end of the war he wrote *Se Questo è un Uomo* (*If This Is a Man*), published by Einaudi in 1947 in which he described the atrocity of his hell in the Lager. The title *If This Is a Man* refers to the dignity and identity which is stripped off the prisoners who are nameless and reduced to numbers. At a moment of extreme psychological exhaustion, Levi tries to remember a few lines from Dante's *Inferno* and to translate them into French for his prisonmate, Jean. It is the chant of Ulysses. In the twenty-sixth chant of the Inferno, in the eighth pit of the inferno of the eighth circle, Dante and his guide Virgilius encounter the souls of the false counselors, Ulysses and Diomede, in the form of a two-tongued flame. Ulysses tells Dante of his untamable desire to know the world beyond the Pillars of Hercules, the limit of the acceptable. Ulysses says:

Considerate la vostra semenza: Take thought of the seed from which
        you spring.

Fatte non foste a viver come bruti,   You were not born to live as brutes,
Ma per seguire virtute e conoscenza.   but to follow virtue and knowledge.[16]
                         (*Inferno*, XXVI, 118–20)

Dante here makes Ulysses speak after his death, from the perspective of the conscious sinner, who now considers his journey as a '*Folle volo*' (mad flight). Dante's journey, in search of religious virtue, mirrors that of Ulysses for knowledge. While Primo Levi attempts to teach Italian to his friend, through Dante's chant of Ulysses, he realizes that his destiny is the result of an interrupted relationship between virtue and knowledge. Digging into his memory and into the cultural leftovers of his disintegrated soul, Primo Levi finds in Dante's lines on Ulysses the moral admonition to rise up from the animal state to which he has been reduced ("You were not born to live as brutes"). It also allows him to strive for the restitution of his dignity, his humanity, his physical integrity ("But to follow virtue and knowledge").

Abebà is faithful to the same kind of humanity. She does not want to allow her oppressors to dent her pride as a woman and as a patriotic warrior. For the cultivated Levi Dante is the epitome of memory and cultural belonging as much as the *aghelghel* is for Abebà. While the one clearly indicates Primo Levi's access to the great literature of the Italian nation, the woven basket indicates the realm to which Eritrean women were relegated in their participation in the making of the nation and of tradition. The disruptive act of repeating a female task while being sentenced to death as a woman-warrior represents the intricacy and the paradoxes in which Eritrea finds itself in the total confusion of civil war. As often in war, or in revolution for independence, women fulfilled an indispensable function in which they trespassed their traditional role. Having the chance to acquire freedom from gender restrictions as never before, women in Eritrea joined the ELF (Eritrean Liberation Front) or EPLF (European Popular Liberation Front) to fight the enemy and also to escape the risk of sexual mutilation which awaited them if they stayed at home. Abebà, and also Ribka, are heroines of this necessary phase of transition in which women were assertive agents, responsible for their lives and for those of others. It is in this moment of self awareness that Abebà can peacefully endure her destiny and transform her prison into a site of resistance and escape. The cell is turned into a domestic realm, a house which stands for identity, that is primarily a cultural identity. It is a female place which strives for an intimacy in which contact can be established with ancestral energies of survival.

It is in this trespassing metaphor of space that Sibhatu's domestication of the prison cell must be interpreted, thereby amplifying Parati's interpretation of the basket-weaving as a exorcism of external threat. It is in this strategy of elision and effacement of space, time, and fears, that Abebà's prison transforms itself from a confining locus into a trope of escape from gender and ethnic repression.

Within this context Sibhatu's background as a woman in flight and her touching story of Abebà are testimony to two exemplary destinies of resistant women, exemplary in the sense that they were not unique or sporadic, but on the contrary similar to those of many other women engaged in the construction of a new independent African country. These two life stories speak for many others, part of a repertoire of national memory that celebrates courage, collective responsibility, and this memento mori as a turning point for acquiring knowledge.

CULTURAL TRANSLATION

The presentation of *Aulò* as a text traveling between languages and cultures requires some references to that intense field of studies which is called "translation studies." This academic area established itself around the 1970s and has undergone a remarkable expansion during the last decade with a considerable complexification of theoretical analysis.

The recent reflection on cultural diversity and the increased awareness of the hegemonic role played by Western languages upon other languages has moved translation studies increasingly towards cultural studies. This new approach has made the interconnection between language transcodification and its cultural implications inextricable facets of translation practices. Translation comes to be seen as one of the strategies for dealing with the Other. This "cultural turn" taken by translation has offered new insights into the cultural manipulation operated through an apparently faithful translation. Through translation, the culture of a given society can be constructed and this latter approach is of vital importance for postcolonial studies. For postcolonial critics it is important to analyze why certain texts are chosen for translation instead of others,[17] to analyze the role in the selection played by the translator, the editor, and the publisher, and to analyze the techniques employed for translation. The evaluation of these elements is fundamental in the unmasking of those cultural institutions that serve to marginalize minority voices.

An act of linguistic translation is an act of cultural translation, and more so in the case of Third World texts since translating a Third World text into English implies an inherent ethnocentric position. To avoid cultural dyslexia, which means the failure to "read" other cultures and come to term with differences, it is necessary to do a lot of homework before attempting translation of texts embedding different cultures.

The classical approach to translation usually provides three models: the Horation model, in which the translator tends to be faithful to the target audience (this implies that the negotiation is slanted towards language—i.e., Latin—and the negotiation does not take place on absolute equal terms); the Jerome model, in which the translator tends to be faithful to the source text, in this case the Bible; and the Schleiermacher model, which emphasizes the preservation of the alterity of the source model for the target reader (this is usually done for texts that constitute cultural capital). The Schleiermacher model emphasizes the importance of foreignizing translation so that the alterity of the source text is preserved in the receiving language.[18] The parallels between Horace's time and English today are interestingly close. Translations into English, particularly from Third World languages, are almost invariably slanted towards English.

According to Susan Bassnett and André Lefevere the study of translation is necessary "to better relativise the present, the study of post-colonial translation to better re-evaluate Eurocentric models, and the study of different kinds of criticism, anthologies, reference works, as well as translations, to see how images of texts are created and function within any given language" (Bassnett and Lefevere, 1998: xiii). This new interdisciplinary approach to translation shows what Lawrence Venuti calls "the ethnocentric violence of translation" by showing how cultures construct "images" of writers and how texts become cultural capital for the ruling élite.[19] This process of hegemonic dismantling is necessary within a postcolonial discourse since language encodes power relations. Today, traditional notions of translation as a copy of the original are ideologically loaded. Translation is always enmeshed in a set of power relations that exist both in the source and target language. As Bassnett writes,

If translation studies has been increasingly concerned with the relationship between individual texts and the wider cultural system within which those texts are produced and read, it is therefore not surprising that within cultural studies, and in post-colonial theory in particular, translation is increasingly being seen both as actual practice and as metaphor.[20]

Sibhatu's text in two languages creates a case of "autotranslation," the kind that the Nobel Prize winner and Calcutta poet Rabindranath Tagore used to practice with his own poetry, translating his Bengali into English, causing a stir in the cultural scene at the beginning of the nineteenth century. However, Sibhatu's autotranslation presents an ulterior form of deviance since she needs the mediation of a priest to construct her "authentic self." Despite this obfuscation of the original, the reader can still determine the text he/she chooses to rely on. This choice leaves space for speculations on the ambivalence between the reciprocity of meanings. We can assume that Ribka translated herself, albeit with the help of an Eritrean Vatican priest. How much of the agency inscribed in the original text has been lost in the translation? How much of her gendered specificity and voiced silence has been erased in the Italian version? She says that she needed help to render her "Roman" Tigrinya into a more "Tuscan" Tigrinya, a task which was performed, with much love, by Dott. Kinfè Tesfagabre of the Vatican Radio.

Paradoxically enough Sibhatu must first translate herself into Italian. It is for Ribka natural to appropriate the local language first, which is Roman, the language spoken on the streets, in the buses, in the markets. To purify this into standard Italian (Tuscan), she needs help. This act of translating the self from the immediate mother tongue into the familiar but not perfectly commanded Italian language is a process mediated by a male Eritrean. But to illustrate the intricacy and the hidden traces of agency that might have been lost in translation, it is important to discuss an article on translation by Gayatri C. Spivak, which better illustrates the political implications of such acts. The difficulty of this mediation can be better expressed with the Italian proverb *traduttore, traditore* (translator, traitor) to which anthropologists have added the questions of ethnographic accuracy. Spivak offers further insight into the debate around minority discourses, on the politics of language which establish hierarchies within the postcolonial literatures.

The act of translation of postcolonial literatures has more political and feminist implications than it would appear for Western texts. This is because the minority language inscribes a very different cultural world and responds to the problem of representation and agency with codes often unknown in European languages, for example. Sibhatu's text illustrates this. Her deliberate self-translation helps to erase the act of hegemonic intervention that usually occurs in the act of translation, but not completely, since language escapes the control of the master.

The Politics of Translation

Gayatri C. Spivak's article "The Politics of Translation" (1993: 170–200) deepens the problematic mentioned by Susan Bassnett and André Lefevere concerning the ideological manipulation that takes place when translating a

Third World text into a dominant language. Spivak points out that the female agency inscribed in a language can become subsequently erased by the translator (usually a white feminist) who does not know enough of the cultural aspect of female agency engrained in the language to be translated.

In her article Spivak first points out the various meanings of translation, from translation as reading to the implications of these acts. Translation "takes on a massive life of its own if you see language as the process of meaning-construction" (p. 179) and as Spivak continues, language may be one of many elements that allows us to make sense of things, of ourselves. Making sense of ourselves is what produces identity. According to Spivak, one of the ways to avoid enclosure and essentialism, "to get around the confines of one's 'identity' as one produces expository prose is to work at someone else's title, as one works with a language that belongs to many others. This after all is one of the seductions of translating. It is a simple miming of the responsibility to the trace of the other in the self" (p. 179).

Spivak offers a vision of language as something which inscribes the agent, the writer, even if the intention of the writer is not fully present. And "the task of the feminist translator is to consider language as a clue to the workings of gendered agency." The writer is written by her language but it has to be kept in mind that the "writing of the writer writes agency in a way that might be different from that of a British woman/citizen" (pp. 170–80). Therefore, here Spivak advocates the political responsibility in translating Third Women's texts in which agency is differently inscribed in the language used. To properly perform the act of translation, you have to surrender to the text, since translation is one of the most intimate acts of reading. But between the language as semantic construction and language in which rhetoric and figuration disrupt logic and linearity, the translator has to be capable of making distinctions and of facilitating the breaking of the surface:

> The task of the translator is to facilitate this love between the original and its shadow, a love that permits fraying, holds the agency of the translator and the demands of her imagined or actual audience at bay. The politics of translation from a non-European woman's text too often suppresses this possibility because the translator cannot engage with, or cares insufficiently for, the rhetoricity of the original. (p. 181)

Spivak implies that it is exactly in the rhetorical system of a language that sometimes the experience of silence and otherness is embedded, as a possible space outside language. "Absolute alterity or otherness is thus differed-deferred into another self who resembles us" (p. 181). Spivak makes, therefore, a distinction between the logic of language that allows us to pass from word to word and make connections and the rhetoric of language that must work in the silence between and around words. The relation between rhetoric and logic, between the condition and effect of knowing, is a relation by which a world is made for the agent, so that the agent can act in a political and ethical way. "Unless one can at least construct a model of this for the other language, there is no real translation" (p. 181). Therefore, an act of discipline and responsibility is necessary in order not to produce irresponsible translation which erases the agency of the other, creating a neocolonialist construction of the non-Western scene.

Western feminists often give the opportunity to Third World women to speak in the language of the majority, English: *"it is merely the easiest way to be 'democratic' with minorities"* (p. 182). Under the democratic ideal hides the law of the strongest. A rhetorically unconscious translation can lead to confusing situations in which the translation into English of literature by a woman in Palestine, adds Spivak, can resemble the translated writing of a man from Taiwan. "The rhetoric of Chinese and Arabic! The cultural politics of high-growth, capitalist Asia-Pacific and the devastated West Asia! Gender difference inscribed and inscribing in these differences!" (p. 182).

Therefore, a good translator has to surrender to the text and must solicit the text to show the limits of its language because that rhetorical aspect will point to the silences. This requires a profound commitment to the learning of another language and to remaining open to what is around language in order to translate identity and agency as much as possible. That the writer and the translator are both women or both feminist is not sufficient to translate responsibly the space of rhetoric that hides a gendered voice. "The experience of contained alterity in an unknown language spoken in a different cultural milieu is uncanny" (p. 181). An irresponsible act of translation can silence the author even more; therefore Spivak rightly advocates that the depth of commitment to correct cultural politics, felt in the detail of personal life, is sometimes not enough: "The history of the language, the history of the author's moment, the history of the language-in-and-as-translation, must figure in the weaviness" (p. 186). Spivak also sees obstacles in the translation of languages like Bengali in which the rhetorical devices work differently from English. Another crucial point made by Spivak is that the translator from a Third World language should be sufficiently in touch with what is going on in literary production in that language to be capable of distinguishing between good and bad writing by women, resistant and conformist writing by women: "She must be able to confront the idea that what seems resistant in the space of English may be reactionary in the space of the original language" (p. 188). The person who is translating has to have a tough sense of the specific terrain of the original so that she can fight the racist assumption that all Third World women's writing is good.

This discussion is relevant for Sibhatu's text since it highlights her uncommon solution to the risk of appropriation through translation by the dominant group. Sibhatu has chosen to keep her voice in her mother tongue and also in Italian, which even though it does not have the resonant power of English, still contains a series of hegemonizing characteristics. Sibhatu's open text becomes an act of resistance against the ethnocentric appropriation of the Italian language and also a disconcerting way of responding to the white gaze, by literally facing the text in Italian. This direct confrontation creates the space for an alternative politics of resistance in which the act of linguistic translation is not fully accomplished but undermined by a *testo a fronte* in Tigrinya. It represents the impossibility of a cultural translation that privileges the dominant language by hosting the immigrant in its own democratic linguistic assimilation. The traces of difference are visually present, and yet this *testo a fronte* also reveals an act of dialogism and not only of resistance. The continuity between original and translation practically conveys Bakhtin's concept of heteroglossia, the multiplicity of languages and heritages within the discourse used.

Hopefully Ribka Sibhatu did her homework properly before translating her text into Tigrinya, avoiding the implications of complex cultural analysis rightly advocated by Spivak. The hand that helped Sibhatu to translate herself is not only male but also part of a religious discourse. Padre Kinfé Tesfagabre helped Sibhatu to purify her Tigrinya use in order to improve its literary quality. Strangely enough in this case the editorial help is not offered for her Italian, which is not her mother tongue, but for her real mother tongue that, because of her flight to Ethiopia (where she had to speak Amharic) and then her exile first in France and then Italy, is no longer fluent. Her oral form dominates the written one and the authority of a learned priest helps her out. Sibhatu's living in translation has allowed her to use her own tools to translate herself at all levels, as a sexed, gendered postcolonial subject whose agency evades the language she uses. She keeps, in fact, her linguistic nomadism also in her mother tongue. Probably since she is not being perfectly bilingual, her text is not the kind of faultless translation that Spivak strives for. Still, Sibhatu proceeds in her "worlding of a (split) world" (Spivak, 1990: 1–16) through a double inscription of herself. Sibhatu's *testo a fronte* must be read as an ambivalent space, as a challenge to the enclosure of the Italian language by using Tigrinya to make the Western reader the Other who is not capable of entering that cultural and linguistic system. At the same time Tigrinya is a homage and a contribution to her literature as much as to the new Italophone space in the Italian literature. In this case the use of more languages really represents what George Steiner has defined in his *After Babel* (1975) as the need for privacy and territory, noting that every people has in its language a unique body of shared secrecy (Steiner, 1975: p. 473).

By locating herself outside one monolithic linguistic and cultural system, Ribka Sibhatu attempts to live across boundaries, searching for her freedom by wearing several "language-skins," both dominant and minor, shifting her focus from private to public, from oral to written, from local to global, from the relics of the past wars to the future dynamic of children's visions. Her approach to multiculturalism has the taste of transculturation, of reciprocal influences of modes of representation. The term *transculturation* was first used by ethnographers to describe how marginal groups select and invent from material transmitted to them by the dominant cultures. However, Mary Louise Pratt reinterprets transculturation as a "phenomenon of the contact zone" which are "social spaces where disparate cultures meet, clash and grapple with each other, often in highly asymmetrical relations of dominance and subordination" (Pratt, 1992: 4).

Ribka Sibhatu's children's text is an accomplished example of how language translation assumes the breadth within a postcolonial discourse of cultural translation. On the one hand, her different languages help her to keep her freedom and territory through the veil of secrecy provided by her language-skins, as Steiner would say. On the other hand the two facing languages and cultures enter into a mutual interpenetration by creating what Mary Louise Pratt calls transculturation. This confrontation between languages creates, in fact, mutual cultural contamination and establishes a process of transformation, both for the Italian audience, the Tigrinya reader, and the citizen of the world.

Chapter 9

Voices in Pain:
Once We Were Warriors

Sirad S. Hassan, *Sette Gocce di Sangue*

One of the things that we have to change is how we think about oppression.
>—bell hooks, "A Conversation about Race and Class," p. 63

CULTURAL ANALYSIS AGAINST SILENCE

On the wave of Sibhatu's communal text on Eritrea this chapter will also deal with resistant writings, which denounce a widespread form of oppression. The text, *Sette Gocce di Sangue: Due Donne Somale (Seven Drops of Blood: Two Somali Women)*. was published in Italy in 1996. Sirad S. Hassan, who is a psychologist of "development growth" born in Mogadishu in 1962, was brought up and educated in the United States. She has worked for UNICEF and lives at present between Italy and the United States. The most important issue of her book is the narration of a taboo, female infibulation, which cripples the life of many women in their bodies and spirits. As she writes in her introduction, this text is "dedicated to all women who suffered infibulation,"[1] and it is the story of two Somali girls, Hawa and Ascia, who could have been, as the writer further explains, "my aunts, my cousins, my girlfriends, or my mother and my grandmothers, who are Somali and all infibulated, which means they have gone through the mutilation of the vulva and the partial suture of the vagina. But atrocious practices as this do not only regard Somalia: more than 100 million women, in thirty countries of the world are sexually mutilated." In this way

185

Hassan explains why she has written this book and the position she takes in relation to its content. She reconstructs, in the form of a painful and compelling narration, the true life stories of two Somali women who are followed in their infibulated *via crucis* through their drama as children, adolescents, and adult women, mutilated in their bodies and in their joy of life. It is a third person narration based on real lives but it expands its content to all women who have suffered a similar destiny. It works as a denunciation of the pain and suffering inflicted on little girls who have had no choice but to obey the social patriarchal systems to which their mothers were also subjected.

Hassan's Inside Stories: Infibulation and Migration

This novel recounts the life stories of two Somalian women, Hawa and Ascia, from their adolescence up to their immigrant status in the city of Rome. Told in the third person, this rather chronological narration offers a double perspective on similar experiences. The narrator alternates the perspective from Ascia to Hawa, conveying the reality both as it is perceived from the outside and from within.

Hassan's intent is to voice the pain and trauma caused at an early age by the practice of infibulation. This is ascribed not only to a physical mutilation but also to a psychological impact whose consequences follow the woman into adulthood. There are basically no direct testimonies about the personal experience of this practice, sexuality remaining for many an obscure area, mined with cultural taboos, loaded with anxiety and fear. This is one of the reasons why genital mutilations provoke violent emotional reactions, both from those in the West who are shocked and indignant, and from those in Africa and in the Middle East who are wounded when these practices are described as barbaric. That is why Africans prefer to minimize the quantitative importance of the practice.

In Africa today women's voices are being raised for the first time against genital mutilations that are still practiced on babies, little girls, and women. These voices belong to a few women, who, from Egypt to Mali, from Sudan and Somalia to Senegal, remain closely attached to their identity and heritage, but are prepared to call it into question when traditional practices endanger their lives and their health. They are beginning the delicate task of helping women free themselves from customs that have no advantage and many risks for their physical and psychological well-being, without at the same time destroying the supportive and beneficial threads of their cultural fabric.

Sirad S. Hassan occupies a privileged position from which to offer her voice. Born in Somalia but residing in Italy and in the United States, she can use both her knowledge as a psychologist and her distance from the countries involved in the practice to engage herself in a quasi-scientific narration of a human experience that afflicts millions of women. She assumes Spivak's positioning as "competent native informant" since she talks about a reality she knows from the inside, but she is located in the West where she can profit from a publishing system interested in her voicing of native women's experience. Her detached position acquired through a narration in the Third Person, plus the fictional content of the novel, grants her a safe space from where she can impartially convey the current practice of infibulation in today's Somalia. Without resorting to the easy sensationalism that the practice has provoked in Western countries, Hassan provides an informative account which erases misunderstanding and recriminations about the practice.

What is striking about this form of narration is the gradual process of cognition to which little girls are exposed as they move from total ignorance of the reasons for the pain inflicted on them, to the disorder caused by the realization that the mother is involved in this betrayal, to the confusions generated by the praise that the community offers for their enduring atrocious pain. The narrative tracks their feelings of disorder caused by the disassociation between perception of the body and communal recognition, by physical amputation on one side and social integration on the other. The disorder is caused by the disbelief in one's own pain, since the family and the village welcome it as a moment of happiness. It is the first stage of mistrust of the signals of the body and at the same time a growing status of insecurity and shame due to the misunderstanding generated between the perception of the self and of the others.

Girls go through the practice of infibulation at a very early age, when the figure of the mother is still the whole world. To disobey her would require strength and a consciousness not usually known in girls of five to nine years old. The mother sets the norms and values to be respected but the experience of pain shatters the girls' confidence in the mother and pushes them into a world of loneliness at a very precocious age. The father is usually completely removed from this practice even though he usually covers the costs of the operation and shares the general patriarchal understanding that all respectable women must go through the practice of infibulation. The reasons for such a practice are often false, since infibulation is not a guarantee of virginity or against unfaithfulness.[2] But it does certainly amputate sexual enjoyment. Even the most "mild" clitoridectomy (excision of the clitoris) implies the removal from a woman's body nerves of vital importance for sexual enjoyment. Furthermore the age at which the practice is performed has in the last decade decreased, showing very little of the ritual of initiation and showing no change in the life of the child before and after the operation. The description available of the reactions of children—panic and shock from extreme pain, convulsion, and possible death—indicate a practice comparable to torture. The different implications of this practice will be later taken into account both from a Western point of view and from the point of view of communities where the practice continues to be performed even if declared illegal.[3]

A Question of Standpoint

The positioning within the discourse of sexual mutilation is therefore of the utmost importance to postcolonial studies. The dilemma that bell hooks defines as a "question of standpoint" must be faced: "how can we locate ourselves from standpoints that allow us to be inclusive of difference while also appreciating the similarities of experience? How can we displace paradigms of domination that, in fact, establish authority through exclusion through asserting one people as having knowledge and other people as not having something?"[4]

To escape this impasse, it is necessary to analytically demonstrate the production of women as a socioeconomic political group within particular local contexts. This will be achieved by engaging with texts in order to detect the gender and race biases that are hidden under the literary representation of cultural phenomena and relating them to ethnicity, religion, and psychosexuality.

The discursive strategies within which infibulation has come to exist in Africa are different from the discursive strategies which condemn it in the Western countries. Often this creates a paradoxical situation that stifles communication and dialogue. To explain this asymmetric misunderstanding and incompatibility, the religious, psychosexual, and sociological motivations for the existence and perpetration of the practice will be illustrated here, but mostly the consequences—medical, psychological, emotional, and cultural—will be explored. The theoretical feminist debate between interventionists and defenders of cultural traditions will be also examined through the close reading and contextualization of Sirad S. Hassan's *Sette Gocce Di Sangue: Due Donne Somale* (Palermo: La Luna, 1996).

Hassan's text is exemplary because it puts the issue of female genital mutilation in the foreground rather than making it secondary to the main narrative. It is striking to note that there are almost no literary texts coming from African writers on the issue of female mutilation. If, on the one hand, we can understand the silence on an issue exploited by Western feminists to interfere in the affairs of the African society, it is also discouraging to notice that through silence African writers become accomplices in the perpetration of a practice on girls who are younger and younger, a practice that can no longer represent a rite of passage into adulthood.

The position of African women who choose to keep the issue to themselves is more than understandable. They are wary of overtly enthusiastic radical Western feminists who think they have the right to condemn the practice *tout court*. African women suspect Westerners of concentrating too much on the issue of sexual mutilation instead of on so many other socioeconomic problems that are equally urgent, such as demographic explosion, famine, diseases, and infant mortality, to name but a few. As Nawal El Saadawi points out, this is due to the fact that Western women tend to draw sharp distinctions between their own situation and that

> of women in the region to which I belong, and who believe there are fundamental differences. They tend to depict our life as a continual submission to medieval systems, and point vehemently to some of the rituals and traditional practices such as female circumcision. They raise a hue and cry in defense of the victims, write long articles and deliver speeches and congresses. But by concentrating on such manifestations there is a risk that the real issues of social and economic change be evaded or even forgotten, and that the effective action be replaced by a feeling of superior humanity, a glow of satisfaction that may blind the mind and feelings to the concrete everyday struggle for women's emancipation.[5]

Saadawi's refusal to deal with the problem of circumcision in isolation from general economic and social pressure is laudable and her refusal to succumb to Western rehegemonizing and homogenizing positions is absolutely necessary. In keeping with Donna Haraway's claim of situated knowledge—that we have to carry responsibility for our visions and be accountable for our positions—the practice of sexual mutilation will be dealt in an interpretative framework, with all the consequences that this entails. This engagement with the debate is not meant to be interventionist but rather to investigate why the issue of sexual mutilation does not easily appear on the agenda of female African writers and how it is conveyed when it is. African women are afraid of undermining the positive representation that people in their country are trying to achieve against Western cultural interference and reductionism.[6] The silence that important writers like Buchi Emecheta, Ama Ato Aidoo, writers who have fought for the emancipation of the African woman, have decided to maintain on this question is representative of the intricacy that such an issue has within the social contexts of African countries and of the difficulty of assuming a position for or against it. This is particularly true in the context of the condemnation of infibulation by the West, which invokes human rights principles that, despite several international world conferences, such as in Cairo and Beijing, remain firmly grounded in the principles of the Western Enlightenment.[7] Circumcision is obviously articulated as a dilemma for African women because the embrace of emancipation and the denunciation of patriarchal oppression within their societies is seen as conflicting with the process of decolonization and cultural restitution. African feminists retreat into silence in order not to damage the process of constructing a positive representation with which Africa and postcolonial countries in general are engaging against the interference of the dominant countries. African women often say that the debate should be left to them and that they should not accept any Western hierarchical intervention.

In defending the politics of cultural restitution, women put their nation and the general male interests first against their own needs for emancipation, since they attribute to the collectivity and to the balance within it priority over their own individual well-being. The debate over individualism in favor of collectivism (but whose collectivism?) has paralyzed African critics and writers on the subject of female mutilation. As Awa Thiam writes, "there is no longer question of accepting excuses for disregarding these problems, least of all the excuse that is most frequently put forward: that the liberation of black people in general is far and away more important than the liberation of women" (Awa Thiam, 1986: 13). However, Awa Thiam risks essentializing the concept of a universal African woman who needs to be liberated from race and ethnic traditions. It is important to recall Mohanty, who warns us about the exclusivity of experience as inextricably linked to a situated, material position. This leads to the knowledge of the self and the rest of the world as something that cannot be exchanged or replaced by some external, universal assumption.

But following Mohanty's admonitions, how do we get out of the dilemma surrounding the ambivalence of absolutism versus cultural relativism? How do we face the dilemma that Sirad Salad Hassan phrased quoting the Italian writer Ignazio Silone: "I don't feel neutral. I am a human being?"[8] How do we avoid replacing outrage with indifference for a practice that we all feel needs to be eradicated but nobody feels entitled to talk about and act upon without being accused of Eurocentrism or tribalism? Even African women who have personally gone through sexual mutilation, who know all the medical horrors resulting from such a practice, as does the Egyptian physician Nawal el-Saadawi, are criticized for being part of an élite, Western educated and out of touch with people of lower class who are illiterate and who will never be able to read her books. As Françoise Lionnet writes, "There is, in other words a dissymmetry of class and ideology, between them (Western trained feminist intellectuals) and the (uneducated) masses, a dissymmetry that is inevitable, since literary and education remain, to large extent, steps that favor Westernisation" (Lionnet, 1994: 23).

Testimonio

In order to illustrate the complexities of the debate around infibulation, significant narrative accounts of female voices in pain will be explored. It is important to put these texts and voices into dialogue and to emphasize that each voice is located in its own context and that the subject of narration is different from the subject of enunciation. *Seven Drops of Blood* will function as an illustration of the problem of sexual mutilation. Hassan's book is a treatise, an essay on circumcision based on the fictional account of the stories of two Somali women who emigrated to Italy at the time of Siad Barre's regime. Even though Hassan takes the most detached and scientific position towards the problem, the result is very compelling. This intensity is due to the device by which the author's voice is distinct from the narrator's voice, which is distinct from the two Somali women's voices, thus increasing the effect of distress and credibility. Hassan reinterprets a genre that has been identified as *Testimonio* by John Beverly (1992, pp. 91–114), a form which is establishing itself in Central America as the lives of struggling women, often political activists, are reported by a person who interviews them, thus creating a hybrid authoritative voice. The *Testimonio* is neither an autobiography nor a biography but a genre in between since the closeness between source of narration and narrator is an infectious field of mutual influence where orality plays a very important role:

> The word *testimonio* translates literally as "testimony," as in the act of testifying or bearing witness in a legal or religious sense. This connotation is important because it distinguishes *testimonio* from recorded participant narrative, as in the cause of "oral history." In oral history it is the intentionality of the recorder—usually a social scientist that is dominant, and the resulting text is in some sense "data."[9]

Given this situation we are meant to experience both the speaker and the events recounted as real. It implies a pledge of honesty on the part of the narrator that the listener or reader is bound to respect.

In her text Hassan starts her "voice-over" focused on the two girls' early years as they move from cheerful complicitous friends to a painful isolated adulthood. The novel opens with Hawa who is prevented from seeing her best friend Ascia, a nine-year-old who at the beginning of the novel is locked for two weeks in a bedroom to which Hawa is denied access. Ascia's grandmother explains to her that "Ascia had become adult and could not play with her anymore since she had passed, that morning at six o'clock, the test to become adult" (p. 8). Hawa is portrayed as an extroverted and vivacious girl who balances the character of the intelligent but more introverted Ascia. The different class milieus are obvious in the distribution of tasks that the two girls have to perform. While Hawa has to do infinite housework for her brothers and her father, especially during the pregnancy of her mother, Ascia can enjoy a better life, due to the advantages provided by her father's work in Saudi Arabia.

The author describes in the following chapter the events that surround Ascia's rite of initiation. When she wakes up one day, she realizes that strange things are happening and her mother behaves differently towards her. Behaving as the dutiful obedient daughter who does not question her mother, Ascia follows her through the city at dawn. Waiting for them is Mustafà, an influential figure who, thanks to his big glasses and white gown, inspires trust in the mothers who think he is a real doctor, and who is in reality just a nurse getting paid for his operations: "Mustafà was married with three wives, had twelve children, ten of which female, all of them regularly infibulated" (p. 16).

Ascia observes the movements around Mustafà's house that morning. She hears a scream coming from the house which is quickly suffocated. Her mother informs her that they are there to visit the doctor:

> because that "thing" has grown too much and in a short time it will become as big as that of a man and it will cause embarrassment. "If you don't show it to the doctor," the mother continued, "you won't be able to sit down at school anymore, all girls will make fun of you. Furthermore, as a good muslim, you have to cut a bit of that flesh which continues to grow." (p. 16)

The shame for her own body is infused through the vision of the female sex as a monstrous object of ridicule. As Lionnet explains,

> Excision makes clear how power relations are inscribed on the female body by virtue of its subjection to particular sexual traditions. . . . The reasons for this practice have to do with complex definitions of masculinity and femininity that construct the clitoris and the male prepuce as vestiges of the opposite sex which must be eliminated for a "proper" sexual identity to exist. Thus the female body is considered "too masculine" and socially unacceptable when not marked by excision. . . . It is interesting to note that in African context one is not simply born a "woman"; one becomes a female person after having being submitted to a cultural process.[10]

In Hassan's description the words chosen to describe Ascia's operation assume the connotation of a sinister ordeal. In its cold and efficient performance the operation acquires the tint of a slaughtering when seen from the point of view of the little girl:

> Ascia follows the proceeding with terror, she starts sweating and the heart beats very hard, up to her throat. She is already on the table, her legs are separated and tied up like a woman who is giving birth. . . . The two women hold Ascia very tightly because a false movement can cause serious wounds, even deadly ones if some veins are cut by mistake. Ascia is held in such a way that Mustafà can look well at the vulva and starts "operating." (pp. 17–18)

Ascia cannot even express her fear, for she is told to behave like an adult and not to scream. Sometimes little girls are told that her mother and her family will be cursed and die if they scream. The strain to prove courage and loyalty to the mother despite the perception of being literally tortured with her consent provokes a psychological trauma which often makes the girls fall silent.

In Saadawi's text the mother also sets the norms and values to be respected but the experience of pain shatters the girls' confidence in the mother and pushes them into a world of loneliness at a very early age. In this regard Saadawi personally recounts the shattering recognition of her mother among those who were torturing her at the age of six:

> I screamed with pain despite the tight hand held over my mouth, for the pain was not just a pain, it was like a searing flame that went through my whole body. After a few moments, I saw a red pool of blood around my hips. I did not know what they had cut off from my body, and I did not try to find out. I just wept, and called out to my mother for help. But the worst shock of all was when I looked around and found her standing by my side. Yes it was her, I could not be mistaken, in flesh and blood, right in the midst of these strangers, talking to them and smiling at them, as though they had not participated in slaughtering her daughter just a few minutes ago.[11]

Apparently the rite of passage, which should summon the abandonment of childhood and the entrance into adulthood, is signified by the child's nightmarish realization that she is left alone with no one to turn to, the mother distanced and lost in a world that will never return to the way it once was.

As in Saadawi's account, Hassan's Ascia, who also meekly follows her mother because she is unaware of what is awaiting her, experiences the same primal scene of disbelief and shattering of the world: "Her mother observed everything with detachment and coldness" (p. 19). The death of the mother is acknowledged at this stage, and the rite of initiation indeed throws the little girl into womanhood and erases the function of the maternal as protective and caring.[12] The rite of initiation puts the little girl at the center of general attention. Gifts, sweets, and special food are brought. The enormous confusion that arises between the perception of having been wronged and wounded for no reason, and the admiration and praise that it creates instead for the adults marks the beginning of mistrust in the relation between the self and the world. Pain has to be reinscribed as a positive category since it brings beauty and maturity but the loss of love for her own body means also the beginning of a schizophrenic relationship with the self.

The atmosphere of merriment that surrounds Ascia's operation increases her sense of betrayal and disorientation. Women stream into Ascia's room to offer presents, the best food is cooked for her, and the rite of initiation is a moment of celebration which involves the whole community. But men are not allowed to participate:

> Ascia did not dare to complain, but held her breath with tears rolling down her cheeks. She was feeling pain, a pain she had never felt before. She couldn't wait for this to end, that all these women would stop coming with their daughters. She was thinking of the days of convalescence, she could not stand her strapped legs anymore, she was thinking how foolish, stupid those little girls were who were praying to be infibulated too. No! They did not know how painful it was, but maybe they searched for the general approval, for gifts and feasts. (p. 20)

The social approval of the practice is obviously more important than the motivations leading to the need for the operation. The practice is clearly embedded in a cultural context that encodes it as a beautifying and enriching phenomenon without which girls do not become women and will therefore never be able to marry, have some degree of economic security, and lead full female lives. Such a practice forms part of a whole social system which follows the pressure of ethnic customs.

What is not accounted for is the level of pain that girls have to endure not only during the operation but for the rest of their lives. It is not known, in fact, what repercussions a mutilated body can have on the general desire for life. In the novel there is no psychoanalytic reading of the feelings that torment Ascia and Hawa after the operations, but some elements are indicative of progressive introversion and diminished desire for life. Emphasis is placed upon the physical pain and the consequences of the operation, which are mysterious and unexplained. The girls are left in utter ignorance and given no information. The taboo is so strong that not even in the case of serious pain is help called:

> Hawa had always been a very vivacious child, but since she had gone through the operation it was as if something had died within her. She had started talking again but only when strictly necessary, while before she could never restrain herself from talking. (p. 43)

Stepping into silence and becoming diffident about the outer world are the first elements that emerge. As Elaine Scarry writes in *The Body in Pain: The Making and the Unmaking of the World* (1985), for Ascia and Hawa infibulation signifies the death within, the unmaking of their world, and the complete detachment from the possibility to rely on other relatives.

ONCE WE WERE WARRIORS

The Medical Body

Hassan's novel is informed by a controversial view on how a female body should look in order to be considered attractive and healthy. This addresses the first schism between the different conceptions of female body in the Western world and in the Third World. In her essay, "Bringing African Women into the Classroom," Obioma Nnaemeka sharply points out the sensational way in which clitoridectomy is dealt with in Western media and academia.[13] This treatment leads to the pervasive belief in the incompleteness of most African women which in turn denies them humanity. Nnaemeka turns the mirror back and shows how Western women are not in control or free from their bodies either, since plastic surgery is also an abuse of the female body:[14]

> We must not be distracted by the arrogance that names one procedure breast *reduction* and the other sexual *mutilation*, with all the attached connotations of barbarism. In both instances some part of the female body is excised. . . . For the women in areas where clitoridectomy is performed, beauty is inextricably linked with chastity and motherhood. The crucial questions we must ask are: For whom are these operations undertaken? For whom must these women be desirable and acceptable? Women's inability to control their body is not country specific.[15]

By comparing arranged marriage to dating services and comparing polygamy to the Greek origin of the word [poly = many] and the Western hypocritical tradition of men with mistresses, Nnaemeka demonstrates that things are not so simple or "barbaric" as they appear. For example, she shows how women in Africa and in the Arab world have equally condemned the practice of infibulation; there is disagreement however, "about how to wage the war" (Nnaemeka, 1983: 217–20). The critic accuses Western interventionists of making of clitoridectomy a pure question of sexuality and argues that by advocating the enjoyment of sex, such interventionists often contribute to a stricter imposition of certain customs on African and Arab women. The upsurge of religious fundamentalism in the Middle East and in other parts of the Arab world is a sign of resistance to imperialism and other forms of foreign intervention:

> In the name of resisting foreign interventionism, patriarchal societies resort to rigid and heavy handed enforcement of old ways—tradition, religious fundamentalism—which often oppress women. So by fighting our

wars badly, our Western sisters inadvertently collaborate in tightening the noose around our neck.[16]

What a body is and what sexual pleasure should be depends upon the cultural constructions of the medically healthy and aesthetically beautiful body that affect both Western and Third World women.[17]

For example, in Hassan text's, the odyssey Hawa has to go through is described because she cannot diagnose the symptoms of her body. Hawa, discovers only at a very late stage that her ill health is due to the consequences of what she has suffered as a child. She is by now an adult who has already emigrated to Italy and is leading a normal life as a domestic servant to il Signor Gianni. Only the increasing pain in her abdomen, due to the menstrual flow that cannot pass, makes Hawa work less until she becomes seriously ill. Il Signor Gianni decides to take her to the hospital and here begins the bewilderment of the Italian doctors who cannot understand what has happened to her. Hawa, who has made her genital parts taboo, cannot understand the doctor's astonishment. This is the moment of the cultural gap since Hawa thinks infibulation affects all women whereas the Italian doctors treat her as having a monstrous deformation. If Hawa's innocence can be attributed to the taboo which obstructs knowledge about the practice, there are no excuses for the doctors, who should be knowledgeable about the practice since it had been denounced since colonial time. This shows that medicine still accepts the Western vision of the female body and does not contemplate cultural variants within its field of application:

> "I cannot believe what I'm seeing, what happened?" [asked the doctor] "Did you burn yourself? Did you have an accident?" . . . What the doctor saw was a vulva which did not have a piece of female organ, which was scraped and smooth. Perplexed he called another doctor on the phone, leaving the trembling Hawa with her legs in the air. (p. 95)

The Western doctor is horrified by the amputation. He recognizes the deformation without acknowledging the social practices which produced such an altered body. And Hawa who had not been aware of her uniqueness, because the practice is universal in her country, cannot comprehend the doctor's astonishment and begins to think she is victim of an unusual illness. The awareness of her alterity that Hawa has to carry through the streets of Rome because of her different skin color is now replaced by a more delicate and invisible element: her different sexual identity. From the moment of infibulation this issue has being left unspoken, repressed, and Hawa cannot voice or make sense of her diversity.

Hawa hesitates when confronted with the decision of whether to be reopened. Her doubts are interpreted as irrational and meaningless. It will be Bashir, a Somali friend of hers, who will enlighten the Signor Gianni on the

cultural relevance of the practice of sexual mutilation and on the implications
for Hawa if she abandons it:

> If Hawa is opened, everyone will be against her. Fauzia had to fight a lot be-
> cause she had told a close friend she had been opened up for health reasons.
> From that day no acquaintances and even relatives greeted her. This hap-
> pened before we lived together: now we have intercourse which is painful
> for her, since her vagina is still tight after such a long time of artificial clo-
> sure, and could not develop, but especially she does not feel anything during
> intercourse, she is not with me when we make love. (pp. 101–02)

This male perspective about infibulation, the only one in the text, offers no new
insights on the reasons for the practice, but adds to the suffering, which also affects the male partner. No real possibility for change is envisaged, just the pow-
erlessness of men and women in the face of a social practice which is integrated
in an immutable system of values. Migration is one of the possibilities for escape. Being far from home and from social control grants a margin for self-
determination. Nonetheless, the level of disapproval among the immigrant
community toward a woman who resists is still very high. Even though social
control within the emigrated community is reduced, the stigma of having be-
trayed ancient customs remains painful. The diminished dignity and respectability attributed to deinfibulated women strikes a delicate chord since
emigrated woman are, on the one hand, more free to make individual decisions
and, on the other, frightened to step into further isolation.

Caught in a dilemma, Hawa is asked to make a choice, her own choice
since she has no family and no husband by her side. She is free to choose both
for her partial liberation and for the unknown consequences that this might
imply for her. She opts for deinfibulation and the physical and psychological
relief is immediate:

> After the cooking course, she enrolled for an Italian course offered by the
> local authority of Rome, free to all foreigners. But what also changed
> was her attitude towards the others. Gradually she was becoming herself
> again, the one before the infibulation. (p. 103)

The intense menstrual cramps and malaise, which had deprived Hawa of her
sense of life, have disappeared. The price she has to pay is her isolation from
her own community. Now she refuses to see Fauzia and Bashir or to go around
the station because everyone will be gossiping about her. She chooses, therefore, for integration into the Italian society to balance the loss of her community. Learning the language, cutting her hair, and wearing Western clothes, to
divert attention from her status as an immigrant, are all steps she takes towards

self-awareness and a progressive detachment from her community of origin, whose support had been shallow and institutional.

Her employer, who offers the Western gaze, observes all the changes with puzzlement. So small is his knowledge of the Somali women's world that he constantly turns to his cousin, who has spent time in Somalia, for advice. He can now make sense of the pain that had enveloped Hawa in strange silent and quizzical moods, and her physical relief is an explanation for her sudden vitality and her transition towards Italian culture. The cousin explains to him once that when they are depressed or ill, African women pretend to be crazy in order to give vent to their rage and pain. Madness becomes the only form to express dissent and resistance against the prescribed norms of behavior and endurance. Also Hawa's suffering is always silent, as silent as Ascia's suffering during her honeymoon. Only now, after all the years of mutual silence, is Hawa capable of retrospectively understanding the suffering of her friend after her wedding night.

Hawa's situation at the hospital, where the female medical body is constructed, will repeat itself a few months later when her friend Ascia, who in the meantime has fled the civil war in Somalia and emigrated to Italy, is carried to the hospital to deliver her baby. The doctors are stunned and uncomprehending:

> "Oh my god, not another of those!" exclaimed the gynecologist annoyed. "After all we know what to do, doctor!"' the midwife reacted promptly and prepared her for the Caesarian section. (p. 107)

The Western irritation against the practice quickly replaces the initial shock and dismay. The doctor perceives the infibulation of Ascia as an obstacle to his task, a nuisance which hinders the perfect execution of his profession. The midwife, on the other hand, quickly evaluates the situation, intervening in the same way she would have for a difficult pregnancy. She does not emphasize the African body as abnormal but operates within her professional knowledge as if it were one of the many cases.

It is a Western practice to create medical metaphors to construct the female body, usually in reproductive terms, often alienating women from their own bodies which are contemplated as an "otherness machine."[18] It is important to highlight that science is shaped by racial and cultural prejudices that can define what a female body should look like or what a healthy female body is. The view that even an ancient science such as medicine is subject to cultural relativism is the major achievement of Emily Martin's book *The Woman in the Body* (1987), which offers useful insights into the practice of circumcision. Martin argues that an analysis of medical discourse needs to be tackled in order to understand how female mutilation is constructed in the West.

Hassan is highly skilled in showing this aspect through the account of Ascia and Hawa at the Italian hospital. Her voice is not heard but her position regarding the hegemonizing attitude of Italian medicine towards the African female body is resounding.

However, as Hassan has illustrated, the psychological impact of sexual mutilation needs to be not only addressed but expressed. It is indeed the task of this chapter to show the way in which pain destroys language, and without language there is no possibility to express identity. It is necessary to illustrate not only the pain that silences infibulated women, but also the strategies employed to overcome it.

Voicing Pain

Hassan's literary text is among the strategies embraced to fight female silencing. The goal is to offer direct or indirect testimony to a phenomenon that is present in medical and human rights reports but hardly discussed in narrative texts. In their book *Testimony* Shoshana Felman and Dauri Laub pose a question: "What is the relation between the act of witnessing and testifying, and the acts of writing and of reading, particularly in our era? What is furthermore, this book will ask, the relation between narrative and history, between art and memory, between speech and survival?" (1992: XIII). Felman and Laub explore these questions with the Holocaust testimonies but the issues she raises are also valid for the exploration of other experiences of pain, such as those caused by infibulation.

Hassan's literary text is a *testimonio* since it aims at contrasting the silence and taboos surrounding the issue of painful mutilation. The implications of this translation from pain to language are thoroughly investigated by Elaine Scarry in her book *The Body In Pain: The Making and the unmaking of the World* (1985). Scarry argues that physical pain constitutes an assault on language and since it destroys language, it resists verbal objectification and

> Unlike any other status of consciousness has no referential content. It is not *of* or *for* anything. It is precisely because it takes no object that it, more than any other phenomenon, resists objectification in language.[19]

Because the experience of pain is so traumatizing that speech is blocked, "it is not surprising that the language for pain should sometimes be brought into being by those who are not themselves in pain but who speak *on behalf* of those who are" (Scarry, 1985: 6). The difficulty of expressing somebody else's distress, and the motivation for wanting to do so, is obviously overlaid by a political aspect since private experiences enter the public discourse. One realm in which a language of pain is formulated and standardized is medical discourse. There are other verbal documents, such as those by Amnesty International or the language of physical pain used in the courtroom. Other attempts at scientific wording are represented by sociological studies and reports. Another source is art, even though, as Virginia Woolf declared, language falls short when required to express pain. There are very few literary representations and artistic productions that center on the nature of physical pain. The rarity with which physical pain is represented in literature is most striking since art does have referential content and is susceptible to verbal objectification.

Seven Drops of Blood presents artistic accounts of experiences of pain linked to genital mutilation which are often unavailable because of the difficulty of objectifying pain into language.[20] Hassan makes no great claims but rather concentrates on the wording of experiences of pain within an ethnocultural reality. When Hawa asks curiously but also anxiously if Ascia will infibulate Zuleika, Ascia's newly born baby, Ascia replies, "I probably won't infibulate her but I will make her the *sunna* which is compulsory. So she won't suffer as much as I did" (p. 109). The *sunna* is the less radical variant of female circumcision. Hawa notices that Ascia had answered unwillingly and had suddenly aged. She started thinking about the future of Zuleika:

> Maybe she was the luckiest of us all, the *sunna* was not a real mutilation and she would not have all the problems faced by infibulated women. Maybe it was time to change the old customs which only made us suffer. Hawa thought that it was right to do the *sunna* to Zuleika, yes it was right that way. She repeated these last sentences aloud, maybe trying to convince herself, and slowly she fell asleep. (pp. 109–10)

With these closing lines the novel leaves the last words to the African women as it focuses on Hawa and Ascia's thoughts about the future of the practice. It is also the most credible and applicable approach to the problem of mutilation since it is contextualized in a socioeconomic structure which requires time to change traditional customs. It leaves space for optimism and change, a change that will happen slowly, after some generations, as the two protagonists infer. What this ending makes clear is that if changes are to happen, they have to come from the African women themselves, and not from the West, and this requires a work of acculturation and increased level of education among African women. Migration seems one way to get away from repressive practices, as in Hawa's and Ascia's trajectory of life. However, even migration cannot eradicate mutilations: the practice is continued in order to keep the support of the community, even far from home.

Experiencing this practice is apparently not enough to condemn and change a long-established tradition. To change the social practice, a society must revise and rectify all norms and values around it and this demands time and knowledge. If a universalist position cannot be taken from the human rights point of view, a necessity arises among African women themselves, which is the right to health and well-being and this is not culturally or nationally bounded but inherent to the human condition itself.

By searching for consensus and agreement (as Hawa is doing with Ascia about Zuleika), Somali women can create a new social practice to replace the old. This leaves the sense of ethnic identity not diminished but reinforced from a gender perspective and offers a new possibility of changing the prescribed ending, as Rachel Blau du Plessis points out in her book *Writing Beyond the Ending:*

> the rightful end of female quest was fully limited either to marriage or death. These representations offered in eighteenth-century novels see women always ending with a social accomplishment—successful courtship, marriage—or judgmental of her sexual and social failure—death.[21]

This prescribed ending reinforced an ideology in which women were functional to the institution of the family. The emphasis put on the practice of excision to guarantee marriageability is reinforced in its inevitability by the implicit social banning. Nonexcision becomes therefore coterminous with social death. On the other hand, no emphasis is put on the high death rate within the execution of the practice itself. The social death is maximalized in its threat and importance over the physical one, which becomes not only neglected and denied but invisible.

Hawa cannot disentangle her sexual mutilation from marriage. Since marriage reopens the pain of mutilation, Hawa opts for the only possible ending left open for her—nonmarriage—in order to keep her bit of pleasure in life going. She asks Ascia about the possibility of not carrying out this practice on her daughter, thus giving new hope to future generations. Writing beyond the ending has to be turned into a rewriting before the ending, in an accumulation of texts and voices which revise the inevitability of long-lasting customs from within.

PRACTICE AND DISCOURSE ON
FEMALE INFIBULATION

Deconstructing Social Practices: Feminism and Postcolonial Theory

In this last section the focus of analysis shifts from the literary wording of pain to the theoretical controversy concerning Western and Third World feminists on how to wage the war for the eradication of infibulation.[22] Due to its complexities of construction and representation the issue of infibulation requires the development of highly nuanced strategies of discursive analysis that account for locations in multiple places, languages, and experiences. This is all the more necessary when one is dealing with issues of international feminism that tend to foster a global discourse instead of a localized one. The reason forms of localized feminism engage in criticism is to decentralize the monopoly of Western feminism that emphasizes gender difference at the expense of ethnic specificity. In order to undermine this trend, postcolonial feminist discourse has been engaged in the realignment of axes of ethnicity, race, and caste along the privileged Western one of gender through a detailed and situated discursive analysis.

Issues such as the practice of genital mutilation in some African countries, the dowry murders in India, the *Hudood* ordinances in the Pakistani Muslim law, the wearing of the veil, or even the relegation into the confined zone of the house (*zenana*) for women of some Islamic societies, for example, have often been identified by white feminism as a demonstration of female oppression worldwide, and especially in Third World countries where women need strong backing in order to engage in a real resistance and rebellion against the repressive patriarchal system. Often these practices are defined without much thought as barbaric, savage, backward, misogynous, and generally lacking in any consideration of the female being as human and capable of subjectivity. Western activists and feminists have often mobilized to eradicate these practices in the name of human rights and global sisterhood, which put women first across borders, nationality, and historical divides. They advocate politics of abolition by intervening in the so-called Third World societies and communities, thus obliterating any possibility for cultural autonomy. Also by imposing "acculturation" according to Western standards, they reducing Third World women to an object status, making them victims twice over.

This intervention lead to the paradox that Caren Kaplan warns of in her article "The Politics of Location" (Kaplan, 1994: 148): in an effort to deconstruct hegemonic, global universals, quite often theorists of difference (read: Western feminists) have reinstituted hegemonies, thereby involuntarily creating a hierarchy between white feminism and the rest of women, constructed as a homogenous alterity. To avoid constructing "monoliths," Chandra Mohanty argues, criticism must accurately describe differences in culture and create new words to express similarities and common ground (Mohanty, 1995).

Mohanty criticizes Western feminism in the first place for its assumption that Third World women are identical regardless of place or ethnicity. Secondly, Mohanty attacks Western feminism for its uncritical use of particular methodologies involved in the first assumption. As an example Mohanty cites the way a critic isolates a religious or kinship system in her analysis of writing. Finally she points out the problems of the politics that these two frames of analysis create. This involves the self-representation of Western women in literature and other disciplines as modern women with some degree of control over their bodies and sexualities and Western feminists' "*re*-presentation" of women of the Third World as domestic or uneducated victims (Mohanty, 1995: 337).

In writing about genital mutilation, Mohanty argues that the Western feminist representation of Third World women is a coherent one. In these texts women are defined as victims of male violence (Fran Hosken); victims of the colonial process (Maria Cutrufelli); victims of the Arab familial system (Juliette Minces); victims of the economic development process (Beverly Lindsay); and finally victims of the Islamic code (Patricia Jeffery). This mode of defining women primarily in terms of their *object status* (the way in which they are affected by certain institutions and systems) characterizes this particular use of "women" as a category of analysis.

Western feminists appropriate and colonize the complex literary, oral, and body production of women of different classes, races, and castes in the Third World, according to Mohanty, creating one of the most bizarre paradoxical conditions of feminism:

> What binds women together is a sociological notion of *sameness* of their oppression. It is, at this point that an elision takes place between "women" as a discursively constructed group and "women" as material subjects of their own history.[23]

According to this elision, Western feminists construct themselves as referents in a binary analytic model. They create a homogenous and coherent *re*-presentation of Third World women as objects (read: ignorant, poor, uneducated, tradition-bound, domestic, family oriented, and victimized), while the *self*-representation of white women is implicit (read: educated, modern, in control of their own bodies and sexuality, and free to make their own decisions). The Western standard is the norm and referent opposed to the Third World status as Other according to their socioeconomic diversity. In the context of Western women writing or studying women in the Third World, such objectification, however benevolently motivated, needs to be both named and challenged since such discourse defines women as archetypal victims, freezing them into "objects-who-defend-themselves" versus men as "subjects-who-perpetrate-violence." To engage in a positive dialogue with women of different backgrounds, it is necessary to locate the standpoint of analysis and also the place used as field of investigation since "difference is constructed differently within various discourses. These different meanings signal different political strategies and outcomes" (Brah, 1991: 53–72).

Adrienne Rich critizes, "that only certain kinds of people can make theory; that the white-middle class femisism can know for 'all women'; that only when a white mind formulates it is the formulation to be taken seriously: Feminism's double bind is that it cannot speak for other women, nor can it speak 'without' or 'apart from' other women" (Rich, 1987: 230). Adrienne Rich's explication of the limits of feminism does not suggest a barrier between the global and the local but rather insists upon a politics of location in order to be able to know, judge, and analyze without further oppressing.[24]

Notions such as global feminism have failed to respond to such needs and have increasingly been subject to criticism. Conventionally, global feminism has stood for a kind of Western cultural imperialism. The term *global feminism* has elided the diversity of women's agency in favor of a universalized Western model of women's liberation that celebrates individuality and modernity. Anti-imperialist movements have legitimately decried this form of feminist global-izing (albeit often for a continuation of their own agendas). Many women who participate in decolonizing efforts both within and outside the United States have rejected the term *feminism* in favor of *womanist,* as Alice Walker does, or have defined their feminism through class or race or other ethnic, religious, or regional struggles.

As Carole Boyce Davies illustrates in her introduction to *Ngambika: Studies of Women in African Literature,* African feminism is a hybrid, which seeks to combine African concerns with feminist concerns, an act of balancing women's own issues with a common struggle with African men against imperialism. Davies acknowledges the "inequities and limits" within traditional, often feu-dal societies, and she cites Molara Ogundipe Leslie's important point about the struggle against women's own internalized oppression: "Women are shackled by their own negative self-image, by centuries of the interiorization of the ide-ologies of patriarchy and gender hierarchy."[25]

Even as one acknowledges the necessity for solidarity among Third World men and women and rejects a separatist feminist movement, it is crucial not to romanticize this solidarity. For Third World women, feminist struggles aim for the full dignity of women along with men. Filomena Steady's articulation that "African feminism combines racial, sexual, class, and cultural dimensions of oppression to produce a more inclusive brand of feminism through which women are viewed first and foremost as human, rather than sexual beings" mystifies the specifically sexual aspects of women's oppression.[26]

On the Western front the critic Françoise Lionnet has also tried to find a way out of the theoretical impasse presented by the issue of infibulation. In her ar-ticle "Dissymmetry Embodied: Nawal El Saadawi's *Woman at Point Zero* and the Practice of Excision" (Lionnet, 1995: 129–53), she enters the debate on universalism and particularism by briefly naming the discursive contexts that construct the phenomenon of female excision and infibulation.

There is no easy way out of this dilemma, neither theoretical nor practical. As Lionnet would put it, the condition of dissymmetry within international feminism shows that incoherences are embedded in the signifying text of cul-ture, a paradoxical situation which entails the permanence of conflicts and dis-sonances despite the possibility of sharing common ground and bonding. She identifies the impasse generated by universalistic positioning on the one hand

and cultural relativism on the other. She distances herself from both, avoiding any possible positioning in favor of or against the practice of female infibulation, showing that the dissymmetries within the social cultural terrains cannot be solved with an either/or approach.

Feminism and the defense of women's rights do not have a universalistic appeal but need to be positioned and located within specific cultures, religions, and classes. In a later article "The Limits of Universalism: Identity, Sexuality, and Criminality,"[27] Lionnet goes further with her critical investigation of the reception of the practice of excision:

> The debate opposes two apparently conflicting versions of human rights, one based on the Enlightenment notion of the sovereign individual subject, and the other on a notion of a collective identity grounded in cultural solidarity.[28]

The pressure of ethnic customs and the ways in which such a practice as infibulation forms a part of a whole social system needs to be considered before using terms such as "barbaric mutilations." But even though the practice finds its raison d'être in a psychosexual context that sees excision as a beautifying and enriching phenomenon without which girls do not become women and wives, the cultural contexts in which this practice is embedded can be changed if we listen to the voices of girls and women who have felt the pain and humiliation in their bodies and souls. If native female voices are added to the debate, one which is not prejudiced by Western universalistic assumptions about the rights of women but nuanced and located within the social traditions under investigation, then a revision is possible in which women remain part of a specifically African system of values while health and well-being are increased for all men, women, and children.

However, we should also acknowledge the value of silence and understand its implications and consequences. Sometimes the issue is addressed but not openly, not explicitly, and we Western readers do not listen properly to these texts. It is necessary to reread many African texts for the significance of their silences, to be able to read across the omissions, the gaps, and the unheard voices for the implicit cultural information which is conveyed according by their specific narrative modes.

As Mieke Bal concludes in her book *Death and Dissymmetry*, "This mode of reading was part of a strategy. It was meant to enhance what usually passes unseen, to relativize what is usually emphasized. Focusing on characters rather than on storyline, on practices rather than on events, those motifs that in traditional commentary tend to be passed on as a part of the bargain became the central issue, *the bargain*" (1988: 231). Therefore the violence implied in the perpetration of ritual practices has to be made central and given voice, pushing the domestic, individual stories into the foreground beyond a political interest which uses violence to objectify female bodies.

The analysis of Hassan's text has been fuelled by the necessity to avoid the objectification and the victimization of infibulated women. The narrative strategies deployed are different and yet converge around the political goal of wording the experience of pain as a way of breaking free from the conspiracy of silence. With this target in mind the interests of the various streams of feminism can be considered as converging towards future transversal coalition politics, in which a horizontal mobilization of women helps to establish affiliation despite different backgrounds.

Hassan's text helps women escape from the weight of alienation and separation. Language plays a fundamental role in coming to terms with the self and with the other. It is therefore important to assess how women fight silencing within different cultures and in this regard a quotation by Maxine Hong Kingston's novel *The Woman Warrior* comes to mind:

> when we Chinese girls listened to the adults talking-story, we learned that we failed if we grew up to be but wives or slaves. We could be heroine, swordswomen. Even if she had to rage across all China, a swordswoman got even with anybody who hurt her family. Perhaps women were once so dangerous that they had to have their feet bound.[29]

The goal is to untie the tongue in order to retrace an identity that has never been lost and that persists in the new subject. This closing quotation encompasses all the paradoxical conditions that women writers in the diaspora have to face: at home in the world and yet burdened by invisible legacies of tradition and collective duty that tie them to past. The authors here discussed have learned how to appropriate and dismantle those tricks of belonging without choosing clearcut positions as they embrace the constant transformation of the self, a shifting of fixed categories, and a life of continual movement, both physically and critically. By reimagining language, identity, and location, the authors offer representations that, while never fully accomplished or totally graspable, envision and inspire many generations to come.

Chapter 10

Conclusion

Every voyage can be said to involve a re-siting of boundaries . . . an undetermined journeying practice.
> —Trinh T. Minh-ha, "Other than Myself/My Other Self," p. 9

POSTCOLONIAL JET LAGS

As Minh-ha reminds us, no journey has closure or a definite point of arrival.[1] The itinerary undertaken in this cultural voyage that is this book is aimed at opening up new routes of analysis without having the certainties of new methods or binding conclusions.

The venture into this journey has fulfilled a twofold requirement. First, it has reopened an important chapter of Italian history with all of its complicities and responsibilities—that of colonialism—a history marked by disavowal and denial. Second, it has explored the tension within postcolonialism that stems from a structure of totality and its parallel politics of fragmentation. Approached as a monolithic category, postcolonialism, in fact, fails "'to grasp the specificity' of the location or the moment," since the "discursive legacy of 'colonization/decolonization' is radically non-diachronic" (Frankenberg and Mani, 1996: 271–93).

These two predicaments have been merged in this comparative framework in which narratives of affiliation are grafted onto histories of difference. Drawing from different disciplinary fields including colonial history, English, Italian, and postcolonial literature, and using different parameters of analysis such as narratology, postcolonial theory, feminism, and cultural analysis, a set of questions around temporal asynchronies and spatial dislocations have been articulated and answered.

The representation of identity offered in novels by women writers of the diaspora is central since the specificity of postcolonial experience is inevitably

207

gender-encoded. The female version of this postcolonial paradigm has not as yet been sufficiently tackled from different perspectives. Here, diaspora has functioned as a trope to express conditions of dislocation and (post)colonial belatedness, which has brought two different streams of migrant literatures (the Indian and the Afro-Italian) under the same spectrum of analysis. Through this, a contact zone has been created for histories that until now have been separated and differentiated in time and space. Here in dialogue with each other they reveal an astonishing set of common concerns.

The journey undertaken has accomplished a double purpose. In the first place it legitimates a new corpus (Italian-language postcolonial women's writings) in a comparative frame, and it sets up new criteria by which it can be assessed and approached. It then examines the category of the "postcolonial" as an analytic and as a normative tool. The comparative perspective both calls and allows for this critical reappraisal.

The problems raised here have required new frames of analysis which touch upon the literary as much as the historical, cultural, and political background of the material. With this comparative approach it has become clear that the increasing marketability of the term postcolonial is not without its drawbacks. Postcolonialism runs the risk of becoming too entangled in its own formulations, thus jeopardizing its canon-breaking impact. It is, therefore, important to reinterpret and renovate the fully-fledged discourse of postcolonialism in the light of new agendas, such as the inclusion of the emerging Afro-Italian tradition, and thereby show its internal variances.

A PASSAGE TO INDIA OR *OUT OF AFRICA*?

Power differences are always situated and relational, and therefore what can be marginal and subaltern in some discourses becomes dominant and oppressive in others. The focus of this study has therefore been on dissymmetries, discordances, and obliquities in order to detect the scattering of hegemonies within the new relocations of culture.

Through this transversal reading, the points of conjunction among fields of studies that would never have otherwise entered into collision or dialogue, have been outlined. Reading the Afro-Italian literature within the postcolonial debate as "minor" in relation to the burgeoning Indian literature stakes out some crucial power relationships created by different colonial, linguistic, and market policies. The fruitful tension between these two areas has also allowed for the exploration of feminist concerns along different margins, establishing horizontal lines of solidarity and dislodging the persistence of the center/periphery model of power relation.

This dichotomy is one of the strongest paradoxes postcolonialism is faced with, since a discourse needs a center in order to enact alternative politics against it. Thus the phantom of "colonialism returns at the moment of its disappearance," as Anne McClintock writes (1995: 11). By reassembling the diversity and alterity of colonial realities under the rubric of European history, postcolonialism falls into the pitfall of flattening different temporalities and geographical specificities into the same postcolonial hyphenated formula. To loosen up the constraints that risk afflicting postcolonial studies, the overlooked Italian perspective has been inserted into the context of the more flamboyant aftermath of the British Empire. With its awareness of different temporal and migrant outcomes, this approach provides important postcolonial rereadings of many literary and cultural works, including films such as *A Passage to India* (David Lean: 1984) and *Out of Africa* (Sidney Pollack: 1985).

COMMON SKIES / DIVIDED HORIZONS

The strongest landmark within the postcolonial agenda is the presence of a paradox which comes to light when two different postcolonial conditions, a more canonized one versus a less established one, assume hierarchical positions in relation to each other—the first of an established literature and the second of a minority literature, as Deleuze and Guattari would phrase it.[2]

In order to highlight this dissymmetry, illustrative materials have been gathered including novels, autobiographies, memoirs, essays, and children's books—all of which have been drawn from two literatures that are very distinct as far as narrative strategies are concerned. As Rosi Braidotti argues in *Patterns of Dissonance* (1991), you need to have a strong identity before you can deconstruct it, and this is the stage reached by the Indian migran women writers, whereas the Afro-Italian women are still engaged in the shaping of an identity. Thanks to the fusion between post-structuralist techniques and the postcolonial political agenda, the Indian tradition has reached a sophisticated level of metadiscourse. Intellectuals such as Salman Rushdie, Meena Alexander, and Sara Suleri are writers and critics at the same time, joining primary and secondary literature in a creative and speculative way. Numerous Booker and Nobel Prizes confirm that the Anglo-Indian novel has introduced a very important chapter to English literature, and new labels such as "New Literatures in English" seem to recenter the discourse around the single rubric of British post-imperial literature.

Despite its undergoing a process of multiculturalization, the Italian-speaking literary world has a weaker definition of cultural identity, which is also the result of the greater historical fragility of the Italian nation-state. However, if the multiculturalization of Italy proceeds at the speed of the last decade, the Italian postcolonial tradition will become more influential, not only with respect to sociopolitical goals, but also in terms of its aesthetic and literary achievements, as shown in this book.

The themes addressed are for the main part unexplored or in some cases, underexposed and are not linked to other literature outside the Italian domain. The need persists to put the emerging Afro-Italian literature on the postcolonial agenda and to explore the issues that are addressed in these texts within an international framework. Here this new emergent body of literature has been explored in its double binding aspect: on the one hand, as a weaker example of cultural identity compared with the overpowering Anglo-Indian identity, and, on the other hand, as an empowering discourse that expresses marginal voices in the light of a global relocation of cultures.

"DISTANT VOICES, STILL LIVES"

The issues that have emerged from this study rotate around language, representation, and gendered identity magnified in the condition of diaspora.

Language is of paramount importance since it encodes power relations. This theme has run as a thread through the whole book but for each individual case language presents a different problem according to the different context.

Almost all the authors dealt with refer to the experience of maternity as unfolding the question of identity: "Who are you? Where do you come from? What identity do you have in your child's eyes?" These questions become pressing for a mother who tries to keep her past alive as she enters the new multicultural reality in which her sons and daughters will live. Motherhood becomes the threshold between the self and society, past and future, and it implies the denunciation of colonial negligence and the hope of a more equal and just civil society.

Another aspect that emerges from this comparative configuration is that no matter how empowered women are or how much a part of a dominant discourse they might be (English versus Italian), they still undergo forms of oppression that need to be addressed and exposed. These oppressions range from the more sporadic phenomenon of *sati* in India to the more blatant widespread practice of sexual mutilation of the female in African regions.

Other aspects of convergence can be detected from a close analysis of the novels. For example, Bharati Mukherjee's belief in fluid identities is not far from Ribka Sibhatu's playful notion of identity that constantly shifts between nations, languages and histories. Sibhatu's children's book—about an Eritrean girl turning refugee—echoes Mukherjee's fairy tale of a self-made Indian girl who swaps the gender/caste/religious restrictions of India for the American dream. Both these female bildungsromans deal with diaspora, ethnicity, and assimilation in a complex, daringly optimistic way. Both texts sketch the transition from a specific peripheral colonial condition towards transnational multicultural realities.

Similar aspects are revealed in Sara Suleri's sophisticated analysis of the role of gender in the construction of the nation. Her hybrid nature (Welsh-Pakistani) highlights a postcolonial gendered identity that is shaped by different positionalities. Erminia Dell'Oro's *métisse* children (Eritrean-Italian) also challenge the authority of national and ethnic straightjackets. These positions provide a parallel to Maria Abbebú Viarengo's tortured treasuring of her double parental lineage (Oromo-Piedmontese); yet these writers are profoundly different in conveying the fragmented notion of self, ethnicity, and belonging.

Gupta's challenge of the "secondary position" to which Indian women are relegated, especially within mythology, is not far from the dilemma described by Sirad S. Hassan concerning the practice of female infibulation, a sacred taboo not easily called into question. Mythology may often demonize women and put them in a subservient position, but practices such as infibulation and circumcision physically mutilate and literally prevent women from being masters of their own destiny. Similar issues are tackled by Meena Alexander, whose postcolonial gendered identity is "cracked by multiple migrations," as she writes in her memoir. From her work we gather that things constantly fall apart when a woman's identity is made up of the jarring, jolting, and tossing of mutilated parts. This book deals with the representation of diasporic women in a global world and thus expressly intertwines material issues with fictional ones. As Stuart Hall writes,

> Representation is the production of the meaning of the concepts in our mind through language. It is the link between concepts and language which enables us to refer to either the "real" world of objects, people or events, or indeed to imaginary worlds of fictional; objects, people and events.[3]

Representation is therefore a key notion for interpreting a wide array of texts in which gender, ethnicity, and diaspora figure as touchstones for unleashing the ideological frame of the present world order. As Hall writes, since words and images are nether neutral or innocent, they must be read and interpreted with careful discrimination. The position of the producer or artist is as important as that of the reader or beholder. Between the two fronts a complex web of meanings are produced and circulated. To establish an intertextual reading among the authors themselves and between the authors and their possible readers means tracking down possible itineraries, none of which is exhaustive and exclusive.

A MAP FOR GETTING LOST

The map concerns the establishment of a horizontal mobilization of women where similar problems are dealt with from different angles and with different outcomes and where separate histories suddenly become entangled, be it the condition of exile, migration, diaspora, or cosmopolitanism. The different reasons for choosing expatriation highlight the fact that personal itineraries are grounded in specific political and economic realities, and even though writers such as Bharati Mukherjee and Ribka Sibhatu are postcolonial subjects living abroad, they are not postcolonial in the same way. Thus a complex temporal and spatial repositioning must be occur in order to validate a "feminist post-colonial conjuncturalist reading of the term post-colonial" (Frankenberg and Mani, 1996: 292).

For example, having the status of refugee does not bestow the same privileges as belonging to a migrant intelligentsia, as in the case of South Asian women writers. Most writers from Africa are clearly from a less stable and favorable background. Hunger, civil war, violence, and escape from Africa have all given their writings a very different hue from that of writers from India. India still has internal religious and regional unrest and has yet to solve problems such as illiteracy, the oppression of women, and poverty, but it is nonetheless a country that has experimented in democracy over the past fifty years.

But not all writers from India are privileged or part of a cosmopolitan jet set, contrary to what the works of Sara Suleri and Bharati Mukherjee would suggest. The female writers who have been selected for the Indian part of this book have not been selected because they are members of an élite but because of their remarkable literary achievements and their important contribution to the debate on diasporic identity. The diasporic debate has until now been mainly dominated by male voices, such as those of Salman Rushdie, Rohinton Mistry, Vikram Seth, and Michael Ondaatje, to mention but a few.

But what is the point of this continuous relocation of dominant versus subaltern voices within the discourse of postcolonialism? The aim has been to open up postcolonialism as a global category not only by showing its internal differences, but also by showing that everywhere identities are emerging, identities that are not fixed but are in transition, drawing on different cultural traditions all at the same time. It may be tempting to think of identity as destined to end up in one place or another—either returning to its roots or disappearing through partial assimilation—but this temptation must be resisted, particularly with regard to diasporic writings since they are engaged with a continuous re-siting of boundaries between nativist traditionalism and metropolitan assimilation.

This rapidly changing world can only be assessed by acknowledging the multiplications of power differences, of hegemonic centers and of linguistic resources. This scattering has been addressed by the Italian philosopher Gianni

Vattimo (1988) as *pensiero debole* (weak thought or weak ontology). Through the contact between high and low, dominant and subaltern, canonized and radical, a new order comes into being in which extremities are blunted and perspectives are multiplied. As these narrative excursions have illustrated, diaspora offers the possibility of charting new maps of identity that are formed at the intersections of different power relations, national boundaries, and cultural belonging, multiplying the visions from the edges and from the center and unlocking their opposition to each other.

THINKING BEYOND THE ENDING

This book has offered a contribution to the revitalization of the contentious postcolonial field by opening up new perspectives and by offering new challenges. Despite its many ramifications, postcolonialism is inadequate for addressing the proliferations of more specifically located cultural, social, and political histories, and for rendering internal histories of subordination. New trajectories of analysis have been sketched that aim to assess narratives that are becoming increasingly global. Is there a trasnational literature? Could there ever again be such an all-encompassing category that would revive the pleasure of grand humanism but would reinstall the danger of universalism? How far can we go with assessing difference while claiming the right to global visibility? Is the new global marketplace a positive arena for endangered languages, literatures, and minorities or, on the contrary, a more complex and devious form of neocolonization that celebrates some "selected representative differences" while erasing the possibility for other uncompromising alternative voices? These questions are complex and require highly positioned and contextualized answers. No clear-cut truths or easy solutions are available as we constantly problematize the categories we use to plan a future that is more comforting and inclusive.

In short, this book is a cautionary tale: both feminism and postcolonialism have to be wary of embracing monolithic approaches. They must try instead to establish common politics that can cut across ethnicities, classes, and culture. At the same time an irresponsible defense of origins and local interests at all costs can be to the detriment of women, alienating them from the larger dynamics of restructuring power. This comparative study traces a new trajectory described by Nira Yuval-Davies (1997) where feminists embrace transversal coalition politics. This is particularly urgent in an era when fragmentation, factionalism, and fundamentalism risk driving women apart. It is, therefore, important to describe new axes of connection and negotiate common sites of resistance while all the time keeping in mind the specific socioeconomic variables that produce differences. Identity is, after all, more than a position in language.

This strategy calls for the revision and intersection of various discourses. Several issues have been covered: first, the search for new categories suitable for assessing the emerging Italian multicultural literature; second, the renewal of the postcolonial debate that deals with the specific processes of multiculturalisation; and third, the development of a comparativism in which literatures of different traditions, outside the European fortress, can speak together and for which the rhizomatic aspect of cultural identity described by Deleuze is valuable. This comparative approach can also be extended to the various processes of multiculturalization that are taking place in other minor postcolonial languages, such as Portuguese and Dutch.

This book leaves its own journey unfinished as it opens out to new expansion, or rather explosion. It is perhaps fitting to think of the useful lesson of postcolonialism as being a "big bang" that brings forth radical and more innovative ways of thinking and reading that lead to new horizons.

Notes

INTRODUCTION

1. Avtar Brah, *Cartographies of Diaspora: Contesting Identities*, 1996, p. 208.

2. Italo Calvino, *Invisible Cities*, 1979, p. 125.

CHAPTER 1. TOUCHSTONES

1. Francophone literature, postcolonial literature from French-speaking areas, has also achieved a remarkable presence within French departments.

2. See Gauri Viswanathan, *Masks of Conquest: Literary Study and British Rule in India*, 1989. In this text the author examines the history of English literature instruction in India and the process by which English studies became an instrument of political control. It rests on the assumption that the use of literary works was put to the service of British imperialism.

3. Salman Rushdie, *Imaginary Homelands*, 1980, pp. 61–70. Rushdie criticizes the term for artificially joining writers of disparate origins and aesthetic principles. To quote Rushdie, "By now 'Commonwealth Literature' was sounding very unlikeable indeed. Not only was it a ghetto, but it was actually an exclusive ghetto. And the effect of creating such a ghetto was, is, to change the meaning of the far broader term 'English literature'—which I'd always taken to mean simply the literature of the English language—into something far narrower, something topographical, nationalistic, possibly even racially segregationist" (p. 63).

4. Naipaul represents one of the first resounding postcolonial answers. In his novels and critical travelogues he intertwines questions of personal displacement with cultural and political analyses of the various countries visited, particularly India, his ancestral land.

5. He is obviously part of a wider tradition of "displaced" Caribbean writers including George Lamming, E. R. Brathwaite, Derek Walcott, Jamaica Kincaid, and Michelle Cliff.

6. See Sandra Ponzanesi, "Diasporic Subjects and Migration," in *Thinking Differently. A Reader in European Women's Studies*, Gabriele Griffin and Rosi Braidotti (eds.), 2002, pp. 205–20.

7. Stuart Hall, "When Was the 'Post-colonial'?" 1996, pp. 242–61: 249.

8. Ella Shohat, "Notes on the Post-colonial," 1998, pp. 99–113: 101.

9. The term *postcolonial* differs from *Third World*; the first matter is political, the second linked to capital division. See Spivak, "Can the Subaltern Speak?" 1988a.

10. Gyan Prakash, "Who is Afraid of Post-coloniality?" 1996, p. 188.

11. Sara Suleri, *Meatless Days*, p. 105.

12. Arif Dirlik. In Stuart Hall, "When Was the 'Post-colonial'?" in Iain Chamber and Lidia Curti (eds.), *Post-Colonial Question: Common Skies, Divided Horizons*, 1996, pp. 242–60: 243.

13. Ibid., p. 246.

14. Ibid., p. 243.

15. Stuart Hall, "When Was the 'Post-Colonial'?" 1996, p. 245.

16. Deleuze makes a distinction between the longer, molecular time of becoming (*aion*) and the continuous sense of recorded time (*chronos*) as explained in Braidotti, *Nomadic Subjects*, 1994, p. 120.

17. Fredric Jameson, *Postmodernism, or the Cultural Logic of Late Capitalism*, 1991, p. 154.

18. The word *diaspora* is derived from the Greek verb *speiro* (to sow) and the preposition *dia* (over).

19. For a thorough exposition of social and cultural diasporas through the ages, see Robin Cohen, *Global Diasporas*, 1997.

20. See Paul Gilroy, "Cultural Studies and Ethnic Absolutism," 1992, pp. 187–98.

21. During an African conference a South African writer, Lewis Nkosi, replied to Thiong'o in Zulu, a language Thiong'o could not understand. This provocative mode revealed the ironic ideological effect of Thiong'o's Marxist strategy of using the vernacular, which was to estrange the writing from the needs of the real people. English and French remain therefore, despite all odds, necessary to establish connections among the several African countries, which have different national and ethnic languages.

22. Michael Gardiner, *The Dialogics of Critique: M. M. Bakhtin and the Theory of Ideology*, 1992, p. 186.

23. Wole Soyinka (1986), Derek Walcott (1992) and V. S. Naipaul (2001)—Nobel Prize for Literature; Salman Rushdie (1981), Keri Hulme (1985), Ben Okri (1991), Michael Ondaatje (1992), and Arundhati Roy (1997)—Booker Prize; Nuruddin Farah

(1998) and David Malouf (2000)—Neustadt Prize for Literature; Jumpa Lahiri (2000)—Pulitzer Prize; and many others.

24. See Graham Huggan, *The Postcolonial Exotic: Marketing the Margins*, 2001; and Richard Todd, *Consuming Fictions: The Booker Prize and Fiction in Britain Today*, 1996; and Luke Strongman, *The Booker Prize and the Legacy of Empire*, 2002.

25. See Bill Ashcroft, Gareth Griffith, and Helen Tiffin (eds.), *The Empire Writes Back*, 1989.

26. Gilles Deleuze and Félix Guattari, *Kafka: Toward a Minor Literature*, 1986.

27. Stuart Hall, "When Was the 'Post-Colonial'?" 1996, p. 244

28. Gayatri C. Spivak, "The Politics of Translation," in *Outside in the Teaching Machine*, 1993, p. 189.

29. Homi K. Bhabha, "The Post-colonial and the Postmodern," in *The Location of Culture*, 1994, p. 172.

30. Chandra Talpade Mohanty, "Feminist Encounters: Locating the Politics of Experience," 1987, p. 31.

31. Ruth Frankenberg and Lata Mani, "Crosscurrents, Crosstalk," 1996, p. 292.

32. Gyan Prakash, "Who is Afraid of Post-coloniality?" 1996, p. 199.

33. Teresa de Lauretis, "Feminist Studies, Cultural Studies: Issues, Terms and Contexts," in idem (ed.), *Feminist Studies/Critical Studies*, 1986, p. 8.

34. Charles Bernheimer (ed.), *Comparative Literature in the Age of Multiculturalism*, 1995, p. 8.

35. Gates in Charles Bernheimer, p. 9.

36. Ibid., p. 9.

37. Ibid., p. 9.

38. Mohanty and Rutherford cited in Smadar Lavie and Ted Swedenburg, *Displacement, Diaspora and Geographies of Identity*, 1996, p. 4.

CHAPTER 2. THE EXUBERANCE OF IMMIGRATION

1. Michael Connell, Jessie Grearson and Tom Grimes, "An Interview with Bharati Mukherjee," *Iowa Review* 20.3 (1999): 26–27.

2. In *Harper Bazar*, 1990.

3. V. S. Naipaul, *The Overcrowded Barracoon*, 1976, pp. 30–31; first published by André Deutsch, 1972.

4. Naipaul, *The Overcrowded Barracoon*, 1976, p. 24. A different, but connected issue on language and imposition of landscape stereotypes has been widely debated by the French speaking Martinican critic and writer Aimé Césaire who worked for the cultural and artistic decolonization of the Caribbean by editing a journal with René Menil, *Tropiques: Revue Culturelle* (1941–1945), and by publishing other important works such as *Discours sur le Colonialisme* (1955). In the article "Aimé Césaire's Subjective Geographies: Translating Place and the Difference it Makes" Indira Karamcheti refers to Suzanne Césaire's manifesto for Martinican poetry. In an issue of *Tropiques* Suzanne Césaire criticized the colonial's complicity with Martinican literatures for its use of exoticization and stereotypical tropicalism (paradoxically enough for a journal called *Tropiques*), calling it "Literature of the hammock, literature of sugar and vanilla. Tourism literature. . . . The hell with hibiscus, frangipani, bougainvillea. Martinican poetry will be cannibal or will not be." Choosing hibiscus, frangipani, and bougainvillea as metonyms for exoticism, both Aimé and Suzanne Césaire emblematically represent the problematic, also explored by V. S. Naipaul, of translating a place such as the Caribbean with the language inherited from the colonizer. In *Between Languages and Culture: Translation and Cross-Cultural texts*, Anuradha Dingwaney and Carol Maier (eds), 1995, pp. 181–97: 181.

5. In *Harper Bazar*, 1990.

6. Malashri Lal, *The Law of the Threshold,* 1995. In her chapter on Bharati Mukherjee Lal discusses the subject of the threshold in Mukherjee as a 'timely example of how far the Indian woman's periphery may be extended beyond her home' (p. 145) to the point of downgrading her Indian heritage and affiliations strenuously emphasizing her American citizenship and illustrating the credo of immigrant writing as a 'maximalist' act.

7. Mukherjee, in Timothy Brennen, *Salman Rushdie and the Third World: Myths of the Nation*, 1989, p. 33.

8. See the already mentioned Malashri Lal from the University of Delhi.

9. For further illustration, see Sandra Ponzanesi, "Marginalia: Rearticulating Subaltern Studies Across System Divisions," *Thamyris* 5.1 (Spring 1998): 170–75, which is a review of the important text edited by T. V. Sathyamurthy, *Region, Religion, Caste, Gender and Culture in Contemporary India*, 1996, and a detailed account of India's separatist movements.

10. Elizabeth Bronfen, "A Sense of Strangeness: The Gender and Cultural Identity in Bharati Mukherjee's *Jasmine*," *Baetyl* 2 (1990): 79.

11. Susan Koshy, "The Geography of Female Subjectivity. Ethnicity, Gender, and Diaspora," *Diaspora* 3.1 (1994): 69.

12. Quoted in Michael Connel, Jessie Grearson, and Tom Grimes, "An Interview with Bharati Mukherjee," *Iowa Review* 20.3 (1990) 7–32.

13. Koshy, 1994, p. 76.

14. Ibid., p. 78.

15. In David Theo Goldberg, *Multiculturalism: A Critical Reader*, 1994, pp. 45–74.

CHAPTER 3. THE SHOCK OF ARRIVAL

1. Meena Alexander, *The Shock of Arrival*, 1996, p. 3.

2. See Rosi Braidotti, *Nomadic Subjects: Embodiment and Sexual Difference in Contemporary Feminist Theory*, 1994, pp. 120–21.

3. Manjushree S. Kumar, "Journey Through Time: Meena Alexander's *Fault Lines*," 1995, p. 217.

4. Bella Brodszki and Celeste Schenck (eds.), *Life/Lines*, 1988, p. 14.

5. Ibid., p. 5.

6. For a general overview of the autobiographical genre in relation to feminist questions, see: Barbara Harlow, *Resistant Literature*, 1987; Sidonie Smith, *A Poetics of Women's Autobiography: Marginality and the Fiction of Self-Representation*, 1987; Shari Benstock (ed.), *The Private Self*, 1988; Bella Brodszki and Celeste Schenck (eds.), *Life/Lines: Theorizing Women's Autobiography*, 1988; Françoise Lionnet, *Autobiographical Voices. Race, Gender, Self-Portraiture*, 1989a; Sidonie Smith and Julia Watson (eds.), *De/Colonizing the Subject: The Politics of Gender in Women's Autobiography*, 1992; Liz Stanley, *The Autobiographical "I": Theory and Practice of Women's Autobiographical Writings*, 1992; Sidonie Smith, *Subjectivity, Identity, and the Body: Women's Autobiographical Practices in the Twentieth Century*, 1993; Leigh Gilmore, *Autobiographics: A Feminist Theory of Women's Representation*, 1994; Lynn Broughton and Linda Anderson (eds.), *Women's Lives/Women's Times: New Essays on Auto/Biography*, 1997.

7. Caren Kaplan, "Resisting Autobiography: Outlaw Genres and Transnational Feminist Subjects," in Sidonie Smith and Julia Watson (eds.), *De/Colonizing the Subject. The Politics of Gender in Women's Autobiography*, 1992, p. 119.

8. Nira Yuval-Davies, *Gender and Nations*, 1997, p. 120.

9. Salman Rushdie, *Imaginary Homelands*, 1981, p. 12.

CHAPTER 4. ALIENATION AND NARRATION

1. The birth of Pakistan, which in Urdu means "land of the pure," is simultaneous with the declaration of Indian independence from the British regime. The solution to the Muslims' demand for a separate state was opposed by the Mahatma until the end, whereas it was considered inevitable by Mountbatten, Nehru, and Jinnah who struggled for the transformation of the Muslims' minority status within India into a political self-determining state. The moment of Partition, which celebrates this historical happening, was marked by diaspora, exile, and violence. Many families were suddenly made

refugees, finding themselves on the wrong side of the freshly sketched border. The birth of Pakistan is, therefore, marked by a history of dislocation and uprooting. Gandhi was consequently assassinated in 1949 by a Hindu. Suleri writes, "When in 1947 Mountbatten's scissors clipped at the map of India and handed over what Jinnah fastidiously called a moth-eaten Pakistan (we had been unrealistically hungry for the whole of the North, and Delhi too, I think), the more energic Muslims of the subcontinent winced to see that they could push and push at their cuticles, only to discover meager half-moons" (p. 74). For more historical background, see Romila Thapar, *A History of India,* 1990; Burton Stein, *A History of India*, 1998; Urvashi Butalia, *The Other Side of Silence: Voices from the Partition of India*, 2000.

2. The following is Jinnah's speech to the crowd, as reported in *Meatless Days*, after the constitution of a separate Muslim state: "It has always been taken for granted that the Mussalmans are a minority, and we have got used to it for such a long time that these settled notions sometimes are very difficult to remove," (p. 114).

3. Suleri, *The Rhetoric of English India*, 1992, p. 15.

4. Oliver Lovesey, "'Post-colonial Self-Fashioning' in Sara Suleri's *Meatless Days*," 1997, p. 47.

5. There are many definitions of postmodernism. Here McHale's classification of how postmodern narratives are usually conveyed in opposition to features of modernism is briefly reviewed. Defining modernism as period A and postmodernism as period B, he lists the following schematic distinctions:

Modernism:	*Postmodernism:*
Hierarchy	Anarchy
Presence	Absence
Genital	Polymorphous
Narrative	Anti-narrative
Metaphysics	Irony
Determinacy	Indeterminacy
Construction of a World-model	Deconstruction of a World-model
Ontological certainty	Ontological uncertainty

Postmodernism concentrates therefore on the ontological uncertainties in which the search for truth is replaced by a sense of provisionality and reality assumes a constructivist character according to linguistic patterns. However, McHale points out the importance of postmodernism not in its opposition to but in its continuity and transformation of modernism. Brian McHale, *Constructing Postmodernism*, 1992, pp. 7–8. See also Hans Bertens, *The Idea of the Postmodern,* 1995.

6. Julia Kristeva, "Women's Time," 1986, p. 192.

7. Susan Koshy, "Mother-Country and Fatherland.: Re-membering the Nation in Sara Suleri's *Meatless Days*," 1997, pp. 45–46.

8. For the challenge of feminism as a foreign ideology imposed in Third World countries, see Kumari Jayawardena's study, *Feminism and Nationalism in the Third*

World, 1986. In this text Jayawardena demonstrates how women in many Third World countries have been active in the movement for national liberation and socialism, independently from Western indoctrination: "In the West, too, there is a Eurocentric view that the movement for women's liberation is not indigenous to Asia or Africa, but has been a purely West European and North American phenomenon, and that where movements for women's emancipation or feminist struggles have arisen in the Third World, they have been merely imitative of Western models" (p. 2). By analyzing the history and the participation of women's organizations in the making of the national identity in many countries of the Middle East and Asia from the late nineteenth century onwards, Jayawardena shows how feminist consciousness and the concept of women's activism were developed specifically within the reality of those societies. She makes a distinction between the use of the words *feminism* and *feminist*, which are considered to be rooted in the Western society of the nineteenth and twentieth century, even though an awareness of women's oppression which was very present in those centuries and before in other parts of the world. Much of the feminist consciousness was linked in the Third World with the struggle for national independence. Jayawardena states therefore that "feminism was not imposed on the Third World by the West, but rather that historical circumstances produced important material and ideological changes that affected women, even though the impact of imperialism and Western thought was admittedly among the significant elements in the historical circumstances" (p. 2).

9. Chandra Talpade Mohanty, "Under Western Eyes: Feminist Scholarship and Colonial Discourse," 1991, p. 67.

10. Gayatri C. Spivak, *In Other Worlds: Essay in Cultural Politics*, 1988, p. 150.

11. Sara Suleri, "Woman Skin Deep: Feminism and the Postcolonical Condition," 1995, p. 137.

12. In "Woman Skin Deep" Suleri states:

> While current feminist discourse remains vexed by questions of identity formation and the concomitant debates between essentialism and constructivism, or distinction between situated and universal knowledge, it is still prepared to grant an uneasy selfhood to a voice that is best described as the property of 'post-colonial woman.' Whether this voice represents perspectives as divergent as the African-American or the post-colonial cultural location, its imbrications of race and gender are accorded an iconicity that is altogether too good to be true. Even though the marriage of two margins should not necessarily lead to the construction of that contradiction in terms, a "feminist center," the embarrassed privilege granted to racially encoded feminism does indeed suggest a rectitude that could be its own theoretical undoing. The concept of the post-colonial itself is too frequently robbed of historical specificity in order to function as a preapproved allegory for any mode of discursive contestation. The coupling of *post-colonial* with *woman*, however, almost inevitably leads to the simplicities that underlie unthinking celebrations of oppression, elevating the racially female voice into a metaphor for the "good". (pp. 135–36)

13. The Hudood ordinances were enforced by General Mohamed Zia-ul-Haq. They added five new criminal laws to the existent legal system. The second ordinance, Zina (adultery or fornification), is of particular importance since the addition concerns the rule of evidence according to which a woman's testimony is worth half of a man's. If a woman is raped and there is no evidence of eyewitnessing by four Muslim males, then rape turns easily into *Zina*. Women, even children, can now be accused for having been raped; laws of mutual consent may easily convert a case of child abuse into a prosecution of the child for *Zina*, for fornication.

14. Inderpal Grewal writes that Suleri's representation of women as heterogeneous and powerful agents, which is in line with her predicament of poststructuralist thought, has almost no connection with the feminist oppositional practices to resist patriarchal order and that there is little belief in feminism of any kind except for a strong concern for how women live with each other within and outside families. Suleri conveys her desire to dissociate herself from the Anglo-American analytic models of feminist subject by escaping classifications and creating an exemplary text of postmodernism that rejects the unitary subject and delineates a diasporic, multiple subjectivity. However, Grewal concludes, "Suleri's text does not address the complicated nature of feminist practices that are demanded by the positionings of post-colonial female subjects in various locations." For Grewal, Suleri's text does not enable any practices of feminist resistance. Inderpal Grewal, "Autobiographic Subjects and Diasporic Locations: *Meatless Days* and *Borderlands*," 1994, p. 242.

15. Sangeeta Ray observes in her article that even if Suleri's text makes us reflect on too easy ideological categories, she does not pay enough attention to the particular intersections of different social spaces that pluralists make us believe have equal value. Addressing Mohanty, Ray concludes that simple plurality will not facilitate a genuine dialogue between the spaces if the modalities that characterize territorial affiliations are not deterritorialized. This is necessary to celebrate the contingent nature of cultural identities within the margins. Sangeeta Ray, "Memory, Identity, Patriarchy: Projecting a Past in the Memoirs of Sara Suleri and Michael Ondaatje," 1993.

16. Daniel Wolfe wrote in his review of *Meatless Days* that "Sara Suleri expertly paces out the boundaries of her subject without giving the reader the pleasure of getting inside" ("Talking Two Mother Tongues," *New York Times Book Review* 4 June 1989, p. 30).

17. Judith Woolf, "Silent Witness," 1997, p. 211.

18. Ibid., p. 206.

19. Benedict Anderson, *Imagined Communities*, 1983, p. 4.

20. For Benedict Anderson the nation is imagined as *limited*. This means that it has finished even if elastic boundaries since beyond it lie other nations. It is imagined as *sovereign* because the concept was born in an age in which Enlightenment and Revolution were destroying the legitimacy of the divinely ordained, hierarchical realms. Even

in a period when the nation was confronted with pluralism of religions, it is free from any divine superstructure. *Imagined Communities*, 1983, p. 6.

21. See Anne McClintock, "'No Longer in a Future Heaven': Gender, Race and Nationalism," 1997, pp. 89–112.

22. Timothy Brennan, "The National Longing for Form," 1990, p. 52.

23. Homi K. Bhabha, *The Location of Culture*, 1994, p. 2.

24. Nira Yuval-Davies, *Gender and Nation*, 1997, p. 2. In *Women-Nation-state*, 1989, Nira Yuval-Davies and Floya Anthias (eds) indicate five major ways in which women are implicated in nationalism:

1. as biological reproducer of the members of national collectivities;
2. as reproducers of the boundaries of national groups (through a restriction of sexual and marital relations);
3. as active transmitters and producers of the national culture;
4. as symbolic signifiers of national difference;
5. as active participants in national struggles.

25. Anne McClintock, "No Longer in a Future Heaven," 1997, p. 91.

26. Homi K. Bhabha, "Dissemination," 1994, p. 150.

CHAPTER 5. FLOATING MYTHS

1. Sunetra Gupta, *Memories of Rain* (London: Orion, 1992); *The Glassblower's Breath* (London: Orion, 1993); *Moonlight into Marzipan* (London: Phoenix House, 1995); *A Sin of Colour* (London: Phoenix House 1999).

2. Claire Messud criticized Gupta in her review for her "latinate words, convoluted complexities and paragraph-long, ill-punctuated sentences." She claims that this style should not be misleadingly interpreted as poetic writing, since unlike Virginia Woolf, Gupta does not manage to grasp the inner working of minds and moments "with pretentious, rococo descriptions of banal details" ["No Skull beneath the Skin," *The Guardian*, 29.6 (1993): 13].

3. Georges Gusdorf, "Conditions and Limits of Autobiography," in James Olney (ed.), *Autobiography: Essays Theoretical and Critical* (Princeton: Princeton University Press, 1980), p. 29.

4. Madhava Prasad, "On the Question of a Theory of (Third) World Literature," 1997, p. 143

5. Teresa de Lauretis, *Alice Doesn't: Feminism, Semiotics, Cinema*, 1984, pp. 118, 119.

6. Colin Falck, *Myth, Truth and Literature: Towards a true Post-modernism*, 1989, p. 150.

CHAPTER 6. A SHORT STORY ABOUT
THE ITALIAN EMPIRE

1. See Frances Gouda, *Dutch Culture Overseas: Colonial Practice in the Netherlands Indies 1900–1940*, 1995.

2. See Patrick Chabal, with Moema Parents, et al, *The Postcolonial Literature of Lusophone Africa*, 1996.

3. See Yemane Mesghenna, *Italian Colonialism. A Case Study of Eritrea, 1869–1934: Motive, Praxis, and Result*, 1988.

4. Robert Young, "Colonialism and the Desiring-Machine," 1994, p. 16.

5. Centro Furio Jesis (ed.), *La Menzogna della Razza*, 1994; Barbara Sorgoni, *Parole e Corpi: Antropologia, Discorso Giuridico e Politiche Sessuali Interrazziali nella Colonia Eritrea (1890–1941)*, 1998; Alberto Burgio (ed.), *Nel Nome della Razza: Il Razzismo nella Storia D'Italia 1870–1945*, 1999.

6. For a more thorough background on Italian Colonialism, see also the following texts: G. Rochat, *Il Colonialismo Italiano: Documenti*, 1974; Angelo del Boca, *Gli Italiani in Africa Orientale: La Conquista dell'Impero*, vol. 1–4, 1979; John Markakis, *National and Class Conflict in the Horn of Africa*, 1987; Tekeste Negash, *Italian Colonialism in Eritrea, 1882–1941: Policies, Praxis, and Impact*, 1987; John Markakis, *Nationalities and the State of Ethiopia*, 1989; Roy Pateman, *Eritrea: Even the Stones Are Burning*, 1990; Gianpaolo Calchi Novati, *Il Corno D'Africa nella Storia e nella Politica. Etiopia, Somalia e Eritrea fra Nazionalismi: Sottosviluppo e Guerra*, 1994; Nicola Labanca, *Oltremare: Storia dell'Espansione Coloniale Italiana*, 2002.

7. During the fascist regime cinema was considered a powerful weapon of propaganda and persuasion. In 1924, a special center for the production of documentaries was created in Rome (Istituto Luce). Many documentaries were made as propaganda for *le gesta d'oltremare* (the colonial expansion). Mario Camerini's *Kiff Tebbi* (1928) celebrated the conquest of Libya in 1912, and *Lo Squadrone Bianco* by Augusto Genina (1936) also celebrated the heroic gestures of the Italian soldiers against the Libya rebels of the deserts. Augusto Genina also made *Bengasi* (1942), which narrates the occupation of Bengasi by the British army. Another kind of film, such as Guido Brignone's *Sotto La Croce del Sud* (1937), focused on the rhetoric against *métissage* and considered the racial degeneration brought about the encounter between Italian man and local women. Numerous are the filmic representations of the battle of El-Alamein, which took place in 1942 in Libya. These refer to the position of an Italian battalion in the *settore sud* of the Libyc desert where the climatic and logistic conditions were intolerable, where many minefields made advancement impossible, where provisions never arrived, and, most important, where no news arrived about the fate of the Italo-German army under Rommel in the north as it fought against the British under Montgomery. The whole battalion was annihilated in the desert after a confrontation with the British army. The first film, *El-Alamein* (1957) by Guido Malatesta, has been followed by *La Battaglia di El-Alamein* (1968) by Giorgio Ferroni and by the more recent *El-Alamein: La Linea del Fuoco* (2002) directed by Enzo Monteleone. The bombastic fascist rhetoric present in the first

two films is replaced in *La Linea del Fuoco* by a subtle pyschological tone among the soldiers, who narrate stories in which glory consists more of loyalty to companions than to the fatherland. *La Linea del Fuoco* has more of the literary undertone of Buzzati's *Deserto dei Tartari* than the realism of a war film. *El-Alamein* presents strong characters and beautiful images of the desert. The film came out with *I Ragazzi di El-Alamein*, which, sixty years after the battle, collects interviews with the survivors. *El-Alamein* reveals a very different picture from the official version of the period. Another postcolonial response to the fascist representations comes from the epic *Lion of The Desert* (1981), which portrays the heroic gestures of the famous Libyc leader Omar Mukhtar, the Arab hero and guerilla fighter who for twenty years coordinated the rebellion against Benito Mussolini. The film, directed by Moustapha Akkad, has a dazzling international cast, including Anthony Quinn as Omar Mukhtar, along with John Gielgud, Oliver Reed, and Rod Steiger. The film was financed with a stellar budget by the Libyan dictator Muammar Qaddafi. See James Hay, *Popular Film Culture in Fascist Italy: The Passing of the Rex,* 1987; Gianpiero Brunetta, *L 'Ora D'Africa del Cinema Italiano,* 1990; Jacqueline Reich and Piero Garofalo (eds.), *Reviewing Fascism: Italian Cinema, 1922–1943,* 2002.

8. The historical background of colonial India has been overlooked here not because it is not important for the understanding of the literature of the Indian diaspora, but because it is not directly relevant to this comparative study, which focuses on the undermining of the British-India axis within postcolonial studies. There is, obviously, an enormous scholarly literature on the topic. Here are a few examples: Bernard Cohen, *Colonialism and Its Forms of Knowledge: The British in India,* 1996; Matthew Edney, *Mapping and Empire: The Geographical Construction of British India, 1765–1843,* 1997; Margaret MacMillan, *Women of the Raj,* 1988; Romila Thapar, *A History of India,* 1990; Burton Stein, *A History of India,* 1998.

9. In Italian cultural memory this event is associated with Verdi's opera *Aida* (1871). Edward Said attempted to read this opera as a product of Europe's developing imperialist culture. However, as Paul Robinson argued, the music itself was far from the orientalist modes that characterized French composition. Moreover, the content of the opera composed by Italy's most strenuous defender of the Risorgimento ideals (the liberation of Italy from foreign domination) is very sympathetic to the Ethiopians (represented by the figure of Aida) who struggle against the supremacy of the Egyptians (which is an allegory for the Italian Risorgimento and its resistance to the Hapsburgs). See Paul Robinson, "Is Aida an Orientalist Opera?" in *Revisioning Italy,* pp. 156–66.

10. The defeat of Adwa constitutes a national stigma. Various historical studies have described the impact of the event on the national prestige and have read the War of Ethiopia in 1935 as partly motivated by a desire to avenge the Italian defeat of 1896. See Nicola Labanca, *In Marcia Verso Adua,* 1993. An interesting note is the film in Ahmaric made by the leading Ethiopian director Haile Gerima, *Adwa: An African Victory* (1999), which was presented at the Fifty-Sixth Mostra Internazionale di Arte Cinematografica (Venice Film Festival 1999) in the section "Nuovi Territory." The film chronicles the epic Battle of Adwa of 1896, in which the Ethiopians defeated an invading Italian army against great odds. An ancient, historic city nestled in mountainous northern Ethiopia, Adwa was saved by the leadership of King Menelik, who disproved

Italian claims that Africans were inferior and easily subjugated. The Battle of Adwa became a source of national pride for Ethiopians and an important symbol of anticolonial resistance for all Africans.

11. Robert Young writes, "Clearly the ideology and procedures of French colonialism, based on an egalitarian enlightenment assumption of the fundamental sameness of all human beings and the unity of the human race, and therefore designed to assimilate colonial people to French civilization, differed very substantially from the indirect-rule policies of the British which were based on an assumption of difference and of inequality, or from those of the Germans and Portuguese" (*Colonial Desire*, 1995, p. 164).

12. Aldobrandino Malvezzi, *La Politica Indigena Nelle Colonie*, 1933, p. 236.

13. This moment was sealed by Mussolini's march to Rome. In 1924 Mussolini took responsibility for the political assassination of Matteotti, the leader of the opposition, which confirmed the nature of his authoritarian régime in 1925.

14. See Peppino Ortoleva and Marco Revelli, *La Società Contemporanea*, 1983.

15. Tekeste Negash, *Italian Colonialism in Eritrea, 1882–1941*, 1987, p. 110.

16. Ennio Flaiano, *A Time to Kill*, trans. by Stuart Hood (London: Quartet Encounters, 1992), p. 26. Original title *Tempo di Uccidere* (Milano: Longanesi, 1947).

17. The question of the Italian identity is a rather difficult one. As Antonio Negri said, perhaps no country other than Italy has seen a third of its population leave in the space of fifty years. From the moment of unification in 1861 until the 1920s, when fascism closed the door to Italian emigration, a third of the population left, ten million out of the thirty million inhabitants that Italy had at the time (*Revisioning Italy*, 1997, p. 45).

18. Beverly Allen and Mary Russo explain:

> An interrogation of class and "racial" components of Italianicity within the United States points in two directions: 1) toward an acknowledgement of Italian Americans as a group marked ethnically and by class, and 2) toward an acknowledgement of the structural position of Italian Americans as a borderland of racialized distinction: the last "white" and "racial" category in a sweep from "white" to "black." The films of the African American film maker Spike Lee, for instance, acknowledge the intriguing dangerous nature of this proximity in their stories of racial violence and interracial love. (*Revisioning Italy: National identity and Global Culture*, 1997, p. 7)

19. Because of his opposition to fascism, the Jewish Carlo Levi, painter, doctor, and writer, was banished (*mandato al confino*) at the start of the Abyssinian War (1935) to a small primitive village in Lucania. With an incredible talent for creating characters and sensibility for the human condition, Levi wrote a powerful compassionate novel about this region forgotten by God. See Carlo Levi, *Christ Stopped at Eboli*; first published in Italy by Einaudi in 1945.

20. For more information on the complex construction of the Italian identity, see the important work of David Forgacs and Robert Lumley, *Italian Cultural Studies: An*

Introduction, 1996. A very good general introduction to Italian contemporary society is Paul Ginsborg, *Italy and Its Discontent 1980–2000,* 2002. See also Stephen Gundle, *Between Hollywood and Moscow: The Italian Communists and the Challenge of Mass Culture, 1943–1991,* 2000, and the collections *Revisioning Italy: National Identity and Global Culture,* ed. by Beverly Allen and Mary Russo, 1997, and *Writing New Identities: Gender, Nation, and Immigration in Contemporary Europe,* ed. by Gisela Brinker-Gabler and Sidonie Smith, 1997.

21. "Reinventing Britain" was an academic conference organized in London by the British Council, 21 March 1997. Stuart Hall made the opening and closing remarks while Homi Bhabha presented a "Manifesto for Reinventing Britain."

22. See on the issue Alessandro del Lago, *Non-persone: L'esclusione dei Migranti in una Società Globale,* 1999. Alessandro del Lago investigates the process through which the Italian system constructs *emergenza immigrazione* by representing migrants as social threat and as the source of social disorder. The migrant becomes an ideal target for outing the frustrations of a nation, which considers itself stable and civil, were it not for the "migrant invasion."

23. *L'indice dei Libri del Mese,* 1992, n2, in Maria Cutrufelli's review of Erminia dell'Oro's *L'Abbandono: Una Storia Eritrea,* 1991.

24. One essay by Vinicio Ongini is ironically entitled *"Cenerentola è nata in Cina"* ("Cinderella Was Born in China"). In it he traces the connection between the little foot of Cinderella that establishes her nobility and the practice of foot binding in China. Apparently the oldest version of the fairy tale seems to have been written by a Chinese officer, according to the Italian historian Carlo Ginzburg in *Storia Notturna* (Torino: Einaudi, 1989). This proves the extraordinary capacity of fairy tales to present themes of cultural similarities and differences. As cultural subtexts they can generate an amazing number of uprising textualities. See Maria Antonietta Saracino, *Altri Lati del Mondo,* 1994, pp. 165–76.

25. Maria Antonietta Saracino, "In Casa D'Altri," in *Altri Lati del Mondo,* 1994, p. 16.

26. This is well illustrated by Firdous Azim in *The Colonial Rise of the Novel,* 1993. In this critical text Azim sets the beginning of the English novel back in time and shows that the novel as a genre has clearly excluded both women and people of color. In an attempt to break down the universality of the novel, Azim offers an important contribution to postcolonial and feminist studies.

27. Very interesting on this subject is the collection of essays edited by Marie-Hélène Caspar, "L'Africa e l'Italia Contemporanea: Miti, Propaganda, Realtà," 1998.

28. Gabriele D'Annunzio, *Più che L'Amore* in *Tutte le Opere di d'Annunzio* (Milano: Mondadori, 1932).

29. Gabriele D'Annunzio, *Teneo te Africa: La seconda Gesta d'Oltremare* (Roma: Il Vittoriale degli Italiani, 1942).

30. MarieHélène Caspar, *L'Africa di Buzzati. Libia: 1933. Etiopia: 1939–1940,* 1997. See also Sandra Ponzanesi's review of the book "Professionista Magico: Dino Buzzati e l'Africa," in *Incontri, Rivista Europea di Studi Italiani,* 1997, pp. 3–4.

31. Kureishi, *Buddha of the Suburbia* (London: Faber and Faber, 1990), p. 3.

32. Oreste Pivetta, "Multiculturalismo," 1996.

33. Ibid., p. 10.

34. It is known that the colonized traveled and lived in Britain since the beginning of the Empire. In *Extravagant Strangers: A Literature of Belonging* (1997), Caryl Phillips reports the stories of immigrant blacks present in Britain in the early seventeenth century. Indian subjects regularly visited or studied in England (i.e., Gandhi, Nehru, and Jinnah, to mention the most famous), creating the first instances of racial encounter at the heart of the empire. In *At the Heart of the Empire: Indians and the Colonial Encounter in Late-Victorian Britain* (1998), Antoinette Burton offers an investigation of diasporic movement in the colonial metropolis, reporting the presence of important figures such as Pandita Ramabai, Cornelia Sorabji, and Behramji Malabari. Rozina Visran makes in her *Asians in Britain: 400 Years of History* (2002), a real tour de force by telling the history of the Indian community in Britain, from the indentured servants of the seventeenth century to the princes, professionals, students, conscript soldiers, and refuges of the twentieth century. Also Inderpal Grewal's *Home and Harem: Nation, Gender, Empire, and the Cultures of Travel* (1996), Susheila Nasta's *Home Truths: Fictions Of the South Asian Diaspora in Britain* (2001), and Sukhdev Sandhu, *London Calling* (2003) deal with immigration to Britain as a flow which preceded the end of empire.

35. On this issues see critical studies such as Ruth Ben-Ghiat, *Fascist Modernities: Italy, 1922–1945*, 2001; Barbara Spackman, *Fascist Virilities: Rhetoric, Ideology, and Social Fantasy in Italy*, 1996; Victoria de Grazia, *How Fascism Ruled Women: Italy, 1922–1945*, 1993; Karen Pinkus, *Bodily Regimes: Italian Advertising Under Fascism*, 1995; Robin Pickering-Iazzi (ed.), *Mothers of Invention: Women, Italian Fascism, and Culture*, 1995.

36. Graziella Parati, "Living in Translation," 1996, p. 4.

37. Renato Curcio, *Shiv Mahal* (Rome: Sensibile Alle Foglie, 1991). Curcio founded the publishing house Sensibili Alle Foglie from prison. A political activist of the 1970s, he was imprisoned as leader of the terrorist group *Brigate Rosse* (Red Brigade) and released in October 1998.

38. Jesus Maria de Lourdes, *Ricordai: Vengo da un'isola di Capo Verde-Sou de uma ilja de Cabo Verde* (Roma, Sinnos, 1996).

39. See David Bregola, *Da Qui Verso Casa* (Roma Edizioni Interculturali, 2002).

CHAPTER 7. DAUGHTER'S OF EMPIRE

1. Isak Dinesen (Karen Blixen), *Out of Africa* (1937).

2. Doris Lessing wrote *Under my Skin* (London: Harper Collins, 1994), her autobiography which begins with her childhood in Rhodesia and ends in 1949 when she left for London, and *The Grass Is Singing* (1950; republished by Heinemann) which is rec-

ognized as one of the finest postwar novels set against the racial background of Rhodesia. Recently Lessing has published a travel book about her visit to Zimbabwe (the old Rhodesia), *African Laughter: Four Visits to Zimbabwe* (London: Harper Collins, 1992).

3. *Ballata Levantina* (Milano: I Contemporanei, 1961); *Cortile e Cleopatra* (Milano: Mondadori, 1973); *Pamela e la Bella Estate: Racconti* (Milano: Feltrinelli, 1962); *Le Quattro Ragazze Wieselberger* (Milano: Mondadori, 1976); *Il Vento sulla Sabbia* (Milano: Mondadori, 1973). For a study of Cialente's *Le Quattro Ragazze Wiselberger* and its importance for the Italian female autobiographical tradition, see Graziella Parati, *Public Histories, Private Stories: Italian Women's Autobiography*, 1996.

4. The *schiftà* were bandits for the Eritreans and patriots for the Ethiopians. They expropriated many Eritreans' possessions and murdered many civilians.

5. Robert J. C. Young, *Colonial Desire: Hybridity in Theory, Culture, and Race*, 1995, p. 9.

6. For a better understanding of Stoler's important work in which she offers a colonial reading of Foucault's *History of Sexuality*, challenging the marginalization of empire in his genealogy, see *Race and the Education of Desire: Foucault's History of Sexuality and the Colonial Order of Things*, 1995. By engaging in a dialogue with Foucault's resounding absence of race and colonialism in his account of power relationships, Stoler makes his critique productive and removes it from ingrained reception of his ideas.

7. Laura Ann Stoler, "Making Empire Respectable," 1990, p. 35.

8. See Françoise Lionnet, "Métissage, Emancipation, and Female Textuality in Two Francophone Writers," in *Life/Lines: Theorising Women's Autobiography*, Bella Brodski and Celeste Schenk (eds), 1988, pp. 260–81; François Lionnet, "Of Mangoes and Maroons: Language, History, and the Multicultural Subject of Michelle Cliff's *Abeng*," in *De/Colonizing the Subject*, Sidonie Smith and Julia Watson (eds.), 1992, pp. 321–45.

9. *Anghere* is a subtle dough, used as bread.

10. Here it is important to point that the centralization imposed by the Amharic regime has meant not only the obliteration of the Oromo culture, with an Oromo language that was not allowed to be used officially, but also a state of negligent administration. Over the past few decades various liberation fronts within Ethiopia have fought against the dictatorial Ethiopian regime with the aim of reestablishing their autonomy. These liberation fronts were the Oromo Liberation Front (OLF) and the Tigrayan Liberation Front (TLF) with the Tigrayan People Liberation Front (TPLF) as subgroup. The latter was based on the model of the Eritrean Peoples Liberation Front (EPLF).

11. This review is rather multicultural and besides gathering new unpublished short stories offers an interesting panorama on world literatures and cultures. The journal's title *Linea d'Ombra (Shadow Line)* is also significant for its content: the title refers to Joseph Conrad's famous book *The Shadow Line: A Confession* (1917), which was later used by Amitav Ghosh for his novel *The Shadow Lines* (London: Bloomsbury, 1988) set between Calcutta and London at the time of the Bangladesh secessionist war.

12. For a broader critique of Lacan's linguistic psychoanalytic interpretation by Julia Kristeva—in which she divides the symbiotic (the bond mother-daughter) before the entrance into the symbolic system represented by the language of the father—see Kaja Silverman, *The Acoustic Mirror: The Female Voice in Psychoanalysis and Cinema*, 1988.

13. Extracommunitarian means literally someone who is not from the European Union, but it is also a euphemism to address black people, colored people, the Other.

CHAPTER 8. LIVING IN TRANSLATION

1. Graziella Parati, "Living in Translation: Thinking with an Accent," 1997.

2. Tigrinya should not be confused with Tigrè, since these are the two most diffused languages in Eritrea, and they are both of South Semitic origin. Tigrinya is spoken in the Eritrean Highlands, in Asmara, and in the Ethiopian region of Tigray. Tigrè, however, is only spoken in Eritrea. It is used in the lowlands, in the Eastern part of Eritrea on the border with Sudan and along the coast in cities such as Massawa.

3. On this issue see the important text by Ghirmai Negash, *A History of Tigrinya Literature: The Oral and the Written*, 1890–1991 (Leiden: CNWS, 1999).

4. Ribka Sibhatu, "Il Caffé di Abebà," 1994, p. 2.

5. Ibid., p. 2.

6. H. Bruce Franklin, *The Victim as Criminal and Artist: Literature from the American Prison* (New York: Oxford University Press, 1978), pp. 249–50, cited in Barbara Harlow, *Resistance Literature*, 1987, p. 122.

7. Barbara Harlow, *Resistant Literature*, 1987, Preface, XVIII.

8. Ribka Sibhat, "Il Caffè di Abebà," 1994, p. 2.

9. Haz-Haz is a women's prison in Asmara.

10. In the official Tigrinya language Abebà, which is the name of the girl mentioned, means "flower."

11. *Aghelghel* is an Eritrean basket with a conic-shaped lid which is made with leaves of the palm tree *dum* and is meant to bring *hmbascià* to a celebration, in Abebà's case, a mourning.

12. *Hmbascià* is the Eritrean bread which is brought to celebrate an event.

13. Sigmund Freud, "The Uncanny," in *The Standard Edition of the Complete Psychological Works of Sigmund Freud*, Vol. 17, trans. by James Strachey (London: Hogarth; The Institute of Psycho-Analysis, 1955), p. 219.

14. Ibid., p. 220.

15. Primo Levi was born in Turin in 1919 and committed suicide in 1987.

16. Dante Alighieri, *Divina Commedia: Inferno*, trans. by John D. Sinclair, 1939, xxvi: 118–20.

17. Tim Brennan, for example, has argued that those Third World texts and authors deemed the canon "cosmopolitan writers" considered "interpreters and authentic public voices of the Third World." These authors have the function of compliance with a "metropolitan audience's tastes" for certain kinds of postmodern narratives. "Alien yet familiar," these writers straddle two cultures; attached to the specific locales in the Third World, they address their work primarily to readers in the West, whose tastes they both share and/or appeal to. This dual orientation (and, perhaps, allegiance) of their work makes them the privileged mediators and translators of Third World cultures and peoples for Western readers. Indeed one can also argue that, with a foot in each of two cultures, these writers are themselves, to borrow a phrase from Rushdie, "translated m[e]n" (cited in Anuradha Dingwaney and Carol Maier (eds.), *Between Languages and Cultures: Translation and Cross-Cultural Texts*, 1995, pp. 5–6].

18. For the different theories on translation and their evolution with respect to cultural studies, see Susan Bassnett, *Translation Studies*, 1980; Susan Bassnett and André Lefevere (eds.), *Translation, History, and Culture*, 1990; Shantha Ramakrishna (ed.), *Translation and Multilinguism: Post-colonial Context*, 1997; Susan Bassnett and André Lefevere (eds.), *Constructing Cultures: Essays on Literary Translation*, 1998.

19. Lawrence Venuti, "Translation as Cultural Politics: Regime of Domestification in English," *Textual Practice* 7.2 (1993), pp. 208–23; *The Translator's Invisibility*, 1995; *The Scandals of Translation: Towards an Ethics of Difference*, 1998.

20. Susan Bassnett, "The Translation Turn in Cultural Studies," 1998, p. 137.

CHAPTER 9. ONCE WE WERE WARRIORS

1. There are three main types of female circumcision. *Clitoridectomy*, considered to be the equivalent of male circumcision, consists in the removal of the prepuce of the clitoris. *Excision* is the removal of the prepuce, the clitoris itself, and the labia minora. *Infibulation* consists in the removal of the clitoris, the whole labia minora and majora, and the stitching together (suturing) of the two sides of the vulva leaving a very small orifice to permit the flow of urine and menstrual discharge. See Olayinka Koso-Thomas, *The Circumcision of Women: A Strategy for Eradication*, 1987, pp. 16–17.

2. The tradition, which is neither mentioned in the Koran nor in the Bible, seems to date back to Cleopatra's time (it is often also called Pharaonic circumcision) when slaves had to remain virgins before their sale, and men who went to war for long periods of time could guarantee their wives' fidelity through the sewing up of their women's vagina. In the Roman world the chastity belt was more in practice. The reason for the survival of infibulation until nowadays has mostly to do with the belief that it protects virginity in societies which put virginity as an absolute prerequisite for marriageability and where extramarital relationships provoke the most severe penalties. Although the intention of the operation might be to diminish a woman's desire, the facts, from a medical

point of view, are that excision of the clitoris reduces sensitivity, but it cannot reduce desire, which is a psychological attribute. Offering as a reason for infibulation "the preservation of virginity and the prevention of immorality" is odd on a strictly practical level, since reinfibulation is easily done to look like the original one, whereas a ruptured hymen is more difficult to repair.

3. In addition to Africa and the countries of Asia, Europe and Latin America practice female mutilation. Africa: a) sub-Saharan belt (Sudan 85%, Nigeria 60%), b) Horn of Africa (Somalia 99%, Ethiopia 90%, Eritrea 80%, Djibouti, 99%), c) West Africa (Sierra Leone 90%, Mali 75%, Senegal 20%, Ghana 30%, Gambia 80%, Guinea 70%), d) Egypt (60%) and e) Kenya (60%). Asia: (by Muslims groups) in Malaysia, Indonesia, Pakistan and Philippines. Middle East: United Arab Emirates, South Yemen, Bahrain, and Oman. Europe: Recently it has surfaced in certain parts of Europe, such as France, The Netherlands, and Germany where large numbers of immigrants from Africa and Asia have settled. The immigrants have transferred their circumcision culture from their countries of origin to their adopted homelands. Latin America: Brazil (especially Salvador de Bahia where West Africans have settled because of slavery), Mexico. Not only Muslims, but also Copts, Catholics, Protestants, and nonbelievers practice infibulation. It is *not* practiced in the cradle and seat of Islam, Saudi Arabia, where devout Muslims go each year to pay homage. Neither is it practiced in Islamic countries such as Algeria, Iran, Iraq, Libya, Morocco, and Tunisia. These statistics are taken from "Female Genital and Sexual Mutilation," published in *Women's International Network News* (21 January 1995), pp. 34–39.

4. Mary Childers and bell hooks, "A Conversation about Race and Class," 1993, p. 67.

5. Nawal El Saadawi, *The Hidden Face of Eve: Women in the Arab Worls*, 1980, p. XIV.

6. There is obviously a risk of essentializing the concept "African woman." Given its huge cultural and political complexity, such a notion cannot be but homogenizing. However it is strategically useful in order to express the common front that Third World feminists in Africa have made on the issue of infibulation against the imperialistic intervention of Western critics. The term is used here as a temporary binary front, which is not exempt from internal contradictions and differentiations.

7. It is interesting to note that a male writer like the Somali Nuruddin Farah has decided to include the issue of sexual mutilation in his narration *Sardines* (Heinemann, 1992). A modern mother, who has just rejected her cooperation with the new government and is worried about the high position given to her husband, is terrified that her young daughter will be obliged by her grandmother to go through the rite of initiation that has marked the entrance into womanhood for many generations. The topic becomes split in its totality into a generational gap which shows the clashing between old and modern traditions within the country, avoiding the superstructure of labeling the practice as negative only because the West points its finger.

8. Hassan, *La Donna Mutilata*, 1996, p. 13.

9. John Beverly, "The Margin at the Centre: On *Testimonio*," 1992, p. 94.

10. Françoise Lionnet, "The Limits of Universalism: Identity, Sexuality, and Criminality," 1995, p. 163.

11. Nawal El Saadawi, *The Hidden Face of Eve: Women in the Arab World*, 1980, p. 8.

12. In *The Drama of the Gifted Child and the Search for the True Self*, Alice Miller explores the psychological consequences in adulthood of children who repress their deepest and most hidden feelings to fulfill the expectations of their parents. This denial of their own natural enjoyment and narcissistic personality creates in adulthood disturbances due to the loss of contact with the true self. The consequences are emotions such as insecurity and spiritual impoverishment which lead to depression, anxiety, and suicidal drives. Such repression can be seen in the silent obedient infibulated girls who suffocate their own feelings to obey their mothers' and communities' expectations. Submitting to the perpetration of this social practice, in adulthood these women often feel emotionally disordered and are frequently afflicted by serious psychological disturbances like depression and madness (Alice Miller, *Das Drama des begabten Kindes und die Suche nach dem Wahren Selbst*, 1979).

13. In Margaret R. Higonnet, *Borderwork: Feminist Engagements with Comparative Literature*, 1994, pp. 301–18.

14. For a study of the reasons and impact of plastic surgery on the female body, see Kathy Davis, *Reshaping the Female Body: The Dilemma of Cosmetic Surgery*, 1995.

15. Obioma Nnaemeka, "Bringing African Women into the Classroom," 1994, p. 315.

16. Obioma Nnaemeka, "A Statement on Genital Mutilation," 1983, p. 313.

17. For a study on the construction of the female body in paintings, medicine, and literature, see *The Female Body in Western Culture: Contemporary Perspectives*, ed. by Susan Rubin Suleiman, 1985.

18. See Emily Martin, *The Woman in the Body: A Cultural Analysis of Reproduction*, 1987. The anthropologist Emily Martin analyses how medical language about women's bodies reveals cultural assumptions about women and their life's purpose.

19. Elaine Scarry, *The Body in Pain: The Making and Unmaking of the World*, 1985, p. 5.

20. There are instead several Western texts addressing infibulation as the main topic of discussion. See, for example, Hanny Lightfoot-Klein's part travelogue, part ethnographic account of her travels through Africa, *Prisoners of Ritual: An Odyssey into Female Circumcision in Africa*, 1989.

21. Rachel Blau du Plessis, *Writing Beyond the Ending: Narrative Strategies of Twentieth-Century Women Writers*, 1985, p. 1.

22. The details on the psychosexual, religious, and cultural reasons for the perpetration of female mutilation and its medical consequences are taken from the accurate and influential report by The Minority Rights Group in London, *Female Circumcision, Excision, and Infibulation*, edited by Scilla McLean and Stella Efua Graham (Report 47,

1980). For further studies on the subject, see also Efua Dorkenoo, *Cutting the Rose: Female Genital Mutilation, The Practice and Its Prevention* (London: Minority Rights Publications, 1995); World Health Organization, *Female Genital Mutilation: An Overview* (Geneva: World Health Organization, 1998); *Female Genital Mutilations: A Joint WHO/UNICEF/UNFPA Statement* (Geneva: World Health Organization, 1997); Nahid Toubia, *Female Genital Mutilation: A Call for Global Action* (New Tork: Women, 1993); Lewis B. Sckolnick, *Female Genital Mutilation* (Civil Rights Report Series, 1994).

23. Chandra Talpade Mohanty, "Under Western Eyes. Feminist Scholarship and Colonial Discourses," 1995, p. 162.

24. For a further study on Black Feminism and issue of positionality, see Patricia Hill Collins, *Black Feminist Thought: Knowledge, Consciousness, and the Politics of Empowerment*, 1991.

25. Carole Boyce Davies, *Ngambika: Studies Of Women in African Literature*, 1986, p. 8.

26. See Filomena Steady, "African Feminism. A Worldwide Perspective," 1989, p. 10.

27. Françoise Lionnet (ed.), *Post-colonial Representations: Women, Literature, Identity*, 1995, pp. 154–65.

28. Ibid., p. 155.

29. Maxine Hong Kingston, *The Woman Warrior: Memories of a Girlhood Among Ghosts* (London: Picador, 1977), p. 25.

CHAPTER 10. CONCLUSIONS

1. Trinh T. Minh-ha, "Other than Myself / My Other Self," in G. Robertson, et al. (eds.), *Travellers' Tales*, 1994, pp. 9–26: 21.

2. Since it is an *ad hoc* definition for this comparison, this title has been taken from the subheading given by Iain Chambers and Lidia Curti to their collection, *The Post-colonial Question: Common Skies, Divided Horizons*, 1996.

3. Stuart Hall (ed.), *Representation: Cultural Representations and Signifying Practices*, 1997, p. 17.

Bibliography

A. PRIMARY READINGS

Alexander, Meena.

(* Allahabad, India 1951)

Poetry:
The Bird's Bright Ring (1976) Calcutta: Writer's Workshop

I Root My Name (1977) Calcutta: United Writers Selling Agents

Stone Roots (1980) New Delhi: Arnold Heinemann

House of a Thousand Doors (1988) Washington, DC: Three Continents Press

River and Bridge (1995) New Delhi: TSAR Press

Illiterate Hearts (2002) Chicago: Northwestern University Press

Raw Silk (2004) Chicago: Northwestern University Press

Fiction:
Nampally Road (1991) Hyderabad: Disha Books

Fault Lines (1994) New York: The Feminist Press

Manhattan Music (1997) San Francisco: Mercury House

Criticism:
Women in Romanticism. Mary Wollstonecraft, Dorothy Wordsworth and Mary Shelley (1989) Totowa: Barnes and Noble Press

236 BIBLIOGRAPHY

The Shock of Arrival: Reflections on Post-colonial Experience (1996) Boston: South End Press

Gupta, Sunetra.

(* Calcutta, India 1965)   Fiction: *Memories of Rain* (1992) London: Orion

The Glassblower's Breath (1993) London: Orion

Moonlight into Marzipan (1995) London: Phoenix House

A Sin of Colour (1999) London: Phoenix House

Hassan, Sirad Salan.

(* Mogadishu, Somalia 1962)   Fiction: **Sette Gocce di Sangue: Due Donne Somale** (1996) Palermo: La Luna

La Donna Mutilata (1996) Palermo: Sellerio

Mukherjee, Bharati.

(* Calcutta, India 1940)   Fiction: *The Tiger's Daughter* (1972) Boston: Houghton Mifflin Co.

Wife (1975) Toronto: Penguin

Darkness: Days and Nights in Calcutta (1977) Markham, Ont., Canada

The Middleman and Other Stories (1988) New York: Grove Press

Jasmine (1989) New York: Grove Weidenfeld

The Holder of the World (1994) New York: Knopf

Leave It to Me (1977) New York: Knopf

Desirable Daughters: A Novel (2002) New York: Theia

dell'Oro, Erminia.

(* Asmara, Eritrea 1938)   Fiction: *Asmara Addio* (1988) Milano: Baldini and Castoldi

L'Abbandono: Una Storia Eritrea
(1991) Torino: Einaudi

Il Fiore di Merara (1994) Milano:
Baldini and Castoldi

Mamma al Vento (1996) Milano:
Baldini and Castoldi

La Gola del Diavolo (1999) Milano:
Feltrinelli

Children's Book: *Matteo e i Dinosauri* (1993) Torino:
Einaudi

La Pianta Magica (1994) Milano:
E. ELLE

*Lo Straordinario incontro con il
Lupo Hokusai* (1994) Milano:
E. ELLE

Sibhatu, Ribka.

(* Asmara, Eritrea 1962)   Fiction: ***Aulò: Canto-Poesia dall'Eritrea***
(1993) Roma: Sinnos

Essay: "Il Caffé di Abebà." In *Caffé* 1 (Sep-
tember 1994), p. 2.

Suleri, Sara.

(* Lahore, Pakistan (1946?))   Fiction: ***Meatless Days*** (1989) Chicago: University of Chicago Press

Criticism: *The Rhetoric of English India* (1992)
Chicago: University of Chicago Press

Viarengo, Maria.

(* Ghidami, Ethiopia 1949)   Fiction: ***Andiamo a Spasso?*** in *Linea
D'Ombra* 53 (November 1990)

B. CRITICAL BIBLIOGRAPHY

Adam, Ian, and Helen Tiffin. 1991. *Past the Last Post: Theorizing Post-colonialism and
PostModernism*. London: Harvester Wheatsheaf.

Aden, Mohamed. 1997. "Italy: Cultural Identity and Spatial Opportunism from a Postcolonial Perspective." In Beverly Allen and Mary Russo (eds.), *Revisioning
Italy: National Identity and Global Culture*. Minneapolis: University of Minnesota Press, pp. 101–15.

Agnew, John. 1997. "The Myth of Backward Italy in Modern Europe." In Beverly Allen and Mary Russo (eds.), *Revisioning Italy: National Identity and Global Culture.* Minneapolis: University of Minnesota Press, pp. 23–42.

Ahmad, Aijaz. 1992. *In Theory.* London: Verso.

———. 1995. "The Politics of Post-coloniality." *Race and Class* 36.3: 9.

Allen, Beverly, and Mary Russo. 1987. *Revisioning Italy: National Identity and Global Culture.* Minneapolis: University of Minnesota Press.

Alexander, Jacqui, and Chandra Talpade Mohanty (eds.). 1997. *Feminist Genealogies: Colonial Legacies, Democratic Futures.* New York: Routledge.

Amos, Valerie, and Pratibha Parmar. 1984. "Challenging Imperial Feminism." In *Feminist Review* 17: 3–19.

Anderson, Benedict. 1983. *Imagined Communities: Reflections on the Origin and Spread of Nationalism.* London: Verso.

Anthias, Floya, and Nira Yuval-Davies (eds.). 1992. *Racialized Boundaries: Race, Nation, Gender, Colour, and Class and the Anti-racist Struggle.* London and New York: Routledge.

Appadurai, Arjun. 1996. *Modernity at Large: Cultural Dimensions of Globalization.* Minneapolis: University of Minnesota Press.

Appiah, Kwame Anthony. 1992. *In My Father's House: Africa in the Philosophy of Culture.* London: Methuen.

Appiah, Kwame Anthony, and Henry Louis Gates (eds.). 1995. *Identities.* Chicago: University of Chicago Press.

Ashcroft, Bill, Gareth Griffith, and Helen Tiffin (eds.). 1989. *The Empire Writes Back: Theory and Practice in Post-Colonial Literatures.* London and New York: Routledge and Keegan Paul.

———. 1995. *The Post-Colonial Studies Reader.* London and New York: Routledge.

———. 1998. *Key Concepts in Post-colonial Studies.* London and New York: Routledge.

Azim, Firdous. 1993. *The Colonial Rise of the Novel.* London: Routledge.

Bal, Mieke. 1986. *Narratology: Introduction to the Theory of Narrative.* Toronto: University of Toronto Press.

———. 1987. "Myths à la Lettre: Freud, Mann, Genesis and Rembrandt, and the Story of the Son." In Shlomith Rimmon-Kenan (ed.), *Discourse in Psychoanalysis and Literature.* London: Methuen, pp. 57–89.

———. 1988. *Death and Dissymmetry: The Politics of Coherence in the Book of Judges.* Chicago: The University of Chicago Press.

———. 1994. *The Point of Theory: Practices of Cultural Analysis.* Amsterdam: Amsterdam University Press.

Barkan, Elazar, and Marie-Denise Shelton (eds.). 1998. *Borders, Exiles, Diasporas.* Standford: Standford University Press.

Barker, Francis, Peter Hulme, and Margaret Iversen (eds.). 1996. *Colonial Discourse/Post-colonial Theory.* Manchester: Manchester University Press.

Barthes, Roland. 1965. *Saggi Critici.* Torino: Einaudi.

———. 1972. *Mythologies.* New York: Hill and Wang.

Bassnett, Susan. 1998. "The Translation Turn in Cultural Studies." In Susan Bassnett and André Lefevere (eds.), *Constructing Cultures: Essays on Literary Translation.* Clevedon: Multilingual Matters, pp. 123–40.

———. 1980. *Translation Studies.* London: Methuen.

Bassnett, Susan, and André Lefevere (eds.). 1990. *Translation, History, and Culture.* London: Pinter.

Ben-Ghiat, Ruth. 2001. *Fascist Modernities: Italy, 1922–1945.* Berkeley: University of California Press.

Benhabib, Seyla, Judith Butler, Drucilla Cornel, et al. (eds.). 1995. *Feminist Contentions: A Philosophical Exchange.* New York: Routledge.

Benstock, Shari (ed.). 1988. *The Private Self.* Chapel Hill: University of North Carolina.

Bernheimer, Charles (ed.). 1995. *Comparative Literature in the Age of Multiculturalism.* Baltimore: Johns Hopkins University Press.

Bertens, Hans. 1995. *The Idea of the Postmodern: A History.* London: Routledge.

Beverly, John. 1992. "The Margin at the Centre: On *Testimonio.*" In Sidonie Smith and Julia Watson (eds.), *De/Colonizing the Subject: The Politics of Gender in Women's Autobiography.* Minneapolis: University of Minnesota Press, pp. 91–114.

Bhabha, Homi K. 1984. "Of Mimicry and Man: The Ambivalence of Colonial Discourse." *October* 28: 125–33.

———. 1992. "Freedom's Basis in the Indeterminate." *October* 61: 46–57.

———. 1994. "Dissemination: Time, Narrative, and the Margins of the Modern Nation." In Homi K. Bhabha (ed.), *The Location of Culture.* London: Routledge, pp. 139–70.

———. 1994. *The Location of Culture.* London: Routledge.

Bhabha, Homi K. (ed.). 1990. *Nation and Narration.* London: Routledge.

Bloom, Harold. 1973. *The Anxiety of Influence.* New York: Oxford University Press.

Blunt, Alison, and Gillian Rose (eds.). 1994. *Writing Women and Space: Colonial and Post-colonial Geographies.* New York and London: Guildford Press.

Boca, Angelo del. 1976. *Gli Italiani in Africa Orientale. Dall'unità alla marcia su Roma*, Vol. I (1976); *La conquista dell'impero*, Vol. II (1976); *La caduta dell'impero*, Vol. III (1986); *Nostalgia delle colonie*, Vol. IV (1986). Bari: Laterza.

———. 1992. *L'Africa Nella Coscienza degli Italiani: Miti, Memorie, Errori, Sconfitte*. Bari: Laterza.

———. 1995. "Le Leggi Razziali nell'Impero di Mussolini." In Angelo del Boca, Legnani, M.G. Rossi (eds.), *Il Regime Fascista*. Bari: Laterza, pp. 329–51.

Boehmer, Elleke. 1995. *Colonial and Post-colonial Literature: Migrant Metaphors*. Oxford: Oxford University Press.

Boyarin, Jonathan. 1994. "Space, Time, and the Politics of Memory." In Jonathan Boyarin (ed.), *Remapping Memory: The Politics of Time and Space*. Minneapolis: University of Minnesota Press, pp. 1–37.

Brah, Avtar. 1996. *Cartographies of Diaspora: Contesting Identities*. London and New York: Routledge.

Braidotti, Rosi. 1991. *Patterns of Dissonance: A Study of Women in Contemporary Philosophy*. Trans. by Elizabeth Guild. Oxford: Polity Press.

———. 1994. *Nomadic Subjects: Embodiment and Sexual Difference in Contemporary Feminist Theory*. New York: Columbia University Press.

———. 2002. *Metamorphoses: Towards a Materialist Reading of Becoming*. Oxford: Polity Press.

Bregola, David. 2002. *Da Qui Verso Casa*. Roma: Edizioni Interculturali.

Brennan, Timothy. 1989. *Salman Rushdie and the Third World Myth of the Nation*. London: MacMillan.

———. 1990. "The National Longing for Form." In Homi K. Bhabha (ed.), *Nation and Narration*. London: Routledge, pp. 44–70

Brinker-Gabler, Gisela, and Sidonie Smith (eds.). 1997. *Writing New Identities: Gender, Nation, and Immigration in Contemporary Europe*. Minneapolis: University of Minnesota Press.

Brodszki, Bella, and Celeste Schenck (eds.). 1988. *Life/Lines: Theorizing Women's Autobiography*. Ithaca and London: Cornell University Press.

Bronfen, Elizabeth. 1990. "A Sense of Strangeness. The Gender and Cultural Identity in Bharati Mukherjee's *Jasmine*." *Baetyl* 2: 61–79.

Broughton, Lynn, and Linda Anderson (eds.). 1997. *Women's Lives/Women's Times: New Essays on Auto/Biography*. Albany: State University of New York Press.

Brunetta, Gianpiero. 1990. *L'Ora D'Africa del Cinema Italiano: Materiali di Lavoro*. Rovereto: Rivista Studi Storici.

Buikema, Rosemarie, and Anneke Smelik (eds.). 1993. *Women's Studies and Culture: A Feminist Introduction*. London: Zed Books.

Bulbeck, Chilla. 1998. *Re-orienting Western Feminism: Women's Diversity in a Post-colonial World*. Cambridge: Cambridge University Press.

Burdett, Charles. 2000. "Journeys to Italian East Africa." *Journal of Modern Italian Studies* 5.2: 207–27.

———. 2001. "Memories of Italian East Africa." *Journal of Romance Studies* 1.3: 69–85.

Burgio, Alberto (ed.). 1999. *Nel Nome della Razza: Il Razzismo nella Storia D'Italia 1870–1945*. Bologna: Il Mulino.

Burton, Antoinette. 1998. *At the Heart of the Empire: Indians and the Colonial Encounter in Late-Victorian Britain*. Berkeley: University of California Press.

Butalia, Urvashi. 2000. *The Other Side of Silence: Voices from the Partition of India*. Durham: Duke University Press.

Calchi Novati, Gianpaolo. 1994. *Il Corno D'Africa nella Storia e nella Politica: Etiopia, Somalia e Eritrea fra Nazionalismi. Sottosviluppo e Guerra*. Torino: Società Editrice Internazionale.

Calvino, Italo. 1979. *Invisible Cities*. London: Picador.

Carby, Hazel V. 1982. "White Women Listen! Black Feminism and the Boundaries of Sisterhood." In Bill Ashcroft, Gareth Griffith, and Helen Tiffin (eds.), *The Empire Strikes Back: Race and Racism in 70's Britain*. London: Hutchinson, pp. 212–35.

Caspar, Marie-Hélène. 1997. *L'Africa di Buzzati, Libia: 1933. Etiopia: 1939–1940*. Université Paris X Nanterre. Centre de Recerches Italiennes C.R.I.X.

———. 1998. "L'Africa e l'Italia Contemporanea: Miti, Propaganda, Realtà." *Narrativa*, Centre de Recerches Italiennes. Université Paris X, Nanterre, No. 14.

Castells, Manuel. 2000. *The Rise of the Network Society*. Oxford: Blackwell.

Centro, Furio Jesis (ed.). 1994. *La Menzogna della Razza*. Bologna: Grafis.

Césaire, Aimé. 1972. *Discourse on Colonialism*. New York: Monthly Review Press.

Chabal, Patrick, and Moema Parents (eds.). 1996. *The Postcolonial Literature of Lusophone Africa*. London: Hurst Company.

Chambers, Iain, and Lidia Curti (eds.). 1996. *The Post-colonial Question: Common Skies, Divided Horizons*. New York and London: Routledge.

Chatterjee, Partha. 1986. *Nationalist Thought and The Colonial World: A Derivate Discourse*. London: Zed Books.

———. 1989. "The Nationalist Resolution of the Women's Question." In Kumkum Sangari and Sudesh Vaid (eds.), *Recasting Women: Essays in Colonial History*. New Delhi: Kali for Women.

Cheah, Pheng, and Bruce Robbins (eds.). 1998. *Cosmopolitics: Thinking and Feeling Beyond the Nation.* Minneapolis: University of Minnesota Press.

Childers, Mary, and bell hooks. 1990. "A Conversation About Race and Class." In Marianne Hirsch and Evelyn Fox-Keller (eds.), *Conflicts in Feminism.* New York: Routledge, pp. 60–81.

Childs, Peter, and R. J. Patrick Williams. 1997. *An Introduction to Post-colonial Theory.* London: Prentice Hall

Clifford, James. 1988. *The Predicament of Culture: Twentieth-century Ethnography, Literature, and Art.* Cambridge: Harvard University Press.

———. 1992. "Traveling Cultures." In Lawrence Grossberg, Cary Nelson, and Paula Treichler (eds.), *Cultural Studies.* London: Routledge, pp. 96–112.

Cohen, Bernard. 1996. *Colonialism and its Forms of Knowledge: The British in India.* Princeton: Princeton University Press.

Cohen, Robin. 1997. *Global Diasporas: An Introduction.* Seattle: University of Washington Press.

Collins, Patricia Hill. 1991. *Black Feminist Thought, Knowledge, Consciousness, and the Politics of Empowerment.* London and New York: Routledge.

Culler, Jonathan. 1983. *On Deconstruction: Theory and Criticism after Structuralism.* London: Routledge and Keegan Paul.

Davies, Carole Boyce. 1986. *Ngambika: Studies Of Women in African Literature.* Trenton: Africa World Press.

———. 1994. *Black Women, Writing, and Identity: Migration of the Subject.* London: Routledge.

Davis, Kathy. 1995. *Reshaping the Female Body: The Dilemma of Cosmetic Surgery.* New York: Routledge.

de Grazia, Victoria. 1993. *How Fascism Ruled Women: Italy, 1922–1945.* Berkeley: University of California Press.

Del Lago, Alessandro. 1999. *Non-persone: L'esclusione dei Migranti in una Società Globale.* Milano: Feltrinelli.

Deleuze, Gilles, and Félix Guattari. 1986. *Kafka: Towards a Minor Literature.* Trans. by Dana Polan. Minneapolis: University of Minnesota Press. Originally published in 1975.

Derrida, Jacques. 1976. *Of Grammatology.* Trans. by Gayatri C. Spivak. Baltimore: Johns Hopkins University Press.

Dingwaney, Anuradha, and Carol Maier (eds). 1995. *Between Languages and Culture: Translation and Cross-Cultural Texts.* Pittsburgh: University of Pittsburgh Press.

Dirlik, Arif. 1992. "The Post-colonial Aura: Third World Criticism in the Age of Global Capitalism." In *Critical Inquiry*, Vol. 20 (Winter): 328–56.

Donald, James, and Ali Rattansi. 1992. *"Race," Culture, and Difference*. London: Sage Publications.

Dorkenoo, Efua. 1995. *Cutting the Rose: Female Genital Mutilation, the Practice and its Prevention*. London: Minority Rights Publications.

During, Simon. 1987. "Postmodernism and Post-colonialism Today." *Textual Practice* 1.1: 32–46.

During, Simon (ed.). 1993. *The Cultural Studies Reader*. London and New York: Routledge.

Dyer, Richard. 1993. "White." In *The Matter of Images*. London and New York: Routledge, pp. 141–63.

Edney, Matthew. 1997. *Mapping and Empire: The Geographical Construction of British India, 1765–1843*. Chicago: University of Chicago Press.

Fanon, Franz. 1961. *The Wretched of the Earth*. Harmondsworth: Penguin.

———. 1991. *Black Skin, White Mask*. London: Grove Press.

Farah, Nuruddin. 1986. *MAPS*. London: Picador.

Felman, Shoshana. 1985. *Writing and Madness: Literature, Philosophy, Psychoanalysis*. Ithaca: Cornell University Press

Felman, Shoshana, and Dauri Laub. 1992. *Testimony: Crisis of Witnessing in Literature, Psychoanalysis, and History*. New York and London: Routledge.

Fincher, Ruth, and Jane M. Jacobs (eds.). 1998. *Cities of Difference*. New York: Guilford Press.

Forgacs, David, and Robert Lumley. 1996. *Italian Cultural Studies: An Introduction*. Oxford: Oxford University Press.

Foucault, Michel. 1977. *Discipline and Punish: The Birth of the Prison*. Trans. by Alan Sheridan. New York: Pantheon Books.

Frankenberg, Ruth, and Lata Mani. 1996. "Crosscurrents, Crosstalk: Race, 'Postcoloniality,' and the Politics of Location." In Smadar Lavie and Ted Swedenburg (eds.), *Displacement, Diaspora, and Geographies of Identity*. Durham: Duke University Press, pp. 271–93.

Fraser, Robert. 2000. *Lifting the Sentence: The Poetics of Postcolonial Fiction*. Manchester: Manchester University Press.

Freud, Sigmund. 1955. "The Uncanny." In *The Standard Edition of the Complete Psychological Works of Sigmund Freud*, Vol. 17. Trans. by James Strachey. London: Hogarth. The Institute of Psycho-Analysis.

Gandhi, Leela. 1998. *Post-colonial Theory: A Critical Introduction*. New York: Columbia University Press.

Gardiner, Michael. 1992. *The Dialogics of Critique: M. M. Bakhtin and the Theory of Ideology*. London: Routledge.

Gates, Henry Louis Jr. (ed.). 1986. *"Race," Writing and Difference*. Chicago: The University of Chicago Press.

Gellner, Ernest. 1998. *Nationalism*. London: Phoenix.

Ghosh, Bishnupriya, and Brinda Bose. 1997. *Interventions: Feminist Dialogues on Third World Women's Literature and Film*. New York: Garland.

Gilman, Sander L. 1992. "Black Bodies, White Bodies: Towards an Iconography of Female Sexuality in Late Nineteenth-Century Art, Medicine, and Literature." In James Donald and Ali Rattansi (eds.), *"Race," Culture, and Difference*. London: Sage Publications, pp. 171–97.

Gilmore, Leigh. 1994. *Autobiographics: A Feminist Theory of Women's Representation*. Ithaca: Cornell University Press.

Gilroy, Paul. 1987. *"There Ain't No Black in the Union Jack": The Cultural Politics of Race and Nation*. London: Hutchinson.

———. 1992. "Cultural Studies and Ethnic Absolutism." In Lawrence Grossberg, Cary Nelson, and Paula Treichler (eds), *Cultural Studies*. New York: Routledge.

———. 1993. *The Black Atlantic: Modernity and Double Consciousness*. London: Verso.

———. 2000. *Against Race: Imagining Political Culture Beyond the Color Line*. Cambridge: Harvard University Press.

Ginsborg, Paul. 2002. *Italy and Its Discontent 1980–2000*. London: Penguin Press.

Gleick, James. 1988. *Chaos: Making a New Science*. London: Heinemann.

Goldberg, David Theo. 1994. *Multiculturalism: A Critical Reader*. Cambridge: Blackwell.

Gouda, Frances. 1995. *Dutch Culture Overseas: Colonial Practice in the Netherlands Indies 1900–1940*. Amsterdam: Amsterdam University Press.

———. 1998. *Domesticating the Empire: Race, Gender and Family Life in French and Dutch Colonialism*. Charlottesville: University of Virginia Press

Gramsci, Antonio. 1966. *The Southern Question*. Roma: Editori Riuniti.

———. 1971. *Selections from Prison Notebooks of Antonio Gramsci*. Ed. and trans. by Quintin Moore and Geoffrey Nowell-Smith. London: Lawrence Wishort.

Grewal, Inderpal. 1994. "Autobiographic Subjects and Diasporic Locations: *Meatless Days* and *Borderlands*." In Inderpal Grewal and Caren Kaplan (eds.), *Scattered Hegemonies: Postmodernity and Transnational Feminist Practices*. Minneapolis: University of Minnesota Press, pp. 231–54.

————. 1996. *Home and Harem: Nation, Gender, Empire, and the Cultures of Travel.* Durham: Duke University Press.

Guha, Ranajit (ed.). 1982. *Subaltern Studies: Writings on South Asian History and Society.* Delhi: Oxford University Press.

Gundle, Stephen. 2000. *Between Hollywood and Moscow: The Italian Communists and the Challenge of Mass Culture, 1943–1991.* Durham: Duke University Press.

Gusdorf, Georges. 1980. "Conditions and Limits of Autobiography." In James Olney (ed.), *Autobiography: Essays Theoretical and Critical.* Princeton: Princeton University Press.

d'Haen, Theo, and Patricia Krüs (eds.). 2000. *Colonizer and Colonized.* Amsterdam and Atlanta: Rodopi.

Hall, Stuart. 1992. "Cultural Identity and Diaspora." In Patrick Williams and Laura Chrisman (eds.), *Colonial Discourse and Post-Colonial Theory: A Reader.* Hemel Hampstead: Harvester Wheatsheaf, pp. 392–403.

————. 1996. "When Was the 'Post-colonial'? Thinking at the Limit in the Post-Colonial Question." In Iain Chamber and Lidia Curti (eds.), *Common Skies, Divided Horizons.* London: Routledge, pp. 242–61.

Hall, Stuart (ed.). 1997. *Representation: Cultural Representations and Signifying Practices.* London: Sage.

Hall, Stuart, and Paul du Gay (eds.). 1996. *Questions of Cultural Identity.* London: Sage Publications.

Hall, Stuart, and Mark Sealy (eds.). 2001. *Different: A Historical Context. Contemporary Photographers, and Black Identity.* London: Phaidon Press.

Hammond, Jenny. 1990. *Sweeter than Honey: Ethiopean Women and Revolution. Testimonies of Tigrayan Women.* Trenton, N.J.: The Red Sea Press Inc.

Harasym, Sara (ed.). 1990. *The Post-colonial Critic: Interview, Strategies, Dialogues.* New York: Routledge.

Hardt, Michael, and Toni Negri. 2001. *Empire.* Cambridge: Harvard University Press.

Harlow, Barbara. 1987. *Resistant Literature.* New York and London: Methuen.

Hay, James. 1987. *Popular Film Culture in Fascist Italy: The Passing of the Rex.* Bloomington: Indian University Press.

Higonnet, Margaret R. (ed.). 1994. *Borderwork: Feminist Engagements with Comparative Literature.* Ithaca: Cornell University Press.

Hirsch, Marianne. 1989. *The Mother/Daughter Plot: Narrative, Psychoanalysis, Feminism.* Bloomington: Indiana University Press.

Hobsbawm, E. J. 1992. *Nations and Nationalism since 1780: Programme, Myth, Reality.* Cambridge: Cambridge University Press hooks, bell. 1984. *Feminist Theory: From Margin to Center*. Boston: South End Press.

———. 1995. "Representations of Whiteness in the Black Imagination." In bell hooks (ed.), *Killing Rage, Ending Racism*. London, Penguin Books.

Hoving, Isabel. 2001. *In Praise of New Travelers: Reading Caribbean Migrant Women Writers*. Stanford: Stanford University Press.

Huggan, Graham. 2001. *The Postcolonial Exotic: Marketing the Margins*. London and New York: Routledge.

Hulme, Keri. 1985. *The Bone People*. London: Picador.

Humm, Maggy. 1991. *Border Traffic: Strategies of Contemporary Women Writers*. Manchester: Manchester University Press.

Jacobs, Jane M. 1996. *Post-colonialism and the City*. London: Routledge.

Jameson, Fredric. 1981. *The Political Unconscious Narrative as a Socially Symbolic Act*. Ithaca: Cornell University Press.

———. 1986. "Third World Literature in an Era of Multinational Capitalism." *Social Text* 15: 65–88.

———. 1991. *Postmodernism, or the Cultural Logic of Late Capitalism*. Durham: Duke University Press.

Jayawardena, Kumari. 1986. *Feminism and Nationalism in the Third World*. London: Zed Books.

Juan Jr., E. San. 1995. *Hegemony and Strategies of Transgression: Essays in Cultural Studies and Comparative Literature*. Albany: State University of New York Press.

———. 1998. *Beyond Post-colonial Theory*. New York: St. Martin's Press.

Kaplan, Caren. 1987. "Deterritorializations: The Rewriting of Home and Exile in Western Feminist Discourse." In Abdullah Jan Mohamed and David Lloyd (eds.), *The Nature and Context of Minority Discourse. Cultural Criticism* 6–7: 187–98.

———. 1992. "Resisting Autobiography: Outlaw Genres and Transnational Feminist Subjects." In Sidonie Smith and Julia Watson (eds.), *De/Colonizing the Subject: The Politics of Gendering in Women's Autobiography*, pp. 115–38.

———. 1994. "The Politics of Location." In Inderpal Grewal and Caren Kaplan (eds.), *Scattered Hegemonies: Postmodernity and Transnational Feminist Practices*. Minneapolis: University of Minnesota Press, pp. 137–52.

———. 1996. *Questions of Travel: Postmodern Discourses of Displacement*. Durham: Duke University Press.

Katrak, Ketu H. 1989. "Decolonizing Culture. Towards a Theory for Post-colonial Women's Texts." *Modern Fiction Studies* 35.1: 157–79.

Kirpal, Viney. 1988. "What is the Third World Novel?" *Journal of Commonwealth Literature* 23: 144–56.

Koshy, Susan. 1994. "The Geography of Female Subjectivity. Ethnicity, Gender, and Diaspora." *Diaspora* 3.1: 69–84.

———. 1997. "Mother-Country and Fatherland: Re-membering the Nation in Sara Suleri's *Meatless Days*." In Bishnupriya Ghosh and Brinda Bose (eds.), *Interventions: Feminist Dialogues on Third World Women's Literature and Film*. New York and London: Garland Publishing, pp. 45–61.

Koso-Thomas, Olayinka. 1987. *The Circumcision of Women: A Strategy for Eradication*. London: Zed Books.

Krishnaswamy, Kevathi. 1995. "Mythologies of Migrancy: Post-colonialism, Postmodernism and the Politics of (Dis)location." *ARIEL: A Review of International English Literature* 26.1: 125–46.

Kristeva, Julia. 1986. "Women's Time." In Toril Moi (ed.), *The Kristeva Reader*. Oxford: Basil Blackwell, pp. 187–213.

———. 1991. *Strangers to Ourselves*. Trans. by Leon S. Roudiez. New York: Columbia University Press.

———. 1993. *Nations without Nationalism*. Trans. by Leon S. Roudiez. New York: Columbia University Press.

Kumar, Manjushree S. 1995. "Journey Through Time: Meena Alexander's *Fault Lines*." In R. K. Dhawan (ed.), *Indian Women Novelists*, Vol. 3. Delhi: Prestige Books, pp. 208–21.

Laclau, Ernesto, and Chantal Mouffe. 1985. *Hegemonies and the Socialist Strategies: Towards a Radical Democratic Politics*. London: Verso.

Labanca, Nicola. 1993. *In Marcia Verso Adua*. Torino: Einaudi.

———. 2002. *Oltremare: Storia dell'Espansione Coloniale Italiana*. Bologna: Il Mulino.

Lahiri, Jumpa. 1993. *Interpreter of Maladies*. London: Flamingo.

Lal, Malashri. 1995. *The Law of the Threshold: Women Writers in Indian English*. Shimla: Indian Institute for Advanced Study.

Lauretis, Teresa de. 1984. *Alice Doesn't: Feminism, Semiotics, Cinema*. London: Macmillan.

——— (ed.). 1986. *Feminist Studies: Critical Studies*. Bloomington: Indiana University Press.

Lavie, Smadar, and Ted Swedenburg. 1996. *Displacement, Diaspora, and Geographies of Identity*. Durham: Duke University Press.

Levi, Carlo. 1982. *Christ Stopped at Eboli*. Middlesex: Penguin.

Lévi-Strauss, Claude. 1963. "The Structural Study of Myth." In *Structural Anthropology*. New York: Basic Books, pp. 206–31.

Lightfoot-Klein, Hanny. 1989. *Prisoners of Ritual: An Odyssey into Female Circumcision in Africa*. New York: Harrington Press.

Lionnet, Françoise. 1988. "Métissage, Emancipation, and Female Textuality in Two Francophone Writers." In Bella Brodski and Celeste Schenk (eds.), *Life/Lines: Theorising Women's Autobiography*. Ithaca: Cornell University Press, pp. 260–81.

———. 1989a. *Autobiographical Voices: Race, Gender, Self-Portraiture*. Ithaca: Cornell University Press.

———. 1989b. "Dissymmetry Embodied: Nawal El Saadawi's *Woman at Point Zero* and the Practice of Excision." In Françoise Lionnet (ed.), *Post-colonial Representations: Women, Literature, Identity*. Ithaca: Cornell University Press, pp. 129–53.

———. 1992. "Of Mangoes and Maroons: Language, History, and the Multicultural Subject of Michelle Cliff's *Abeng*." In Sidonie Smith and Julia Watson (eds.), *De/Colonizing the Subject*. Minneapolis: Minnesota University Press, pp. 321–45.

———. 1994. "Dissymmetry Embodied: Feminism, Universalism, and the Practice of Excision." In Margaret R. Higonnet (ed.), *Borderwork: Feminist Engagement with Comparative Literature*. Ithaca: Cornell University Press, pp. 19–41.

———. 1995. "The Limits of Universalism. Identity, Sexuality, and Criminality." In *Post-colonial Representations: Woman Literature, Identity*. Ithaca: Cornell University Press, pp. 154–66.

———. 1995. *Post-colonial Representations: Women, Literature, Identity*. Ithaca: Cornell University Press

Loomba, Ania. 1998. *Colonialism/Post-colonialism*. London and New York: Routledge.

Lovesey, Oliver. 1997. "'Post-colonial Self-Fashioning' in Sara Suleri's *Meatless Days*." *Journal of Commonwealth Literature* 32.2: 35–50.

Mack Smith, Denis. 1997. *Modern Italy: A Political History*. New Haven: Yale University Press.

MacMillan, Margaret. 1988. *Women of the Raj*. London: Thames and Hudson.

Malouf, Denis. 1993. *Remembering Babylon*. London: Chatto and Windus.

Mani, Lata. 1989. "Contentious Traditions: The Debate on Sati in Colonial India." In KumKum Sangari and Sudesh Vaid (eds.), *Recasting Women: Essays in Colonial History*. New Delhi: Kali for Women, pp. 88–126.

———. 1990. "Multiple Mediations: Feminist Scholarship in the Age of Multinational Reception." *Feminist Review* 35: 24–41.

———. 1992. "Cultural Theory, Colonial Texts: Reading Eyewitness Accounts of Widow Burning." In Lawrence Grossberg, Cary Nelson, and Paula Treichler (eds.), *Cultural Studies*. London: Routledge.

Markakis, John. 1987. *National and Class Conflict in the Horn of Africa*. Cambridge: Cambridge University Press.

———. 1989. *Nationalities and the State of Ethiopia*. The Hague: Institute of Social Studies.

Martin, Emily. 1987. *The Woman in the Body: A Cultural Analysis of Reproduction*. Boston: Beacon Press.

McClintock, Anne. 1992. "The Angel of Progress: Pitfalls of the Term 'Post-colonialism.'" *Imperial Leather: Race, Gender, and Sexuality*. London and New York: Routledge, 1995, pp.1–17.

———. 1995. *Imperial Leather: Race, Gender, and Sexuality in the Colonial Context*. New York and London: Routledge.

———. 1997. "No Longer in a Future Heaven." In Anne McClintock, Aamir Mufti, and Ella Shohat (eds.), *Dangerous Liaisons: Gender, Nations, and Post-colonial Perspectives*. Minneapolis: University of Minnesota Press, pp. 89–112.

McClintock, Anne, Aamir Mufti, and Ella Shohat (eds.). 1997. *Dangerous Liaisons: Gender, Nation, and Post-colonial Perspectives*. Minneapolis: University of Minnesota Press.

McHale, Brian. 1988. "Some Postmodernism Stories." In Theo D'Haen and Hans Bertens (eds.), *Postmodern Fiction in Europe and the Americas*. Amsterdam and Atlanta: Rodopi Press, pp. 13–25.

———. 1992. *Constructing Postmodernism*. London: Routledge.

McLean, Scilla, and Stella Efua Graham (eds.). 1980. *Female Circumcision, Excision, and Infibulation*. London: The Minority Rights Group, Report No. 47.

Meijer, Maaike. 1996. *In Tekst Gevat: Inleiding tot een Kritiek van Representatie*. Amsterdam: Amsterdam University Press.

Mesghenna, Yemane. 1988. *Italian Colonialism in Eritrea, 1869–1934: Motive, Praxis, and Result*. Diss. Lund.

Messud, Claire. 1993. "No Skull beneath the Skin." *The Guardian*, 29 June.

Miller, Alice. 1979. *Das drama des begabten Kindes und die Suche nach dem wahren Selbst*. Frankfurt am Main: Suhrkamp Verlag.

Minh-ha, Trinh T. 1989. *Woman, Native, Other: Writing Post-coloniality and Feminism*. Bloomington: Indiana University Press.

Modood, Tariq, and Pnina Werbner (eds.). 1997. *The Politics of Multiculturalism in the New Europe: Racism, Identity, and Community*. London: Zed Books.

Mohamoud, Abdullah A. 1996. "Empowering Ethnicity in Ethiopia Reexamined." In *NewsLetter*, Research Centre for International Economy at the University of Amsterdam, Vol. 2.5 (November): 8–10.

Mohanty, Chandra Talpade. 1987. "Feminist Encounters: Locating the Politics of Experience." *Copyright* 1 (Fall 1987): 24.

———. 1990. "On Race and Voice: Challenges for Liberal Education in the 1990's." *Cultural Critique* 14 (Winter): 179–208.

———. 1991. "Under Western Eyes: Feminist Scholarship and Colonial Discourse." In Chandra T. Mohanty, Ann Russo, and Lourdes Torres (eds.), *Third World Women and the Politics of Feminism*. Bloomington: Indiana University Press, pp. 51–80.

———. 1995. "Under Western Eyes: Feminist Scholarship and Colonial Discourses." In Bill Ashcroft, Gareth Griffiths, and Helen Tiffin (eds.), *The Post-Colonial Studies Reader*. London and New York: Routledge, pp. 259–68.

Mouffe, Chantal. 1979. *Gramsci and Marxist Theory*. London: Lawrence and Wishart.

Naipaul, V. S. 1961. *A House for Mr. Biswas*. London: André Deutsch.

———. 1976. *The Overcrowded Barracoon*. London: André Deutsch.

Narayan, Uma, and Sandra Harding (eds.). 1998. *Border Crossings: Multicultural and Post-colonial Feminist Challenges to Philosophy*. Bloomington: Indiana University Press.

Nasta, Susheila. 2001. *Home Truths: Fictions Of the South Asian Diaspora in Britain*. London: Palgrave.

Negash, Ghirmai. 1999. *A History of Tigrinya Literature: The Oral and the Written, 1890–1991*. Leiden: CNWS.

Negash, Tekeste. 1987. *Italian Colonialism in Eritrea, 1882–1941: Policies, Praxis, and Impact*. Diss. Uppsala.

Negri, Antonio. 1997. "Italy, Exile Country." In *Revisioning Italy: National Identity and Global Culture*. Minneapolis: Minnesota University Press, pp. 43–51.

Newman, Judie. 1995. *The Ballistic Bard: Post-colonial Fictions*. London: Arnold.

Nnaemake, Obioma. 1983. "A Statement on Genital Mutilation." In Miranda Davies (ed.), *Third World: Second Sex, Women's Struggles, and National Liberation: Third World Women Speak Out*. London: Zed Press, pp. 217–20.

———. 1994. "Bringing African Women into the Classroom: Rethinking Pedagogy and Epistemology." In Margaret R. Higonnet (ed.), *Borderwork: Feminist Engagements with Comparative Literature*. Ithaca: Cornell University Press, pp. 301–18.

———. 1997. *The Politics of (M)Othering: Motherhood, Identity, and Resistance in African Literature*. London and New York: Routledge.

Okri, Ben. 1991. *The Famished Road*. London: Vintage.

Ondaatje, Michael. 1992. *The English Patient*. London: Picador.

Ortoleva, Peppino, and Marco Rivelli. 1983. *La Società Contemporanea*. Milano: Mondadori.

Palma, Silvana. 1999. *L'Italia Coloniale*. Roma: Editori Riuniti.

Pankhurst, R. 1964. "Italian Settlement Policy in Eritrea and its Repercussions, 1889–1896." In *Boston University Paper on African History*, Vol. 1, pp. 119–156.

Parati, Graziella. 1993. "When the 'Other' is Black: Portraits of Africans by Contemporary Italian Writers." *Romance Language Annual* 5: West Lafayette Ind: Purdue Research Foundation, 272–77.

———. 1996a. "Living in Translation: Thinking with an Accent." In *Romance Languages Annual* 8. West Lafayette, Ind.: Purdue Research Foundation, 1998, pp. 1–7.

———. 1996b. *Public History, Private Stories: Italian Women's Autobiography*. Minneapolis: University of Minnesota Press.

———. 1996c. "Looking Through Non-Western Eyes: Immigrant Women's Autobiographical Narratives in Italian." In Sidonie Smith and Gisela Brinker-Gabler (eds.), *Writing New Identities: Gender, Nationalism, and Immigration the New European Subjects*. Minneapolis: University of Minnesota Press, pp. 118–42.

———. 1997. "Strangers in Paradise: Foreigners and Shadows in Italian Literature." In Beverly Allen and Mary Russo (eds.), *Revisioning Italy: National Identity and Global Culture*. Minneapolis: University of Minnesota Press, pp. 169–90.

———. 1999. *Mediterranean Crossroads: Migration Literature in Italy*. London: Associated University Presses.

Parry, Benita. 1972. *Delusions and Discoveries: Studies in India in the British Imagination 1880–1930*. London: Allen Lane/Penguin Press.

Parry, Benita (contrib.). 1997. *The Politics of Postcolonial Criticism*. Andrew Gurr (ed.) Leeds: Maney for the Humanities Research Association.

Pateman, Carol. 1988. *The Sexual Contract*. Cambridge: Polity Press.

Pateman, Roy. 1990. *Eritrea: Even the Stones are Burning*. Trenton, N.J.: The Red Sea Press.

Pfeil, Fred. 1994. "No Basta Teorizer: In-Difference to Solidarity in Contemporary Fiction, Theory, and Practice." In Inderpal Grewal and Caren Kaplan (eds.), *Scattered Hegemonies: Postmodernity and Transnational Feminist Practices*. Minneapolis: University of Minnesota Press, pp. 197–230.

Phillips, Caryl. 1997. *Extravagant Strangers: A Literature of Belonging*. London: Faber and Faber.

Pickering-Iazzi, Robin (ed.). 1995. *Mothers of Invention: Women, Italian Fascism, and Culture*. Minneapolis: University of Minnesota Press.

Pinkus, Karen. 1995. *Bodily Regimes: Italian Advertising Under Fascism*. Minneapolis: University of Minnesota Press.

Plessis, Rachel Blau du. 1985. *Writing Beyond the Ending: Narrative Strategies of Twentieth-Century Women Writers*. Bloomington: Indiana University Press.

Ponzanesi, Sandra. 1992. *Alla Ricerca del Centro: Viaggio e Self-Discovery nella Narrativa di V. S: Naipaul*. Università degli Studi di Bologna.

———. 1997. "Professionista Magico: Dino Buzzati e l'Africa." *Incontri: Rivista Europea di Studi Italiani* 3–4: 200–06.

———. 1998. "Marginalia: Rearticulating Subaltern Studies Across System Divisions." *Thamyris* 5.1: 170–75.

———. 2001. "All'Ombra della letteratura Postcoloniale: Meticciato e Ibridità Culturale nelle Scrittura AfroItaliana di Maria Abbebù Viarengo." In Liana Borghi (ed.), *Letterature Comparate al Femminile*. Urbino: Quattro Venti, pp. 273–82.

———. 2002. "Diasporic Subjects and Migration." In Gabriele Griffin and Rosi Braidotti (eds.), *Thinking Differently: A Reader in European Women's Studies*. London: Zed Books, pp. 205–20.

———. 2004. "Imaginary Cities, Space and Identity in Italian Literature of Immigration." In Robert Lumley and John Foot (eds.), *Italian City Scapes. Cultural and Urban Change in Contemporary Italy*. Exeter: University of Exeter Press, pp. 156–165.

Prakash, Gyan. 1992. "Post-colonial Criticism and Indian Historiography." *Social Text* 31–32: 8.

———. 1996. "Who is Afraid of Post-coloniality?" *Social Text* 49.4 (Winter 1996): 187–203.

Prakash, Gyan (ed.). 1995. *After Colonialism: Imperial Histories and Post-colonial Displacements*. Princeton: Princeton University Press.

Prasad, Madhava. 1997. "On the Questioning of a Theory of (third) World Literature." In Anne McClintock, Aamir Mufti, and Ella Shohat (eds.), *Dangerous Liaisons: Gender, Nations, and Post-colonial Perspectives*. Minneapolis: University of Minnesota Press, pp. 141–62.

Pratt, Mary Louise. 1992. *Imperial Eyes: Travel Writing and Transculturation*. London: Routledge.

Rajan, Rajeswari Sunder. 1993. *Real and Imagined Women: Gender, Culture, and Post-colonialism*. London and New York: Routledge.

Ray, Sangeeta. 1993. "Memory, Identity, Patriarchy: Projecting a Past in the Memoirs of Sara Suleri and Michael Ondaatje." *Modern Fiction Studies: Fiction in the Indian Subcontinent* 39.1: 37–58.

Reich, Jacqueline, and Piero Garofalo (eds.). 2002. *Reviewing Fascism: Italian Cinema, 1922–1943*. Bloomington: Indiana University Press.

Rich, Adrienne. 1986. "Notes Towards a Politics of Location." In *Blood, Bread and Poetry: Selected Prose 1979–1985*. New York: W. W. Norton: 210–31.

Rochat, Giorgio. 1974. *Il Colonialismo Italiano*. Torino: Loescher.

Rosenblatt, Roger. 1980. "Black Autobiography: Life as the Death Weapon." In James Olney (ed.), *Autobiography: Essays Theoretical and Critical*. Princeton: Princeton University Press.

Roy, Arundhati. 1997. *The God of Small Things*. London: Flamingo.

Roy, Parama. 1998. *Indian Traffic: Identities in Question in Colonial and Post-colonial India*. Berkeley: University of California Press.

Rushdie, Salman. 1981. *Imaginary Homelands: Essays and Criticism 1981–1991*. London: Granta Books.

———. 1981. *Midnight's Children*. London: Picador.

———. 1982. "The Empire Writes Back with a Vengeance." *The Times*, 3 July.

Saadawi, Nawal El. 1980. *The Hidden Face of Eve: Women in the Arab World*. London: Zed Press.

Said, Edward. 1978. *Orientalism*. London: Pantheon Books.

———. 1984. "Reflections on Exile." *Granta* 13 (Autumn): 157–72.

———. 1986. "Intellectuals in the Post-colonial World." *Salmagundi* 70.1: 44–64.

———. 1993. *Culture and Imperialism*. London: Vintage.

———. 2000. *Reflections on Exile and Other Essays*. Cambridge: Harvard University Press

Sandhu, Sukhdev. 2003. *London Calling: How Black and Asian Writers Imagined a City*. London: HarperCollins.

Saracino, Maria Antonietta (ed.). 1994. *Altri Lati del Mondo*. Roma: Sensibili alle Foglie.

Sassen, Saskia. 1999. *Globalization and Its Discontents: Essays on the New Mobility of People and Money*. New York: New Press.

Sathyamurty, T. V. (ed.). 1996. *Region, Religion, Caste, Gender, and Culture in Contemporary India*. New Delhi: Oxford University Press.

Scarry, Elaine. 1985. *The Body in Pain: The Making and Unmaking of the World*. New York: Oxford University Press.

Scott, Joan. 1992. "Experience." In Judith Butler and Joan Scott (eds.), *Feminists Theorize the Political*. New York: Routledge, pp. 22–40.

Shohat, Ella. 1992. "Notes on the Post-colonial." *Social Text* 31–32: 99–113.

Silverman, Kaja. 1988. *The Acoustic Mirror: The Female Voice in Psychoanalysis and Cinema*. Bloomington: Indiana University Press.

Smith, Sidonie. 1987. *A Poetics of Women's Autobiography: Marginality and the Fiction of Self-Representation*. Bloomington: Indiana University Press.

———. 1993. *Subjectivity, Identity, and the Body: Women's Autobiographical Practices in the Twentieth Century*. Bloomington: Indiana University Press.

Smith, Sidonie, and Julia Watson (eds.). 1992. *De/Colonizing the Subject: The Politics of Gender in Women's Autobiography*. Minneapolis: University of Minnesota Press.

Sorgoni, Barbara. 1998. *Parole e Corpi: Antropologia, Discorso Giuridico, e Politiche Sessuali Interrazziali nella Colonia Eritrea (1890–1941)*. Napoli: Liguori.

Soyinka, Wole. 1974. *The Interpreters*. London: Heinemann.

Spackman, Barbara. 1996. *Fascist Virilities: Rhetoric, Ideology, and Social Fantasy in Italy*. Minneapolis: University of Minnesota Press.

Spivak, Gayatri C. 1981. "French Feminism in an International Frame." *Yale French Studies* 62: 154–84.

———. 1982. "Subaltern Studies: Deconstructing Historiography." In Ranajit Guha (ed.), *Selected Subaltern Studies*, Vol. 1. Delhi: Oxford University Press, pp. 3–32.

———. 1983. "Displacement and the Discourse of Woman." In Mark Krupnick ed., *Displacement: Derrida and After*. Bloomington: Indiana University Press, pp. 169–95.

———. 1985a. "The Rani of Simur." In Francis Barker (ed.), *Europe and its Others*, Vol. I. Colchester: University of Essex, pp. 128–51.

———. 1985b. "Three Women's Texts and a Critique of Imperialism." *Critical Inquire* 12.1 (Autumn): 243–61.

———. 1986. "Imperialism and Sexual Difference." *Oxford Literary Review* 8.1–2, pp. 225–40.

———. 1988b. "Can the Subaltern Speak?" In Cary Nelson and Lawrence Grossberg (eds.), *Marxism and the Interpretation of Culture*. Urbana, University of Illinois Press, pp. 271–313.

———. 1988c. *In Other Worlds: Essays in Cultural Politics*. New York: Routledge.

———. 1991a. "Theory in the Margin." In Jonathan Arac and Barbara Johnson (eds.), *Consequences of Theory*. Baltimore: Johns Hopkins University Press, pp. 154–80.

———. 1991b. "Feminism in Decolonization." *Differences* 3 (Fall): 139–70.

———. 1993a. *Outside in the Teaching Machine*. London: Routledge.

———. 1993b. "The Politics of Translation." In *Outside in the Teaching Machine*. London: Routledge, pp. 170–200.

———. 1995. "Acting Bits/Identity Talks." In Anthony Kwame Appiah and Henry Louis Gates (eds.), *Identities*. Chicago: University of Chicago Press, pp. 147–80.

———. 1996. "Poststructuralism, Marginality, Postcoloniality and Value." In Padmini Mongia (ed.), *Contemporary Postcolonial Theory: A Reader*. London: Arnold, pp. 198–222.

———. 1997. "Teaching for the Times." In Anne McClintock, Aamir Mufti, and Ella Shohat (eds.), *Dangerous Liaisons: Gender, Nation, and Postcolonial Perspective*. Minneapolis: University of Minnesota Press, pp. 468–90.

———. 1999. *A Critique of Postcolonial Reason: Toward a History of the Vanishing Present*. Cambridge: Harvard University Press.

———. 2003. *Death of a Discipline*. New York: Columbia University Press.

Spivak, Gayatri, C., and Ranajit Guha (eds.). 1988a. *Selected Subaltern Studies*. New York: Oxford University Press.

Stanley, Liz. 1992. *The Autobiographical "I": Theory and Practice of Women's Autobiographical Writings*. Manchester: Manchester University Press.

Steady, Filomena. 1989. "African Feminism. A Worldwide Perspective." In Rosalyn Terborg-Penn et al, (eds.), *Women in Africa and the African Diaspora*. Washington: Howard University Press.

Stein, Burton. 1988. *A History of India*. Oxford: Blackwell.

Steiner, George. 1975. *After Babel: Aspects of Language and Translation*. Oxford: Oxford University Press.

Stoler, Laura Ann. 1990. "Making Empire Respectable: The Politics of Race and Sexual Morality in 20th-Century Colonial Cultures." In Jan Breman (ed.), *Imperial Monkey Business: Racial Supremacy in Social Darwinist Theory and Colonial Practice*. Casa Monographs 3. Amsterdam: VU University Press, pp. 35–70.

———. 1995. *Race and the Education of Desire: Foucault's* History of Sexuality *and the Colonial Order of Things*. Durham: Duke University Press.

Strongman, Luke. 2002. *The Booker Prize and the Legacy of Empire*. Amsterdam and Atlanta: Rodopi.

Suleiman, Susan Robin (ed.). 1985. *The Female Body in Western Culture: Contemporary Perspectives*. Cambridge: Harvard University Press.

Suleri, Sara. 1992. *The Rhetoric of English India*. Chicago: Chicago University Press.

———. 1995. "Woman Skin Deep: Feminism and the Post-colonial Condition." In Anthony Appiah and Henry L. Gates (eds.), *Identities*. Chicago: University of Chicago Press, pp. 133–46.

Taddia, Irma. 1996. *Autobiografie Africane: Il Colonialismo Nelle Memorie Orali*. Milano: FrancoAngeli.

Taylor, Paul. 1992. *Multiculturalism and "The Politics of Recognition."* London: Routledge.

Thapar, Romila. 1990. *A History of India*. New Delhi: Penguin.

Thiam, Awa. 1986. *Black Sisters, Speak Out: Feminism and Oppression in Africa*. London: Pluto Press. First published as *La Parole aux Négresses* in Paris: Editions Denoël, 1978.

Tiffin, Chris, and Alan Lawson (eds.). 1994. *De-scribing Empire: Post-colonialism and Textuality*. New York and London: Routledge.

Todd, Richard. 1996. *Consuming Fictions: The Booker Prize and Fiction in Britain Today*. London: Bloomsbury.

Tommasello, Giovanna. 1984. *La Letteratura Coloniale Italiana: Dalle Avanguardie al Fascismo*. Palermo: Sellerio.

Vattimo, Gianni. 1988. *The End of Modernity: Nihilism and Hermeneutics in Post-modern Culture*. Trans. by John R. Snyder. Cambridge: Polity Press, 1988. First published in Italian as *La Fine della Modernità*. Milano: Garzanti, 1985.

Veer, Peter van der. 1994. "Sati and Sanskrit: The Move from Orientalism to Hinduism." In Mieke Bal and Inge Boer (eds.), *The Point of Theory: Practices of Cultural Analysis*. Amsterdam: Amsterdam University Press, pp. 251–59.

Venuti, Lawrence. 1995. *The Translator's Invisibility*. London and New York: Routledge.

———. 1998. *The Scandals of Translation: Towards an Ethics of Difference*. London and New York: Routledge.

Verdicchio, Pasquale. 1997. "The Preclusion of Postcolonial Discourse in Southern Italy." In Beverly Allen and Mary Russo (eds.), *Revisioning Italy: National Identity and Global Culture*. Minneapolis: University of Minnesota Press, pp. 191–212.

Visran, Rozina. 2002. *Asians in Britain: 400 Years of History*. London: Pluto Press.

Viswanathan, Gauri. 1989. *Masks of Conquest: Literary Study and British Rule in India*. New York: Columbia University Press.

Wa Thiong'o, Ngugi. 1986. *Decolonising the Mind: The Politics of Language in African Literature*. London: Heinemann.

Walcott, Derek. 1989. *Omeros*. London: Faber and Faber.

Walker, Alice, and Pratibha Parmar. 1993. *Warrior Marks: Female Genital Mutilation and the Sexual Blinding of Women*. New York: Harvest Books.

West, Cornel. 1993. "The New Cultural Politics of Difference." In Simon During (ed.), *The Cultural Studies Reader*. London and New York: Routledge.

Williams, Patrick, and Laura Chrisman (eds.). 1993. *Colonial Discourse and Post-colonial Theory: A Reader*. New York: Harvester Wheatsheaf.

Wolpert, Stanley. 1977. *A New History of India*. Oxford: Oxford University Press.

Woolf, Judith. 1997. "Silent Witness: Memory and Omission in Natalia Ginzburg's *Family Sayings*." In Trev Lynn Broughton and Linda Anderson (eds.), *Women's Lives/Women's Times: New Essays on Auto/Biography*. Albany: State University of New York Press, pp. 203–24.

Young, Robert. 1990. *White Mythologies: Writing History and the West*. London: Routledge.

———. 1994. "Colonialism and the Desiring-Machine." In Theo D'Haen and Hans Bertens (eds.), *Liminal Postmodernisms: The Postmodern, the (Post-)Colonial, and the (Post)-Feminist*, Postmodern Studies 8. Amsterdam and Atlanta: Rodopi, pp.11–43.

———. 1995. *Colonial Desire: Hybridity in Theory, Culture, and Race*. London: Routledge.

Yuval-Davies, Nira. 1992a. "Nationalism, Racism, and Gender Relations." Working Paper Series No. 130. The Hague: Institute of Social Studies.

———. 1992b. *Fundamentalism, Multiculturalism, and Women*. London: Routledge.

———. 1993. *Women, Ethnicity, and Empowerment*. The Hague: Institute of Social Studies.

———. 1997. *Gender and Nations*. London: Sage Publications.

Yuval-Davies, Nira, and Floya Anthias (eds). 1989. *Women-Nation-state*. London: Macmillan.

Index